AMERICAN INDIAN GRANDMOTHERS

AMERICAN INDIAN GRANDMOTHERS

Traditions and Transitions

◆

Edited by
MARJORIE M. SCHWEITZER

University of New Mexico Press
Albuquerque

This book is dedicated to the Grandmothers

Library of Congress Cataloging-in-Publication Data

American Indian grandmothers : traditions and transitions /
Marjorie M. Schweitzer, editor.—1st ed.
    p.   cm.
    Includes bibliographical references and index.
    ISBN 0-8263-2077-5 (cloth)
    ISBN 0-8263-2078-3 (pbk.)
    1. Indian women—United States.   2. Grandmothers—United States.
3. Indians of North America—Kinship.   4. Intergenerational
relations—United States.   I. Schweitzer, Marjorie M.
    E98.W8   A54   1999
    305.9′0432′08997—dc21   98–58152
                                                            CIP

CONTENTS

◆

ACKNOWLEDGMENTS

◈

I speak for all of the authors when I acknowledge first and foremost the Grandmothers, and their families, who are featured in these pages. We have acquired lifelong friends (and relatives) and will never look at the world in quite the same way again. We honor the Grandmothers' endurance, ingenuity, successes, and yes, even their difficulties and failings. We have come to know them as people with whom we have much in common while at the same time recognizing their unique lives and legacies. We thank them for sharing their knowledge, their perspectives, and their friendship with us.

As the organizer of the original symposia on which these chapters are based, it was my responsibility to guide the project through its various stages. It has been a privilege to work with the authors. I appreciate their commitment to the project, their scholarly expertise, and their persistence in seeing it through to the conclusion. *Bien merci à tous.*

This acknowledgment would be incomplete without recognition of my colleagues in the anthropology of aging, especially the members of the Association for Anthropology and Gerontology. They have, over the past 25 years or so, raised questions about the cultural dimensions of aging and sought answers that have enormously broadened our understanding about the later stages of life. In providing me with insights about aging, they contributed much to my understanding of the multiple factors involved in the aging process. For a professional and social network *nonpareil,* I owe much to so many, including Maria Cattell, Chris Fry, Bob Rubinstein, Mark Luborsky, Jay Sokolovsky, Jay Elliott, Eunice Boyer, Otto von Mering, Doris Francis, Dena Shenk, Jacob Climo, Tony Glascock, Ellen and Lowell Holmes, Neil Henderson, the late

Marea Teski, Joel Savishinsky, Maria Vesperi, Phil Stafford, Joan Weibel-Orlando, and Robin Weintraub. Thank you.

My family has necessarily been involved in various ways in the making of this book. They have attended powwows, hand games, and other events with me and have met some of the Otoe-Missouria grandmothers. I thank each one for their love, for family gatherings (and especially the music), and for listening to me talk about Indian grandmothers and the ever-changing stages of the project.

Bob danced gourd dance with Otoe elders. Kit captured Fannie Grant's likeness in a sculpture. Ann Hedlund (my daughter-in-law and one of the authors) has been a valuable sounding board for ideas. Sue Woodard (also my daughter-in-law) proofread pages of a chapter and continues to take her kin-keeping responsibilities seriously. Thanks from all of us. Jehanne shared the secrets of publishing with me and chided me ("Read the manual, Mom!") into finally learning more about my word processor than I ever wanted to know.

Roland reconfigured my computer many more times than one, with almost unending patience, unfailing good humor, and admonitions ("Don't let any-one near your computer again!"). He sent me words of encouragement that I kept on my desk for a very long time. His expertise and support were critical to the completion of this project. Thanks, Rol.

John, my own special *word wizard,* has been my strongest, most enduring supporter through these many years. Thanks for always being there, for the songs—and for making it all worthwhile.

I am indebted to Paul Kutsche for guiding me to Durwood Ball, my editor at UNM Press. His professionalism, editorial guidance, and genial nature have been all that Paul promised. Paul and Durwood, thank you.

Thanks also to the enthusiastic staff at UNM Press and to Karen Bentley for careful and sensitive copy editing. It has been a pleasure to work with you.

Marjorie M. Schweitzer
Taos, New Mexico

GRANDMOTHER

A Definition
Grandmother Turtle, Grandmother Spider, or just Grandma. She brought the people to earth and gave them the rules and knowledge they needed to live. Indian People have many grandmothers, real and mythic. Some are biological relatives, some adopted ones. Grandmothers raise children; they tell stories in the winter and teach children the skills they need for survival. Grandmothers are the central characters in the daily and symbolic lives of Native women—indeed, of Native people (Green 1984:310).

KOKOMTHENA

A Shawnee Creation Story
After the flood that covered all the land, an old Indian woman was walking around—all by herself. She was lonely and she began to cry, "Oh, pity me. I am all alone." Moneto, the Great Spirit, heard her cry and he said to her, "Remember how the first man was made!"

The old woman thought and she remembered: she made small images of children from the earth and she blew into their nostrils to give them life. She was no longer alone! The old woman is known to the Shawnees as KoKomthena, Our Grandmother, the Creator.

Our Grandmother lives in a spacious lodge at the edge of the ocean in a bark house with a central fireplace. Pottery vessels, bark platters and plates, and carved wooden spoons line the walls. From one of the little pots Our Grandmother prepares an inexhaustible supply of food. She paints her face with red paint, a round spot on each cheek, and she parts her hair down the middle. Sometimes, when the moon is full, she wears short skirts, and her shadow is reflected in the moon.

KoKomthena participates in every aspect of Shawnee religion relating to the communal interests of the group, as in prophecy and in ceremonial dances. The origin of most of the elements of nature and culture are attributed to her. KoKomthena spelled out the laws and their purposes for the Shawnee, and she originated all of their major ceremonials. She is omniscient.

When visitors arrive at her house, she gives them bits of knowledge—herbal remedies or sacred ways of making fire for tribal ceremonies. She prepares a sweat lodge for doctoring them.

Today as Shawnee women and men sing during the Women's Cluster Dance, the voice of Our Grandmother is sometimes heard above the brush arbor. (Adapted from Howard 1981:162–70.)

INTRODUCTION

◇

MARJORIE M. SCHWEITZER

This book is about twentieth-century American Indian grandmothers, their cultural roots, the mythic models from which they learn, the historical changes they have experienced, and the modern cultural contexts in which they live. The essays explore cultural persistence and adaptation to change, the varied dimensions of being a grandmother, and contemporary interpretations of the grandmother role. In the late twentieth century, Indian grandmothers encourage the honoring of traditional ways but show how to accommodate to an ever-changing world, blending traditions and transitions into pathways their grandchildren consider and perhaps follow.

THE RESEARCH

The following chapters are based on symposia presented at the 1985 and 1986 annual meetings of the American Anthropological Association: *American Indian Grandmothers: Historical and Contemporary Issues* and *American Indian Grandmothers II: Status, Tradition and Change* (Schweitzer, organizer 1985, 1986).

Six of the chapters—by Pamela Amoss, Ann Lane Hedlund, Sue-Ellen Jacobs, Bruce Miller, Marjorie Schweitzer, and Joan Weibel-Orlando—were originally presented as papers in those sessions. Alice Schlegel, the discussant at our first symposium, agreed to contribute a chapter about Hopi grandmothers, and Karen Ritts Benally offered to write about the content of Navajo grandmothering after attending the second session. Dena Shenk, the discussant for our second session, did not contribute a paper, but she made helpful comments from her perspective as an anthropological gerontologist.

Each of the participants came to this project from a slightly different perspective. Joan Weibel-Orlando and I have done research on aging in American Indian communities and the anthropology of aging for many years (Schweitzer 1978, 1987, 1991; Weibel-Orlando 1986, 1988a, 1989, 1990). Pamela Amoss studied cultural renaissance among Indian elders and coedited a volume on aging in different cultures (Amoss and Harrell 1981). Our chapters reflect our interest in the cultural dimensions of aging and the position of older Indians in contemporary American Indian societies. Other chapters are derived from research that began with a focus on other topics but ultimately yielded ethnographic materials about grandmothers and grandmotherhood.

Ann Lane Hedlund's research focused on Navajo weavers and rug weaving from a variety of perspectives, but the importance of grandmothers in passing on the tradition—as well as the importance of weaving for the economic welfare of grandmothers—became increasingly evident (1989). Bruce Miller interviewed Coast Salish women from Puget Sound who were entering the nontraditional arena of politics; he recognized that they were transferring the attributes associated with their grandmother roles to their political roles (1994). Sue-Ellen Jacobs observed and recorded the changing roles of grandmothers during her extensive longitudinal research on women's roles at San Juan Pueblo begun in 1972 (1982). Alice Schlegel's research on matrilineal families, Hopi adolescent girls, and Hopi gender ideology included documentation on the meaning and content of Hopi grandmotherhood (1984).

Karen Benally's life histories of several generations of Navajo women, including a grandmother who was 100 years old, were ready-made for an analysis of the changes in grandmothering roles (Ritts 1989). Pamela Amoss continued her research on cultural persistence and renewed prestige among Coast Salish elders by exploring the connection of myths to the lives of twentieth-century grandmothers (1978).

Joan Weibel-Orlando's study of Los Angeles retirees returning to their native communities led her to the Pine Ridge Reservation of South Dakota and to a Choctaw community in Oklahoma (1988a). My research on aging in Indian communities included a focus on the lives of grandmothers in the Otoe-Missouria tribe of north-central Oklahoma (1978, 1987).

Although we approached Indian grandmotherhood from different perspectives, we all agreed that two themes characterize the data presented: (1) traditions, the persistence of cultural patterns, and (2) transitions, adaptations related to cultural and historical changes. These ideas may seem obvious and mundane on the surface, but they are intricately related to how women perceive their lives; how they carry out the duties, responsibilities, and pleasures of grandmotherhood; and how they cope with change. The two themes are reflected in the titles of the symposia and in the title of the book. They are explored more fully in each of the chapters.

In framing our presentations, we sought answers to questions related to these themes. What do Indian grandmothers do today? What did *their* grandmothers do? Do contemporary grandmothers interpret their roles in ways that are different from their grandmothers? Another way of asking these questions is: What traditional expectations remain? How do contemporary Indian women adapt these expectations to the changing economic conditions and the social milieus found in their communities?

Other questions had to do with the status of grandmothers. What are the attitudes toward grandmothers in Indian communities? How are they treated? By family members? By their communities? How are they regarded by non-Indians? Are the characteristics of being an Indian grandmother unique when compared, say, with being an Anglo-American grandmother? What are the characteristics expected of an "ideal" grandmother?

The answers to these questions are related directly to the second and equally important area of concordance among the authors, that is, in research methods. Anthropological (qualitative) perspectives and methodologies based on fieldwork frame the research.[1]

To explore the concept of grandmotherhood, to examine the interaction between grandmothers and others, and to determine the relationship of grandmother roles to kinship patterns, family structure, and economic conditions in the community, we became participant observers. To verify events and elicit descriptions of customary as well as innovative ways in which Indian women acted as grandmothers, we relied on formal and informal interviews. And to better appreciate worldviews, beliefs, and values, we explored legends and stories and their influence on behavior. We listened as women described their roles as grandmothers, discussed change, voiced their attitudes about aging, and reflected on their feelings about being a grandmother.

To elicit information about individual lives, we collected and analyzed life histories of grandmothers. The life histories were an exercise in collaboration between the women and the researchers, resulting in documents (often accompanied by a taped narration) that preserved a record of the grandmothers' lives.[2] In these chronicles women identified the strategies they evolved to cope with a rapidly changing social environment.[3] They identified concerns important to themselves as grandmothers, as women, and as Indians.[4]

In the analyses of narrations, it was sometimes possible for us to tease apart the varied influences on the grandmothers' lives, such as the tribal heritages they embraced, historical events over which they had no control, and non-Indian ways that they either welcomed or acquired because they were forced to do so. These disparate strands are the warp and weft of integrated but complex lives.[5]

Anthropological methods do not stop with fieldwork but rather begin with the study of documents, both firsthand accounts and secondhand publications. While fieldwork is undeniably the cornerstone of our studies, the field notes take on greater significance when related to information found in written sources. These sources help to establish a historical and cultural context in which to understand the accounts acquired in the field.[6] The integration of information about historical events (such as the sheep reduction policy on the Navajo Reservation in the 1930s) with field observations and interviews helps clarify the influence of such events in women's lives, identifying the traditions that remain and the transitions that have taken place.[7]

Several of us made photographs and videos of the women whose stories we recorded. Joan Weibel-Orlando's video "Going Home: A Grandmother's Story" is about the return of a Lakota woman to her ancestral home after working for 26 years in Los Angeles (Weibel-Orlando 1986). The catalog that Ann Lane Hedlund prepared to accompany a contemporary exhibit of Navajo weaving features color photographs of several weavers who are grandmothers (1992). The photographs and videos are visual verification of the verbal descriptions of grandmothers' lives and provide a welcome resource for family members.

THE GRANDMOTHERS

We begin with, "Who is an Indian grandmother?" "What defines her role?"

Indian women become grandmothers through the usual biological connections to a grandchild through a male or female offspring. But other, culturally relevant ways of becoming a grandmother are equally important. These interpretations of family and tribal relationships are influenced by the social structure of each society, especially kinship patterns. Cultural constructions (including those found in myths and legends), values, beliefs, and worldview—all prescribe behaviors and attitudes, define roles, and determine who is called "grandmother." Even recognition of the biological connection is influenced by cultural interpretation.

Indian children have many grandmothers. In Hopi society all the women of a grandmother's generation are the child's grandmothers. The behavior exhibited by a maternal grandmother toward her daughters' children (kindly and warm) is different, however, from the relationship toward her sons' children (joking). These differences in behavior are related to Hopi views of the natural world and interpretations of relationships between male and female roles (Schlegel).[8]

Clan membership is a determiner of relationships and responsibilities. In a matrilineal society such as the Navajo, a grandchild shares lineal descent with a maternal grandmother but is "born for" or "born into" the paternal clan (Hedlund). The lumping together of collateral kin (aunts, uncles, cousins) with lineal kin (parents, grandparents) results in a classificatory system that removes the distinctions of collateral relatives. A woman *classified* as a grandmother accepts responsibilities and rights toward sibling or clan grandchildren, allowing her to share in the prerogatives and burdens of being a grandmother and increasing the number of grandmothers a grandchild has (Schweitzer).

Individuals may acquire a grandmother (or become a grandmother) by creating a fictive relationship through formal adoption ceremonies or informal, temporary arrangements. While adoption of a grandchild by a grandmother is common, becoming a grandmother by fictive kinship does not necessarily imply a relationship involving young children. Adults may adopt other adults. When a grandmother dies, another is chosen to "act in her place" (Schweitzer).

"Grandmother" is used in some communities to address any older woman. It is an expression of respect and honor. The chapters on Otoe-Missouria grandmothers, Navajo weavers, and Coast Salish tribal leaders explain in more detail how the terms "elder" and "grandmother" or "older woman" and "grandmother" mesh in these communities. This view of older women, along with the broad kinship interpretations for "grandmother" discussed above, makes gender and grandmotherhood inseparable in many of the communities. Jacobs, on the other hand, argues that in San Juan Pueblo society being an elder is not tied directly to being a grandmother.

Cultural ideologies further define and enhance the concept of "grandmother." Prescriptions for or suggestions about the behavior of grandmothers are found in the myths of several cultures discussed. Spider Grandmother, a legendary figure in Hopi society, is often characterized as mother's mother, kind and warm, acknowledging Spider Grandmother's indulgence of the mischievous War Twins (Schlegel). Models for archetypal Navajo womanhood are found in traditional stories about Changing Woman. These ideals prescribe a conservative keeper of traditions (Benally) and are embodied in the roles of Navajo grandmothers (Hedlund).

Coast Salish myths address both ideal behaviors and those that are unacceptable. By listening to the narratives that are passed down from one generation to the next, women learn how *not* to live, as illustrated by the foolish grandmother in the "Starchild" story, or how *to* live, as evidenced by the good grandmother who was advocate for her grandchild in "Nobility at Utsalady" (Amoss).

The connections that Indian women trace through biological (lineal) relationships, classificatory kinship patterns, clan distinctions, fictive kinship, behavioral constructs, and ideological prescriptions are not necessarily found in each of the communities represented here. Historical events and cultural perspectives are unique to each group. Some communities are patrilineal in descent, some are matrilineal, and others are bilateral. Part of the diversity is related to cultural configurations that evolved in different environments over long periods (as, for example, the relationship between matrilineal descent and sedentary horticulture that evolved on the arid Hopi mesas or the band-level society that proved adaptive among nomadic bison hunters of the Plains).[9] There are, however, significant areas of convergence in the lives of contemporary Indian grandmothers.

Of all of the characteristics we observed, one trait dominates: Indian grandmothers are almost universally engaged in childcare and childrearing (Weibel-Orlando 1990). These activities may be long-term and permanent or short-term and temporary. The extent to which grandmothers are involved in raising grandchildren depends on the circumstances of the child's family as well as the physical and financial capabilities and willingness of the grandmothers.

Grandmothers raise grandchildren full-time as "surrogate" mothers (Schweitzer 1978; Weibel-Orlando 1990) for a variety of reasons. A daughter dies, leaving a widower who can't cope or an orphan (as I describe for Otoe-Missouria grandmothers); a parent is addicted to drugs (as Weibel-Orlando relates for a Choctaw grandmother); a young family has too many children to raise with existing resources; or a family continues to follow the tribal custom of "giving" a child to the grandparents to raise.

On a short-term basis, grandmothers "babysit" their grandchildren while parents are gone for a few hours (as Hedlund describes for Navajo weavers). Temporary fostering is sometimes arranged during an especially difficult time for the family, when, for example, the mother is ill or the parents are out of work. Visits of grandchildren to Grandmother's house may last all summer long.

Weibel-Orlando tells about grandchildren who live in Los Angeles during the school year and spend the summer with their grandmother on the Sioux Reservation. Grandmother attempts, in a few short months, to pass on tribal traditions and values and instill in her young grandchildren a sense of Indianness. Transmitting a sense of what it means to be Sioux occurs more easily within a Siouan cultural milieu than in a large multiethnic city.

Older San Juan Pueblo grandmothers carry on several traditional rituals that ceremonially name and protect infants in a significantly Tewa way. It is part of the San Juan societal expectation that grandmothers indulge in meaningful socialization of their grandchildren (Jacobs).

Childrearing by grandmothers is often a mutually reciprocal exchange with benefits flowing in both directions. Raising grandchildren benefits a woman who needs help with daily chores while easing the burdens of a family where both parents work or there are just too many children. A woman who has raised a grandchild may, in turn, be provided housing, transportation, and meals by the adult grandchild when "Grandma" is old and feeble and can no longer get around on her own.

Women adopt unrelated children to raise, creating fictive grandmother-grandchild relationships. By skipping the parent generation, they pass subtle and specific notions of culture and identity directly to the grandchild. Creating fictive relationships helps to care for orphaned children, intervene when the parent generation fails, assuage grief over a grandchild who has died, maintain a feeble old person in her home, widen the circle of family for a grandmother who is isolated or bereft, broaden the economic base of the extended family, and increase the network of support for special events.

Indian women look forward to becoming grandmothers (Green 1983:12) and to the joys and responsibilities. Many grandmothers find the role satisfying and fulfilling. For others, the happiness experienced at the new status is sometimes mixed with ambivalence.[10] Their joy at becoming grandmothers is balanced with a recognition "that sometimes these children have added to their work-load and consequently are a 'mixed blessing'" (Jacobs), especially when they are faced with the less than appealing position of being a grandmother "in need" (Weibel-Orlando). Overlapping role demands that arise from being a surrogate mother *and* a grandmother for someone who is at the same time her "child" and her grandchild may create a sense of ambiguity for both child and grandmother (Weibel-Orlando).

Whether or not young Indian children are being raised on a long-term basis, are fostered for a few weeks, are watched for a few hours, or have simply "gone to Grandma's" for the summer, Indian grandmothers continue to exert a signif-icant influence on the young of Indian communities. In whatever circum-stances the grandmothers care for grandchildren, they carry on a tradition that has roots deep within their cultural pasts. Their roles in the enculturation of children have always been important, but today their participation in the welfare of future generations may be especially crucial. Weibel-Orlando argues that, faced with issues of cultural survival, the effect of enculturation on grandchildren is conservative and is directed toward promoting and maintaining ethnic identity (1990:125). A grandmother's understanding of Indian identity is an invaluable perspective that she is able to pass on to her grandchildren. Grandmother-as-culture-transmitter may be one of her most significant contributions to the perpetuation of Indian communities.

Contemporary grandmothers' lives have been shaped and directed by events that have occurred over time within the tribal community and in the society at large. Some grandmother roles have changed. The ways in which women see and perform their roles as grandmothers have evolved, and new roles for grandmothers have appeared. Women transfer the values, attitudes, and skills of grandmother roles to positions in the economic sphere, to political leadership, to activities in voluntary organizations, and to participation in public and private ceremonies. In doing so, they expand and enhance their participation in a wider variety of contexts (Green 1980:265).

The life histories of several generations of Navajo grandmothers illustrate the general themes of grandmothering that remain intact but show how changes have occurred in the content. When a great-grandmother (as a young woman) acquired a herd of sheep, she was ensuring the welfare of her family. Now her granddaughter, a modern grandmother, stresses education and getting a good job. These attitudes and patterns of thinking are reflections of the transformations that have taken place in Navajo culture, in part as reactions to external historical influences (Benally).

As Coast Salish women accept positions of leadership in the tribe, they use the skills and know-how honed in their problem-solving managerial experiences as grandmothers (Miller). Other Coast Salish grandmothers are innovators in the way they pass cultural messages to the next generation even though they are not responsible for raising their grandchildren firsthand (Amoss). The monetary contributions of Navajo grandmothers help maintain the viability of the family as well as the community while their childminding activities promote cultural continuity (Hedlund).

Using their power and prestige as grandmothers in the family and the clan, Otoe-Missouria women mediate between traditional and non-Indian ways. These older women have embraced accommodation as a way of life and have "Indianized" non-Indian voluntary organizations and ceremonies (Schweitzer). San Juan grandmothers perform as curing specialists and spiritual benefactors (Jacobs).

Tribal norms and the attitudes of family and tribal members have an enormous influence on the status and treatment of Indian grandmothers.[11]

A cultural trait found in many Indian societies is the notion of autonomy, the recognition that an individual has the right to make her own decisions. Although autonomy implies "self-direction," it is inextricably tied to a web of interdependence. The individual, while granted autonomy of decision, is also responsible for her own behavior, behavior that will ultimately affect the group: family, tribe, and community. Autonomy is related to the development of personhood and suffuses the social and moral consciousness of Indian relationships.

The concept of autonomy is relevant to the lives of Indian grandmothers in primary ways: first, as reflected in childrearing practices, and second, in the prerogatives and responsibilities that grandmothers have to make decisions about their own welfare.

Children learn by observing and copying. Indian grandmothers "teach" their grandchildren by showing. I have watched this process many times as little Otoe girls step and twirl in their diminutive shawls, emulating their elders. After a time, they get the dance just right. Hedlund tells of a young Navajo woman who "learned everything from her grandmother by watching and imitating. Her grandmother never 'taught' . . . her directly." Autonomy and a sense of responsibility for one's actions are instilled at a very early age.

The second example of autonomy refers to the decisions made concerning the welfare of grandmothers. The connection between the concept of autonomy, clearly expressed in English as "it's up to her" (Hedlund), and the interdependence of an individual with the group has been widely explored in Navajo culture (and in other Indian societies as well).[12] An individual does not speak for or make decisions for another.[13]

Autonomy means that grandmothers take responsibility for their own lives over the life course and have the right to decide matters concerning their futures when they reach old age. If a woman decides that she wishes to remain in her own home rather than move to her daughter's or refuses certain kinds of care even though she is frail, the decision is hers to make (Schweitzer field notes; Shomaker 1990:28, 33).

STUDIES OF INDIAN ELDERS—PAST AND PRESENT

Early Ethnographies

Early in the twentieth century, anthropologists wished to document the customs and traditions of Indian societies. They relied a great deal on the oldest members of the tribe to help them record details of earlier lifestyles. Information about the roles of Indian elders was usually included in the description of other aspects of culture. Frances Densmore noted the central positions held by elderly men in the tribal council when she described the functioning of Chippewa tribal government (1920:73). When transcribing stories and describing storytelling among the Omaha, Fletcher and La Flesche explained that elderly men and women recited these stories, myths, and fables during winter evenings, often acting them out with song and gesture (1905–06:370).

Ethnographers of that era clearly were not interested in the sociocultural dimensions of aging as a topic of inquiry. While they focused on childrearing practices and often reconstructed the life cycle, their descriptions of birth, childhood, marriage, the duties of adulthood, and funeral rites seldom included much on the period between early adulthood and death.[14] They recorded only brief descriptions of the lives and influence of elders or the roles of grandmothers and grandfathers.[15]

Leo Simmons made the first systematic analysis of aging from a comparative, cross-cultural perspective (*The Role of the Aged in Primitive Society* 1970), using ethnographies as the basis for his work. He culled information about the elderly from researchers who wrote about peoples from around the world as well as from his own intimate knowledge of the Hopi people (Simmons 1942). In his analyses, he included information from 16 American Indian and Eskimo societies of North America.

Simmons was interested in the status and treatment of old people and wanted to ascertain how the elderly fared in different environmental and sociocultural conditions. He illustrated the diverse ways that societies enhanced the security of old people by measuring property rights, general and specific prestige, the control of political and civil offices and duties, the possession of skills and ceremonial knowledge, and the position of the elderly within the family system.

In assessing the depth and structure of security that old Indians (and the old of other cultures) possessed (or lacked), Simmons provided a glimpse of the variations in attitudes toward the elderly, differences in their status, and how each society defined "old." A functional definition of age, based on roles, behaviors, and physical abilities rather than on chronology, emerged from North American societies. This finding parallels the way old age is defined in contemporary Indian communities. His work remains the best summary and analysis of the ethnographic record concerning the status of elderly Indians to date.[16]

Despite the limitations imposed by the ethnographic record, Simmons's comments on the traditional positions and attitudes of the elderly are an important resource for examining the cultural heritage that influences the social structure and roles of contemporary older American Indian women and men. This information can be used to trace the changes that have occurred. In a comment especially relevant to the study of Indian grandmothers, Simmons observed that the data he analyzed about the elderly "revealed significant contrasts" between the sexes (Simmons 1970:1). Gender was a salient factor in how an individual aged![17]

Contemporary Studies

The burgeoning numbers of people over 65 in all segments of the U.S. population, especially in the last half of the twentieth century, have prompted a similar increase in research on aging.[18] While many studies have focused on the problems of aging from the perspective of "the plight of the old," others have asked, "What is the effect of culture on aging?" and "How might the cultural context ameliorate negative aspects?"

Cultural traits affect attitudes toward the elderly, create or eliminate roles, and influence the way the elderly view themselves. Traditional cultural values and beliefs are further affected by the social context in which aging occurs: the economic conditions in which a person lives, an individual's behavior during the entire life course, idiosyncratic role portrayal, and the extent and nature of the immediate family. These parameters of the aging context can have a negative effect on how a person ages, exacerbating any physical and mental ill health that may occur.

Culture may also sustain the elderly. Studies of ethnicity and aging demonstrate that culturally specific attitudes, roles, and environments can, and often do, provide a powerful and positive resource for accommodating to old age even in the event of physical losses (Cool 1980, 1981, 1987; Weibel-Orlando 1988a; Myerhoff 1987; Schweitzer 1987).[19] Aging is more than a simple biological process (Kent 1971).

Research on the roles and statuses of elderly Indians has focused on these two aspects: (1) the problems and (2) the cultural context in which Indians age.

THE PROBLEMS

Indian elderly face conditions that have been described as "double or triple jeopardy"—old and a minority, or old, a minority, and poor (Dowd and Bengtson 1978; Jeffries 1972). Statistical profiles based on the last three censuses (1970, 1980, 1990) have consistently shown a shorter life expectancy, a lower level of education, higher rates of unemployment, lower income, poorer transportation, more chronic health problems, and a higher percentage of deaths related to disease compared to Whites and, in most cases, other minorities.[20]

Indian and non-Indian scholars, assessing the conditions behind these statistics, characterize them as the "unmet needs" of Indian elderly. Gaining a clear picture of the problems was (and is) complex. Communities are diverse. Aging difficulties and disabilities generally begin for the Indian population (especially for rural elderly) earlier than for the general population, at around age 45 (National Indian Council on Aging 1981:3). Obtaining accurate information about Indian elderly has been hampered by poor census data, particularly prior to the 1990 census (National Indian Council on Aging 1981:3). Compounding the problem of understanding exactly what was happening in Indian and other ethnic communities was a general theoretical perspective arguing that age was a leveler. The "age-as-leveler" theory claimed that as people aged they became more alike, regardless of their ethnicity or the cultural context in which they grew old (Gelfand and Barresi 1987:10; Dowd and Bengtson 1978; Bengtson and Morgan 1987; Gelfand 1994:16, 28).

Studies of the needs of Indian aged have covered a range of concerns.[21] They include assessments of how services are delivered to the Indian population, the physical and mental health of elderly American Indians, and critiques of policy issues (e.g., Bell, Kasschau, and Zellman 1978; Association of American Indian Physicians 1979; Joos and Ewart 1988; Red Horse 1982; Manson and Callaway 1988). Recognizing the unique and special needs of Indians, some researchers advocated the creation of policy and delivery of services geared to the specific characteristics of Indian families and communities (e.g., Shomaker 1981). Another study describes the cultural context of aging in a kin-based society as it moves from family support for the elderly to institutional support (Kunitz and Levy 1991).

Following the 1971 White House Conference on Aging, which first drew national attention to the predicament of American Indian elderly, tribal leaders convened the National Indian Council on Aging in 1976. The conference attendees, with the participation of over 1,000 tribal elders, described the most flagrant conditions and long-standing problems faced by Indian elderly, including health care, housing, and transportation.[22]

Meeting the needs of Indian elderly continues to be a major concern (National Indian Council on Aging 1979). The National Indian Council on Aging's requests for changes in the way that Indians are served range from asking for greater understanding and tolerance in urban service centers to maintaining tribal sovereignty in the administration of funds. They seek amelioration of adverse conditions that appear to be perennial problems: housing, employment, and transportation as well as health care.[23] As the major health problems for Indians shift from infectious diseases to chronic and degenerative diseases, the need for long-term care of elders assumes prime importance (John and Baldridge 1996).[24]

Underlying the unmet needs of Indian elderly are long-standing conditions that affect the American Indian population *as a whole:* family incomes are low, more families are in poverty than in all other populations, levels of education are low, and prejudice and discrimination continue to exist.[25] Remote reservations present special challenges, especially during severe winter weather.[26] It is unrealistic to expect the problems of the elderly to be alleviated if families and communities are not functioning well (Kramer 1991:209, 213–15). Unfortunately, the problems that affect Indian communities have resisted easy solutions (John and Baldridge 1996).[27]

These problems are reflected in ambivalence toward grandmothers. While grandmotherhood is generally recognized as important in the structure of Indian families and in the functioning of the tribe (see Red Horse 1980a, 1980b; Medicine 1981; Green 1984:310) families and communities do not always provide a supportive and caring milieu for their elderly. Some grandmothers are treated badly. This is particularly problematic when an old person becomes frail (Amoss, Schweitzer, Schlegel, Hedlund, Jacobs, Miller, Benally).

The ambivalent status of the *frail elder* is a worldwide phenomenon (Schweitzer, Amoss, Miller).[28] The lives of frail elders in contemporary Indian societies become more fragile when alcoholism and drug abuse are present. Family or tribal factionalism adds further disruption. These conditions render culturally prescribed positive behavior toward the elders, whether they are frail *or* healthy, difficult or impossible. Even "benign" neglect can be hurtful. These conditions are amplified by economic deprivation where lack of money means lack of food, fuel, and housing, creating hardships for all members of the family.[29] Elder abuse may result.[30]

Miller, describing the grandmothers who occupy the fringe of Coast Salish society, portrays them as disadvantaged. Grandmothers with few family connections are characterized as old, poor, isolated, and powerless.

Nonconforming interpretation of roles and eccentric personalities may lead to negative responses from others. Women who do not follow the cultural behavioral norms expected of grandmothers are not necessarily accorded prestige just because they have become grandmothers. Big Gap Woman refused to follow the expectations of Navajo society and gain the prestige that a Navajo grandmother is expected to achieve (Benally). Some women who are now grandmothers engaged in unacceptable activities when they were younger; some are simply unpleasant people (Benally, Schlegel, Schweitzer).

THE CULTURAL CONTEXT—ETHNICITY AS RESOURCE[31]

The recognition of *grandmother* and *grandfather* as highly esteemed members of the family and the tribe is basic to Indian culture. The relationship between grandmothers and grandfathers and their grandchildren is often characterized as the most cherished within the family (e.g., in Navajo, Hopi, and Otoe-Missouria societies—Hedlund, Schlegel, Schweitzer). Traditional cultural values teach children an attitude of respect and honor toward their elders.

Building on these traditions, Indian communities today are places where expression of Indian identity can be a positive component of growing old. "Successful aging" occurs in spite of difficulties (Amoss 1981a, 1981b; Hedlund 1992; Red Horse 1980a, 1980b; Schweitzer 1987; Weibel-Orlando 1986, 1988a, 1989).[32] Elders who take pride in their heritage participate by filling ceremonial roles, becoming political leaders, performing tribal rituals, functioning as heads of families and clans, and acting as knowledgeable repositories and transmitters of tribal history, traditions, and identity. Several conditions contribute to positive contexts for contemporary Indian grandmothers.

The current positive regard for Indian elders, by Indians and non-Indians alike, is due in part to the resurgence of ethnic identity begun during the Indian Renaissance of the 1970s (Williams 1980). Laws passed since the 1960s have favored Indian sovereignty and self-determination, and young men and women, encouraged to be proud of their Indian heritage, have turned to their elders to learn more about tribal beliefs and customs, about being Indian (Deloria and Lytle 1983).

The social climate of the first half to two-thirds of the twentieth century was not congenial to being Indian, and many Indians grew up either ashamed of their heritage or unwilling to acknowledge their Indian ancestry. Understandably, then, some Indians ignored the teachings of their parents and grandparents until it was too late to learn. Now, as today's tribal elders, they lament their lost heritage. Some return to their native communities and enter again into Indian social and ceremonial life, learning as retirees what they had missed when they were young.

Others preferred to learn non-Indian ways when they were young and do not regret their choices. Many of today's elders attended a government boarding school, where they were taught White skills for competing in a White world. But even those elderly who today are not tribal sages with traditional knowledge are respected for their experiences and for their success in adapting to a non-Indian world.

Grandmothers with economically secure families whose members follow the mores of their community fare better than those who have few or no relatives or whose relatives do not fulfill their family and community roles.[33] Contemporary Indian families and tribes can and do provide successful economic support to elders in favorable environmental locations (Amoss, Schweitzer, Schlegel, Hedlund, Jacobs, Miller, Benally). Relationships built over a lifetime amid notions of reciprocity help to secure a safe haven and a cared-for old age when grandmothers become somewhat frail (Hedlund). The nature of that haven is molded by an individual's interaction with the group during her entire life cycle.[34]

In the cultural revitalization enjoyed by the Coast Salish, Miller describes innovative roles that foster a high status for contemporary grandmothers. Salish grandmothers who are successful political leaders find their success has a clear relationship to their families' strong economic underpinnings. Even those who are frail are able to contribute as "how-to" advisers. Grandmothers no longer physically able to perform ceremonies or practice their skills of sewing dresses, making shawls, beading moccasins, weaving rugs, or making pottery share their knowledge with others. They pass on the "know-how" and meaning of ceremonies to those eligible to receive the information. They give advice about the learning of a skill, interpret the meanings of customs, or translate the significance of historical events to younger members of the family (Amoss, Jacobs, Hedlund, Schweitzer). Some elder grandmothers still weave but require the help of family members, often their grandchildren, for doing various household tasks or driving them to tribal events (Hedlund, Schweitzer).

A woman's behavior is a widely recognized dimension of an Indian grandmother's status, which includes her demeanor during the early stages of her life as well as her interactions with her grandchildren. A woman must *behave* like a grandmother (according to cultural mores) to be *regarded* as a grandmother (Hedlund). In Otoe-Missouria society, a woman who leads a "moral" life (e.g., if she raises her children well and refrains from using alcohol) is more likely to be respected when she becomes a grandmother than a woman who does not follow the norms of the community.

Grandmothers who have successfully carried out their roles and have been above reproach in their behavior are admired, respected, and revered by their families and by their communities. The women call upon various aspects of their ethnicity as they fill respected positions in community affairs, are honored with special dances and ceremonies, perform tribal rituals, serve on the tribal governing board, or carry out the traditional responsibilities of encul-turating their grandchildren.[35]

INDIAN GRANDMOTHERS AND THE CONTEXTS OF AGING

This brings us to the *paradox of aging*. Aging for American Indians is often characterized in conflicting terms. On the one hand, written accounts, video documentation, public and private events, ceremonies and rituals, and affirma-tions by Indian people offer strong evidence for a cultural context that is rich and supportive, providing multiple roles and prestige for the elderly amid family and tribal networks. On the other hand, demographic and statistical data and needs assessment studies show depressing hardships facing elderly Indians.

Positive and negative aspects of aging are found in all Indian communities in varying degrees. Assessing conditions in these distinctive cultural contexts is further complicated by ever-evolving differences: in reservation/nonreserva-tion environments, urban/rural locations, full-blood/mixed-blood heritage, and more traditional/more acculturated lifestyles. Complicating the issues are the unique legal relationships that Indian people have with the federal govern-ment and the particular history that Indian groups have experienced (Deloria and Lytle 1983).

How do the grandmothers described here relate to the paradox of a rich cultural context that offers recognition of ethnic identity through family and tribal connections *and* the real and often difficult conditions facing aging Indians? How do these conditions bear upon the traditions the grandmothers represent and the transitions they have adopted?

The lives of the grandmothers reflect the traditions, attitudes, and values of honor and respect traditionally reserved for the elderly.[36] The many grand-mother roles that women fill today and the coping strategies they have adopted illustrate the positive cultural dimensions of aging for older Indian women. These contemporary roles are based on traditions that continue as well as on the transitions that have occurred. The importance of grandmothers in earlier times is echoed in grandmothers' lives today. The many examples in this volume are testimony to the enduring strength of Indian communities and to the continuing importance of the grandmother role.

By the same token, the lives of the grandmothers mirror the difficulties detailed in contemporary needs assessment research. Some have little income and are in poor health. Others are isolated either in rural areas (e.g., in widely spaced homesteads on the Navajo Reservation or in sparsely inhabited counties of rural Oklahoma) or in corners of large cities (National Indian Council on Aging 1996a). They are all ultimately affected by what happens to their families and by the general welfare of their communities. The trends charted in the social profiles continue to be part of the context in which grandmothers attempt to fulfill their diverse family and community roles.

The difficulties faced by aging Indians and the supportive cultural contexts are like two sides of a coin, inseparably connected. They are *not* mutually exclusive, and families often find themselves encountering both conditions at the same time. Even though Indian communities are strong and continue traditional tribal activities, families and others in the community are not always able to take care of the needs of their elders. Indian elders who find ethnicity a potential resource for participating in tribal and intertribal events in old age may nonetheless have problems, such as lack of transportation or poor health. For many reasons, families may fail to provide proper care for their family elders when they become frail (Kramer 1991:212; John et al 1993).

Assessing the problems that Indian elders face acknowledges the real conditions in which grandmothers live. Recognizing the successful aging of grandmothers acknowledges the persistence of Indian culture and communities. These two aspects of Indian life are integrally connected parts of a complex, ever-changing whole.[37]

NOTES

1. Guides to standard anthropological techniques can be found in Spradley (1979, 1980); Pelto and Pelto (1975, 1991); and Bernard (1988). *New Methods for Old Age Research,* edited by Fry and Keith (1986), describes qualitative methods for use in aging research. See also Reinharz and Rowles (1988). Holmes and Holmes reiterate the research concerns of anthropologists who study aging: the sociocultural perspective; comparative analysis; holistic analysis; the emic-etic perspectives; the relativistic, small group–case study approach; and interest in process analysis (chapter I 1995).

2. Langness and Frank (1981); Frank and Vanderburgh (1986:185). A life history is but one of many possible scenarios, each expressing a version of the truth. As a collaborative endeavor between the individual and the researcher, the life history that is recorded is in part determined by the circumstances under which the collaboration takes place. Results are also influenced by the goals of both interviewer and interviewee and by the subjects on which the person being interviewed wishes to comment or, alternatively, does not wish to discuss. See also Watson and Watson-Franke (1985) and Geiger (1986). Life histories of Indian women include Blackman (1989, 1992), Cruikshank (1990), Lurie (1961), and Underhill (1979). See

the annotated bibliographies by Bataille and Sands (1991) and Green (1983) for a more complete list.

In addition to the life histories, other publications discuss the lives of older Indian women. Marla Powers describes the traditional roles of old Lakota women (1986); chapter 6, "Old Age," comments on life today for "elderlies," as old Lakota women and men are called (178–81). Beverly Hungry Wolf (1980) characterizes the lives of old Blackfoot women as she recounts tribal customs. The relationship between grandmothers and grandchildren is particularly evident in Hungry Wolf's descriptions of Blackfoot traditions. D. Lee Guemple has reported on the roles of elderly women and men in Eskimo society and the dilemmas aging Eskimos face (1969). Nevertheless, the latter part of the life cycle continues to be a neglected stage in the study of the life course.

3. As Fry points out, each cohort of grandmothers varies in size, in opportunities available, and in the historical events encountered (1990:131).

4. Writings about American Indian women have ranged from romantic portrayals of Indian princesses to studies of menstruation huts and role deviance (particular aspects of Indian lives that seemed to fascinate early non-Indian researchers). Recent research about Indian women is broader and benefits from the contributions being made by Indian women. Their perspectives on the roles and statuses of Indian women from both a historical and a contemporary point of view promote greater awareness of the issues of concern to them (e.g., Allen 1989, 1991; Green 1984, 1992; Ohoyo 1981).

While feminist authors have raised questions regarding the roles and statuses of Indian women vis-à-vis their male counterparts, contemporary Indian women, for the most part, see their concerns embedded in the broader issues of tribal sovereignty rather than in the feminist concerns of non-Indian women. LaFromboise and Parent (1985:782–85) discuss the perspectives of Indian women in regard to feminist views and the retraditionalization of Indian women's roles. See Green (1980:264, 1983:13), LaFromboise and Heyle (1990), and especially Tsosie (1988) for commentary on feminist concerns. Changes continue to occur that will thrust Indian women into new positions, similar to the events described for the Coast Salish tribe by Miller.

Rayna Green (1980, 1983) gives a critical analysis of American Indian women studies, as do Gretchen Bataille and Karen Sands (1991).

5. In chapter 6, "Women's Life Histories," Watson and Watson-Franke (1985) argue that anthropologists have the responsibility to attempt to elicit a life history that takes account of a woman's viewpoint rather than imposing other (male?) categories of what is deemed important.

6. Richard G. Fox proposes what he calls a "nearly new culture history" that pursues the questions of "who people are" and "how they have come to be" and "conserves current anthropology's intention of getting the native point of view in the broad sense" (1991:95).

7. Some authors in this volume include descriptions of traditional grandmother roles and trace changes that occurred over time. Others focus on contemporary role interpretations. Benally includes a synopsis of cultural and historical changes and discusses their effects on the grandmother role. Her remarks provide background information for the description of contemporary Navajo grandmothers discussed in Hedlund's chapter. The cultural and

historical information in the chapter by Amoss provides an expanded perspective for interpreting Miller's chapter.

8. Examples drawn from the authors of this volume are indicated in parentheses without date or page numbers.

9. Band-level society on the Plains was organized around a core of siblings and other close relatives of a male leader. The size of the band varied from 150 to 500, according to the fortunes of warfare and hunting and gathering activities. During most of the year the bands camped and hunted independently of one another and only met as a tribal group at one time of the year. One frequently cited example of a tribal gathering is the Sun Dance.

10. Not all Indian grandmothers wish to be involved in childcare. Many Coast Salish grandmothers say (emphatically) they do not wish to provide childcare—they did that for their own children and for their siblings and do not wish to continue (Bruce Miller, personal communication 1993).

11. Simmons (1945) cites American Indian ethnographies that describe fear of elderly people. Some, especially frail elders, were accused of witchcraft. Shomaker (1990) gives examples from Kluckhohn (1944) and Leighton and Kluckhohn (1947) of accusations of witchcraft among the Navajo but states that the cases where she had contact with frail Navajo grandmothers did not reflect this phenomenon.

12. See Lee (1959:5–14, 15–26, 59–69), Weltfish (1965), Shomaker (1990), and Kluckhohn and Leighton (1946).

13. Specific and appropriate occasions *do* occur where one person speaks for another (or others). One example is the funeral feast. "The one who speaks for" is asked by the family of the deceased to relate whatever they wish to tell the people gathered for the ceremony (Schweitzer field notes).

14. When Edward Dozier describes the village of Hano, for example, he includes several pages on birth and childhood but very little on the rest of the life cycle (1966).

15. One topic concerning frail old people did, however, hold special interest for ethnographers and the general public: the practices of Eskimo people and other North American cultures in dealing with the hardships of the frail elderly. Everyone has heard the story of "putting grandmother out on the ice floe" (although the tale is usually told inaccurately and without adequate interpretation). Hoebel (1954) includes a discussion of senilicide in different cultures, with a special focus on the practices and attitudes of the Eskimo. Guemple (1969) gives a culture-specific explanation of the Eskimo tradition of senilicide.

16. Although it is true that ethnographic records contain sparse information about the elderly, Simmons's analyses of the data available in the mid-1940s into eight categories is an important contribution to the understanding of aging in different cultures.

17. Rubinstein argues that the study of gender and age should be situated in cultural meaning rather than in an "acultural" approach that blurs gender and age, or in what he terms the "culturalized" approach that uses ethnocentric categories and fails to take advantage of the data in ethnographic sources (1990:115–22).

18. "Since 1900, the percentage of Americans 65+ has more than tripled (4.1% in 1900 to 12.8% in 1995), and the number has increased nearly eleven times (from 3.1 million to 33.5 million)." Administration on Aging (1997:2).

19. Ethnicity is multidimensional, varies in intensity, and is situational. All of these characteristics exist in the interaction of ethnicity and aging. The shared history, place of origin, language, dress, and food preferences are subject to the expansions and contractions of inclusive boundaries; i.e., ethnic identity is situational, particularly in an urban environment or in a nonreservation (rural) location. On many levels, ethnic identity has potential as a powerful force in the lives of elderly Indians whether in urban areas or rural areas (Weibel-Orlando 1991:33–43).

With continuing changes in the "rules" governing Indian identity, the concept and expression of ethnicity will inevitably undergo change. For example, the Iowa Tribe of Oklahoma changed its blood quantum requirement from 1/4 to 1/8 a few years ago (Schweitzer field notes). To claim membership in the Kaw Nation of Oklahoma one must be able to trace lineage back to the 1902 membership roll, but there is no blood quantum requirement (*The Denver Post* 1997). As the bloodlines become more and more diluted, increasing ambivalence will inevitably be introduced into the question of "Who is an Indian?" (the *Santa Fe New Mexican* 1997).

20. Statistics for Indian elderly based on census data from 1990 and later can be found in John and Baldridge (1996). Kramer (1991), Kramer, Polisar and Hyde (1990), and Hyde (1990) cite statistics based on census data from the 1980s. Statistics for earlier decades can be found in Schweitzer (1987) and in the references listed in Schweitzer (1991).

21. For summaries of needs assessments of the elderly in Indian communities see Schweitzer (1987) and Weibel-Orlando (1989). See also Schweitzer (1991), Roberts (1990), and John (1993).

22. Recommendations included improving income, responding to language and cultural differences, increasing availability of nursing home care, providing better housing, supplying funds for transportation, increasing the availability of legal services, improving nutrition, and making funds available to meet health care and mental health needs (Lyon 1978:6–19).

23. The 1992 National Indian Council on Aging conference emphasized a need for long-term care, improved services from the Indian Health Service, and greater flexibility in the administration of Medicare, Medicaid, SSI, and the VA (National Indian Council on Aging 1993).

24. The mortality rates for heart disease, cancer, and cerebrovascular diseases are lower for Indian elders than for the non-Hispanic White population. The mortality rate for all other causes of death—pneumonia and influenza, diabetes mellitus, and accidents—is higher for elderly Indians than for Whites. Many of these conditions are directly related to a lower economic status, poorer housing and transportation, and alcoholism (John and Baldridge 1996:49–53).

25. Schaefer (1997) gives a summary of the historical events and special status that American Indians occupy in relation to the federal government. See also John and Baldridge (1996:75) and Pasaino (1997:2).

26. Indian Health Service Media Advisory, HEALTH SERVICES FOR AMERICAN INDIANS IN GREAT PLAINS REMAIN INTACT THROUGH BLIZZARD (1997:1–3). Although the headline sounds positive, many of the more than 100,000 Indians living in North and South Dakota were finding it difficult to get the help they needed because the roads were closed or

impassable. This area of high Indian population often endures severe winter weather. Harsh weather conditions are exacerbated by the high rate of poverty and poor housing.

27. Private individuals attempt to address some of the needs of at-risk Indian elderly. One such endeavor got its start as the "Adopt-a-Grandmother" program. Begun as a program of practical assistance to grandmothers living in remote areas of the Pine Ridge Reservation in South Dakota, it soon expanded to the "Adopt-a-Grandparent" program. The program is funded by voluntary contributions from interested individuals. While it does not foster reciprocal relationships with grandchildren or other family members and lacks the face-to-face meetings that family aid would take, the program does facilitate the transfer of food, clothing, medical supplies, and fuel funds. Similar programs are being organized to serve Indian grandparents in other regions of the country (*The Taos News* 1993; Russell 1993; Nowell 1996).

28. Glascock (1990) describes the ambivalent position that frail elderly occupy in the United States and makes comparisons with the treatment of frail elderly in other cultures. See also Shomaker (1990:27) on frail Navajo grandmothers.

29. Sokolovsky cites Maxwell and Maxwell (1980), whose worldwide comparative study found that negative treatment of the frail elderly increases when family support systems are weak or lacking (1990:291).

30. Maxwell and Maxwell studied elder abuse in two Plains tribes. They assert that "abuse or neglect of elderly" occurred in association with other indicators of community disorganization, such as unemployment and substance abuse (1992:9–12). See also Shomaker (1990: 26–27).

A session entitled "Elder Abuse: What, Where, Why" at the 1996 National Indian Council on Aging biennial conference identified indicators of elder abuse from simple neglect to physical abuse and made suggestions on how tribes can recognize and deal with these problems (National Indian Council on Aging 1996b). An example of a tribal program that addresses the concerns of elder abuse is supported by the Oneida Senior Center in Oneida, Wisconsin (Oneida Senior Center n.d.).

31. Anthropologists first became interested in the study of the elderly (including the elderly in American Indian communities) in the 1960s and 1970s. They brought to aging studies a multidimensional approach: qualitative field techniques, a comparative approach, and an interest in what the elderly had to say about growing old—the subjective perspective. Fry (1980:20) summarizes the initial involvement of anthropologists in the study of aging.

32. The multiethnic study on aging and ethnicity by Myerhoff, Simič, and Weibel-Orlando sought to "discover those cultural features, strategies, and social and psychological conditions that provide for well-being, that is, a sense of competence, autonomy, accomplishment and contentment in old age. . . . An individual who expresses and embodies these traits is said to be aging successfully" (Weibel-Orlando 1989:155). See also Howard Rainer's essay that urges Indian people to have positive attitudes, take advantage of their culture, and look to the future, echoing the thoughts of many of the grandmothers in this volume (1996:5).

33. Simmons (1945) shows that this connection between functioning-nonfunctioning families and old age was also true in the past.

34. Simmons argued that the family was the safest haven for elderly people (1945:177).

35. See note 19 for a definition of ethnicity.

36. Significant information in the introductory paragraphs in the chapters comes from early ethnographies that describe the roles of traditional grandmotherhood.

37. Thanks to Ann Lane Hedlund, Teddy Hoobler, and Shirley Shepherd for reading and commenting on the Introduction. I also want to thank Penny Raife Durant for a detailed critique as well as a generous dose of moral support.

THINKING GOOD
The Teachings of Navajo Grandmothers

◆

KAREN RITTS BENALLY

NAVAJO GRANDMOTHERS: ORIGINS OF THE IDEAL

In Navajo origin narratives, Changing Woman is a kind of quintessential "earth mother" who matures and changes like the seasons, always within a process of renewal. It is Changing Woman who creates The People (*Diné*, Navajo) from the epidermis of her own flesh, stabilizes and enriches the world in which they are to live, and provides them with the knowledge and skills necessary for maintaining a good life. It is Changing Woman's *kinaaldá* that serves as the model for the traditional puberty ceremony for young Navajo women. It is Changing Woman's twin sons, born as a result of her relationship with the Sun God, who rid the earth of the destructive monsters that inhabit it. And it is Changing Woman who, in maturity, travels to the West, where she provides a home and resting place for her husband, the Sun.

In the tradition of Changing Woman, the ideal Navajo woman is simultaneously wife, mother, homemaker, teacher, kin keeper, and preserver of tradition. For the Navajo, the ideal life is one that is long and filled with *hozhó;* that is, with harmony, peace, happiness, and beauty (Kluckhohn and Leighton 1946; Kluckhohn 1949; Vogt and Albert 1966; Witherspoon 1975; McNeley 1981; Farella 1984; Wyman 1970). The Navajo grandmother, or *masání* (literally "old mother"),[1] is the embodiment of those two overlapping ideals.

THE PLACE OF THE GRANDMOTHER IN NAVAJO LIFE

In Navajo society, where relationships are traced matrilineally and where the preferred residence pattern even today is matrilocal, it is around the mother—

and most specifically, around the old mother, or *masání* (maternal grand-mother)—that the family establishes residency. Her *hooghan* (hogan, home)—figuratively, at least—is central, with the homes of her daughters (and occasionally her sons) close by.

Historically, sheep have been the focal point of what we think of as the "traditional" Navajo social and economic system. Within this system, women were the "owners" of the sheep, tending and expanding the herds. The need to range the animals over a large area served to define a mother and her daughters as the ones who "tamed" and held the land *(kéyah)*[2] for their family. Sheep were a critical economic resource for the family as a whole, providing a woman with the means to meet many essential needs of her family. Sheep were used not only as a source of food but also as a source of household goods such as bedding, shoes, and rawhide ropes and as a marketable resource for sale or exchange—as raw wool, as handsome handwoven rugs, or as stock. A woman's skill in effectively managing these resources was basic to the survival of her family, and her children and grandchildren—who began herding at an early age—learned primarily through observing her in action.

Women were also responsible for the activities on the inside of the hogan, including primary responsibility for childrearing. Typically they shared these responsibilities, in reciprocal fashion, with other female kin. One woman often served as the primary caregiver for the entire family. Quite commonly she was either a young woman who was particularly adept at homemaking or an old woman well past the age of childbearing. Sometimes the *masání* "adopted" one or more of her grandchildren, with the hope of ensuring continuing support throughout her old age.

Although women participated in ceremonial activity, generally men functioned as the *hataałii*, or singers. Occasionally postmenopausal women served in this capacity. Older women, however, often functioned as diagnosticians of illness or distress—as stargazers, hand tremblers, or crystal gazers. Particularly skilled diagnosticians might service a broad area and become quite well known for their talents; others might limit their practice to their own family and relatives, fearing repercussions from the community in terms of gossip or possible accusations of witchcraft if, by chance, the patient ultimately died or the problem worsened. Having developed an intimate knowledge of the land and the plants that grew on it, older women were often skilled herbalists, and they passed this knowledge on to their daughters and granddaughters.

Drawing on the values they had been taught as well as on what they had learned through personal experience, Navajo grandmothers taught their children and grandchildren about "good thinking" *(yá'át'ééh ntsáakéés)* and "for-ward thinking" *(naas ntsáakéés).* Their teachings focused on establishing and maintaining a good life, one in which you have everything you need—no more, no less—and one in which family, relatives, and neighbors live and work together in harmony. Basic to these teachings was an understanding of clanship, the maintenance of close kin ties, an appreciation and acceptance of the concept of reciprocity, an awareness of the importance of land and livestock for survival and sustenance, and a willingness to work hard toward current and future goals.

FACTORS INFLUENCING THE CONTENT
OF NAVAJO GRANDMOTHERING

Although the general themes in Navajo grandmothering have remained intact over time, changes have occurred in the specific *content* of this grandmothering. Many of these changes reflect transformations in Navajo society. Navajo women born before the turn of the twentieth century grew up when government influence on the lives of the people was minimal. Their grandparents and parents, however, were likely to have been incarcerated at *Hwéeldi* (Fort Sumner) between 1864 and 1868, and the memories of those years of enforced captivity shaped the view of the future that these elders passed on to their children and grandchildren. As Helen Claschee, a Navajo elder, said:

> The stories I heard, from people who came back from *Hwéeldi,* were scary stories. So that's why I just put all of my energy in the sheep, how to get the herd started. Livestock was very dependable for future use. That's why I focused my energy on it.

Since the turn of the century, the traditional Navajo lifestyle has undergone dramatic change. Many factors have played a role in this change. The influence of the dominant white culture on Navajo life grew rapidly during the first two decades of the century as trading posts opened all over the reservation and as agency towns became established, bringing government in the form of schools, hospitals, jails, and the like. In general, this Anglo influence was perceived by the Navajo as positive, ensuring increased protection from enemies, providing access to material goods such as farm implements and wagons, and opening new markets for the finely crafted handwoven rugs. At the same time, however, there was an expansion of rules and regulations that served to restrain and reshape social behavior. Some of these changes were resented and resisted by the Navajo; particularly loathsome to many was the use of Navajo police to round up young children and force them to attend school, generally off reservation.

By the third decade of the century, sweeping economic and social reforms were enacted across the reservation, and the pace of change multiplied significantly. The 1930s and early 1940s were the years in which John Collier was Commissioner of Indian Affairs. Although he was committed to improving the quality of life for Native Americans without destroying their culture, Collier instituted reforms that profoundly affected the Navajo's established way of life. The most traumatic of these was the introduction of enforced stock reduction.

The stock reduction program was designed to bring livestock numbers into balance with the available rangeland; to improve the quality of the remaining stock and thus its value; to strengthen alternative sources of income-producing activity, such as farming; and to redistribute wealth, eliminating the *ricos'* (rich Navajos') control over the vast majority of the land use areas. The speed at which stock reduction occurred was overwhelming: over a period of approximately eight years (1933–40), the government forcibly reduced livestock numbers by half, with the primary burden of reduction being borne by those who had devoted their lives to expanding and developing their herds. As Ruth Underhill has said,

> The Navajos . . . were subjected to an accelerated program of betterment. Plans about the land, about education, and about self-government, which should have been slowly unfolding for forty years, had to blossom in four. The People were confused, then resentful, and, in the end, bitter, for this was not their way of change (1983:235).

For the women who married and began raising families during the post-stock-reduction era, maintaining a lifestyle based on sheep and land was not an easy option. The government policies that Collier implemented forced Navajo men and women throughout the reservation to search for alternate means of economic support for their families. As members of a population that was still largely nonliterate, Navajo women had few choices. They increasingly relied, therefore, on such traditional skills as weaving to support their families, supplementing the income of their menfolk who, at the same time, were forced to look off reservation for sources of wage work, whether as railroad workers, as transient pickers of agricultural crops, as ranch hands, or in the mines.

These post-stock-reduction women are representative of a transitional period in which almost everything seemed to be in flux. The world around them began to change almost by the minute. Navajo veterans returning from World War II sought major educational reform. The federal government responded to their demands by opening special off-reservation programs merging academic and technical training and began expanding the on-reservation school system, building local schools in even quite remote communities. Congress approved the Navajo-Hopi Long Range Rehabilitation Act, and $85.5 million began pouring onto the reservation, stimulating a rapid growth in tribal government. Uranium was discovered on the reservation, and mining activity—particularly in the northeastern section—became the work of choice for many hardworking and ambitious men who, at the time, had no knowledge of the health dangers inherent in this activity. The Native American Church (Peyote), which had begun to take root on the reservation during the stock reduction era, grew in membership and influence. Pentecostal tent meetings sprang up everywhere.

For this new generation of women, raised in a traditional manner but educated during a period of rapid change, the concepts of "good thinking" *(yá'át'ééh ntsáakéés)* and "forward thinking" *(naas ntsáakéés)* acquired new meaning. Although these women—now grandmothers—continue to stress the importance of family and the maintenance of supportive kin ties, they also emphasize the need to get an education, to secure a job that will provide a steady source of income, and to provide one's family with a "modern" way of life (for example, a rectangular home that includes running water and electricity instead of a hogan, along with a vehicle for transportation needs). Finally, with increasing frequency, they identify as important a belief in the Christian God (although the latter may be emphasized alongside participation in traditional Navajo healing ceremonies).

In the following discussion, the life history approach is used to illustrate the emergence of these new patterns of thinking as they are reflected in the attitudes and content of Navajo grandmothering. The discussion centers on the life story of Helen Claschee,[3] born during the 1880s. I collected Helen's life story over a period of three years, beginning in 1984, eventually also collecting the life histories of 14 additional members of her extended family, including her sister, her cousin, two of her husband's "brothers," several of her daughters, her one living son, and several grandchildren. My goal was to produce a "diachronic ethnography" of the Navajo experience. By focusing on one Navajo family, I hoped to illuminate the way events and conditions in "historical time" had interacted with and influenced the life experiences of members of the family, both individually and collectively, ultimately creating major shifts or "turnings" in the nature of the group as a whole. Most of these stories, including Helen's, were told to me in Navajo and were translated through two field associates (Helen's granddaughter and grandson), both of whom are fluent in Navajo and English. Since few of the stories were told in direct chronological order, a historical ordering of the data was necessary, as was a merging of segments of stories that may have been narrated and added to during different interview sessions. Quoted material, however, is very close to the original text as translated.

The story that follows is a product of that research. The narrative—told in Helen's words and in the words of her children and grandchildren—also encompasses the stories of Helen's great-grandmother, *Asdzáán Biké* (Moccasin Woman), and grandmother, Big Gap Woman *(Asdzáán Tsétah Hatsoh)*, and of the establishment of the *Táchii'nìi* (Red Streak Running Through Water) clan in the community that I call Wide Wash. In the telling, the stories of Helen's daughters, who are now grandmothers in their own right, become apparent.

The stories of these grandmothers—a small sample of women representing a single kin group—illuminate how Navajo grandmothering is partially a reflection of traditional cultural values, partially an expression of the individual characteristics of each woman, and partially a product of external, historical factors.

A TRADITIONAL NAVAJO WOMAN: HELEN CLASCHEE

When I first met Helen Claschee, during the summer of 1984, she was approximately 100 years old.[4] Her mind was extremely alert, but her body was frail. Aware that a vast store of historical knowledge about the family, the community, and the area in which she lived was at risk of forever being lost, one of her grandchildren had arranged to have me collect her life history. Helen had agreed, and late in the interviewing process explained why:

> One of the reasons that I told my story was because I wanted to show how big a land we had used, where certain people used certain parts of the land. In the future, I wanted to have my voice heard: "This was the land. People lived *here*. So-and-so lived *here*. Their grandkids lived *here*. Before there was a lot of intermarriage and the grandkids coming in, all these people were related, and this is how they used the land."
>
> I wanted to show on record that we're still all related. We cannot say, "Move away. This is ours. This is yours. This is how much is mine." We cannot say these things because we are all so related that it is impossible to say, "No, you cannot live here."
>
> It was all shared. I hear people say, "This is my land" and "This is not yours." So that's one of the reasons why I want the land to be laid out like that. That people should hear how they lived then. Just to show that.
>
> People are intertwined, like weaving. If some start pulling at the

Helen Claschee. Photograph by Timothy Benally, Helen Claschee's grandson.

threads, like some of those people who are pushing are, they may pull the whole fabric apart. I see that in the future there's going to be a lot of people saying no to their relatives. And I just want to make sure that people who are related will learn that they have to share.

Helen told her story as she and her granddaughter and I visited each of the places that had meaning in her life. Among others, these included the place

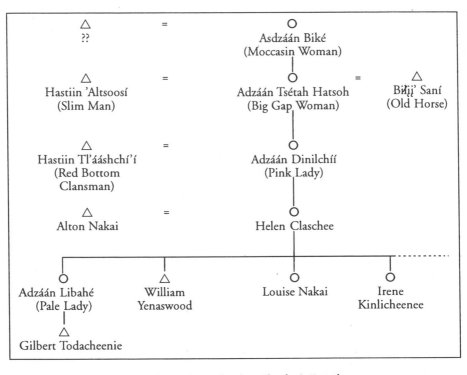

FIGURE I   *Abbreviated Genealogy of Helen Claschee's Family*

where she was born, the place where she was married and established her first hogan, each of the camps where she lived, the farm in Wide Wash, and her family's land on the banks of the San Juan River.

As we traveled the "crosscut"[5] road from Wide Wash to *Tó'ligai* (White Water), Helen told me that she was born at the winter camp of her family, at the base of a canyon called *Tsé Alchíí Naagai* (Two White Rocks Come Together). Her date of birth—an estimate—occurred somewhere between 1880 and 1889. It is from Two White Rocks Come Together that her kin group left when the Navajo were taken to *Hwéeldi* (Fort Sumner) in 1864, and it is to this place that they returned when they were released, in 1868.

The first stories she related were about these years before her birth and about her grandmother, Big Gap Woman *(Asdzáán Tsétah Hatsoh),* and her great-grandmother, *Asdzáán Biké* (Moccasin Woman). These stories were a legacy from having listened carefully to tales told by *Asdzáán Biké* and another elderly relative, *Asdzáán Bíínei* (Lively Lady) (see fig. 1).

Helen began by relating the following:

Big Gap Woman was my maternal grandmother. She was at *Hwéeldi,* and she had her first child—a son—there. Later, my mother was born at *Tó'ligai* (White Water). My grandmother used to live on the side of a stone ridge, and that was where my mother was born.

After my grandmother came back from *Hwéeldi,* her first husband, Slim Man *(Hastiin 'Altsoosí),* left her. He was an all right thinker; he was nicer than my grandmother. When my grandmother got angry, for no reason she always beat up her husband. She would get on top of him and pin down his arms and punch his face, hit his face. She was so strong that Slim Man could not stand it any longer, so he left her. After that, my grandmother married Old Horse *(Biłį́į́' Saní).*

When my grandmother was young, she went all over the place, to Albuquerque and other places; she never stayed at home. Her kids stayed home and took care of the sheep, but she was always on the go. No one knew where she was all this time. My mother, *Asdzáán Dinilchíí'* (Pink Lady), was raised by my great-grandmother, *Asdzáán Biké,* the mother of my grandmother. *Asdzáán Biké* knew how to make moccasins, and that's how she got her name, Moccasin Woman.

After she got old and started to have gray hair, my grandmother came back and stayed home. If there was a visitor, she would tell stories about where she went, how she went, what she did. She did not stay under my roof [at this time], but she lived nearby. She lived down by where my wedding house was (at Big Gap), near the spring lambing camp.

My grandmother was like a mean dog: careless, irresponsible. She was not a wise lady, not a thinking lady. She had a younger daughter, my mother's younger sister. [One day] my mother was out herding sheep with this younger sister; they were together.[6] They had an aunt who lived close by. When my mother was bringing in the sheep, my grandmother said, "I will bring in the herd. You go and get some water." So my mother went on her horse to get some water. The younger sister said, "Let me come with you," but my mother said, "No. Go over to your aunt's house and stay over there." So the little girl, who was walking, running, and talking, went over there.

In the meantime, the family was building a corral nearby. My grandmother was not watching her youngest daughter, and the little girl was just out wandering around. The little girl went over and got some dry cedar stripping. She folded it and folded it, and she made a long straw. There was a fire, and she got fire on the straw and she went and she started a fire in the tall white grass. There were three areas of grass and she caught fire on one, then another of them.

The wind caught the fire on the little girl's skirt. My grandmother had made sash belts for her daughters, and so when the skirt caught on fire, it stopped at the waist because of the belt. It was the aunt that heard the little girl screaming, crying. She ran out there and tried to help her.

When my mother came back, she brought the water into the house. When she came in, she saw what had happened. As soon as she came through the door, my grandmother got mad, and she grabbed my mother's hair and pulled her around and flopped her to the ground. And the little girl just died because she had such bad burns.

That was the kind of mother my grandmother was. So my mother was the one that told her kids, "Do not leave matches around where kids can get them. Do not leave the fire burning when you are going out. Do not leave children alone, all by themselves."

My mother was about the same size that I am and our values similar. She was very nice, the extreme opposite of my grandmother, and very much like my grandmother's sister, Laughing Lady *(Asdzáán Anadloohí)*. They had the same character.

The canyon where Helen was born was typical of the temporary base camps for other Navajos of the same period. There was no permanent hogan or corral; simple lean-to shelters were built and rebuilt as needed, with the canyon shelter serving primarily as protection from inclement weather for both people and livestock. Water sources were some distance away, out on the plains.

Helen was the firstborn child in what was to become a family of 13 siblings. She had an elder sister through the marriage of her mother to an earlier husband but had no contact with her.

My mother was married twice. Her first husband was *Ta'neeszahnii* (Tangle) clan. They had a girl child; just one. This [half] sister was the oldest then, this sister from the first marriage. My mother's first husband left when he saw another lady. My mother and her daughter were alone for a long time before my father came along.

My father was a tall, husky man; *Tl'ááshchí'í* (Red Bottom; Red Cheeks) clan. He and his sisters were orphans. Because they were orphans, they raised themselves. Their mother's brother, who lived near them, made sure that they had plenty of firewood, water, and food, but they lived at their own hogan and their mother's brother just came and checked on them. Pretty soon the eldest of the girls started to learn how to make bread and fix food, and she started to take care of the younger ones. That was how they lived, on their own. Nobody taught them; they learned by observation.

They learned how to take care of the sheep. Each of them had their own herds later, so they were good people.

My father had a grandmother who was just like *my* grandmother, Big Gap Woman. She was at *Hwéeldi*, too. This grandmother would grab him by the hair and put his head between her knees, and she'd get out a switch and spank his bottom. So his teaching was, "Do not be abusive. It is very hurtful to be abused." His teaching was like that.

So my mother and my father were married. I remember them as being capable of doing many things. They were both good thinkers, farsighted, with plans for the future, for the children. They were able to start something and to make a go of it. They were very compatible.

After my grandmother got old and could not have kids anymore, she wanted the daughter from my mother's first marriage to be with her so that she could raise her. My mother did not want Big Gap Woman to raise her daughter, but my grandmother was persistent and that is what happened.

When this half sister was old enough to be married, my grandmother went and asked my mother's second husband—my father—to be the husband of this oldest daughter, too. So he was married to this daughter. From this marriage of my half sister and my father, there were two children, a daughter and a son.

When this happened, my mother took her herd and went away from my father and away from her daughter's herd, and she lived on her own, herding sheep year-round. She was alone, but all of her children took care of her. My father would go over and take care of her, too. He would haul water and bring firewood. [In addition to the sheep] the family had horses and cattle. They had so much herd that each child was given four lambs each time they lambed.

When she was just a small child, Helen's parents migrated to a farm along the southern edge of the San Juan River, not far from the agency town of Shiprock, leaving Helen in the care of her great-grandmother, *Asdzáán Biké* (Moccasin Woman). Helen remained on the *Tó'ligai* plains throughout her growing years. She began herding rams—typically the first herding task given young children—at approximately age six. Within a couple of years she began herding sheep, and that task became the central activity in her young life, filling nearly every waking hour and consuming her thoughts.

Later, when Helen's siblings began to be born in Shiprock and became old enough to help herd, her parents sent them out to her, and she took care of them as well as the sheep. In this manner, she became the person primarily responsible for tending the family's herd, including the sheep belonging to her great-grandmother, *Asdzáán Biké;* her mother's brother; and her grandmother, Big Gap Woman. In time, she also began to establish a small herd of her own.

Helen became very comfortable with her way of life, and she began to see sheep as a means by which to accumulate things you wanted, as an economic resource that was dependable for the future. As she moved the sheep, daily and seasonally, from one grazing area to another, she developed a deep feeling of intimacy with the land, an understanding of its ability to provide, and an appreciation and acceptance of the rhythmic cycles of storm and drought, seasonal change, and the impact of these natural phenomena on land use. For Helen, land became the abiding symbol of a good life.

During this same period, Helen learned to weave. Her first rugs, copied after those she had seen her great-grandmother and other female relatives produce, were small ones, roughly textured and simple in design. Although her rugs improved technically and stylistically over the years, they were never "fine." Their production served a distinct purpose: Helen could make two or three small rugs during a summer, sell them to the trader when she came down from the mountain in the fall, and use the money she obtained from the sale for the purchase of goods such as coffee, flour, sugar, and salt.

Asdzáán Biké died somewhere around the turn of the century. As was the ideal, she had lived a long life and one of happiness. At this point Helen's grandmother, Big Gap Woman, became a more significant person in Helen's life. Their relationship, however, was not a good one. In contrast to her descriptions of her great-grandmother, mother, and aunts as kind and gentle women, Helen's descriptions of Big Gap Woman were extremely negative. Helen said that Big Gap Woman was "not a wise lady, not a thinking lady," and she went on to provide examples of the way Big Gap Woman interacted with the family. One of these stories will suffice to illustrate the kind of relationship they shared:

> My grandmother, Big Gap Woman, was not a very loving person. She was mean. One day before I was married, I was herding four different herds— my grandmother's, my mother's, my mother's brother's, and my own—in the area near the canyon where I was born. My grandmother came and said that she was hungry for some meat. She asked me to get a certain goat from her herd for her to butcher.
>
> There were two goats in the herd that looked the same. I went out to the herd. The rock ledges were at my side. One of the goats was up on the rocks, lying on the ledge. When I came out, I looked over the herd. I saw the goat lying on the ledge and I thought it was the one my grandmother

wanted. So I started to crawl up the rocks. But my grandmother saw the goat that she wanted down below, and she started yelling from below, "The goat is over here."

I didn't hear her; I was busy crawling up the rocks. So my grandmother ran over and got a big rock and threw it at me. It hit me on the hip. It hurt so bad that I couldn't stand up, couldn't do anything. My grandmother got very mad again and started to cuss, started to scream. She got another rock and threw it at me, but she missed. She yelled, "I'm going to kill you and leave you for the wolves. I'm going to kill you and leave you for the crows to poke out your eyes."

I was a mature girl at this time. I was very hurt. I crawled on the other side of the rock. Later, when the pain was not so bad, I crawled up on the ledge again. I saw that my grandmother had caught and butchered the goat.

All of my brothers and sisters had run away from the camp in the meantime. Every time they saw Big Gap Woman coming, they would run into the woods and hide.

We were all afraid of Big Gap Woman, except for my mother's brother. I don't know why he wasn't afraid. She would scold him and he would just ignore her. Because we were always afraid of her, we never got close to her. We always stayed away. My grandmother's sister, Laughing Lady (Asdzáán Anadloohí), was a very kind woman. All of them were nice except Big Gap Woman. She was the only one. Maybe she was just born that way.

In time, Helen married Alton Nakai, one of the middle sons in a family from the neighboring community of Wide Wash. There were already links between her kin group and his: Helen's mother's oldest brother was married to one of Alton Nakai's oldest sisters. The marriage was arranged for the two extremely reluctant young people—Helen believed it was intended as a way to get her away from her abusing grandmother—and the traditional marriage ceremony was held. Helen and Alton moved to Big Gap, where a hogan had been built for them by relatives, and began their lives together.

In the beginning, Helen and Alton lived awkwardly with each other, uncomfortable with the pairing, not even sharing the same hogan. In time, however, Alton began bringing foods to her from the trading post, and they began making tentative overtures of friendliness. Their relationship grew and eventually, as she said, they "got together."

Helen had been frightened of having children; this was one of the reasons she had resisted getting married. Big Gap Woman had told her stories about the difficulties of childbearing and had warned her about getting pregnant.

When Helen finally decided she wanted children, however, she was unable to conceive. Over the dire warnings of her grandmother, Helen eventually consumed a medicinal herb that she was told would stimulate ovulation. Soon after, the first of what were to be 12 children was born. The older women in the community helped with the childbirth, holding her with woven straps in a squatting position over the birthing fleece until the child was born, tending and caring for her during the first few weeks of the infant's life, while she was still weak and while her "insides healed." Helen laughingly said that her mother used to tell the children that they had "come from plants."

With the birth of her children, Helen entered a new phase in her life. During our interviews, Helen spoke with me about childrearing and about how she had learned to be a mother:

> After I had children, I observed that some people were better off than others. They had more sheep, more food, better houses. So I took the good from what I saw and tried to teach it to my children.
>
> Both the boys and the girls were kept at home. They had to stay at home; only fathers did the traveling. The teaching was that if you were to go out to social gatherings, you might encounter bad thinking. You might be pressured by what others were saying. You might get involved in their troubles. Thinking right was to stay at home and be responsible around home.
>
> I don't know how I was taught to be a mother. I was taught to be modest as a girl, as part of my training. But to be a mother, the lecture simply was, "Be a good mother. Be a good provider. Think right."
>
> The teaching was that if you were not a thinking person, the smoke just came out of the chimney. The teaching was that you need to work hard with the sheep so that you never want and so that your children never come back later and say, "I am hungry. You did not teach me how to take care of myself."
>
> I don't know how you learn these things, except by observation and listening you begin to know that some things are good and some things are bad. I just tossed the bad things away and concentrated on the ones that were good. I just chose the right ones, the ones that were of value to me, and I lived accordingly, tried to do my best accordingly.

Helen's children confirmed this view she had of herself. Her son, William Yenaswood, described Helen's mothering as part of a larger discussion of the roles played by both his parents in his upbringing.

Our mother was a sheepherder all her life, and she taught us about sheepherding. She also wove rugs and supported us with that. When people came to visit, she gave them things—mutton, produce, wool.

She was a good mother. She never scolded us, never whipped us. She was our primary teacher. She set the limits. We were not punished. The stress was on sheep, accumulating and taking care of sheep for our own future. For my sisters, they had the sheep to take care of all the time.

Our father was a farmer, and he raised produce. He was responsible for the horses. We also had some cattle during this time. He did not herd sheep much, just now and then. He mostly tended the farm, taking care of the planting, cultivating, and hoeing. He taught us boys about these things, including about fencing and irrigation. He did not go looking for work. There was never any talk of [wage] work outside the family.

We lived very traditionally. Our family's livelihood came from the sheep, the farm, and the rugs my mother wove. The weaving and the shorn wool provided for most of our needs—our clothing and food from the trading post—the things that needed to be purchased.

Education was not stressed by our parents. But my older sister, Pale Lady, went to school, and I also went to school for a short time.

The family practiced traditional religion and participated in healing ceremonies. When I was young, I had a sickness, and I was handicapped by this. My father's brother, *Hataałii Sani* (Old Singer), was a singer of the Beautyway *(Hoozhónee)*. He performed a ceremony for me and I was cured.

When I was growing up, children never went to ceremonials. These days these things are forgotten; children attend ceremonials all the time. My parents thought it was unwise, that it made for "not good thinking" *(doo 'áhojilyáah da)*.

Of the three children I interviewed, Helen's daughter Irene was the youngest. Now a teacher of traditional arts and crafts as well as a fine weaver, Irene's memories echoed and elaborated those of her older brother:

Our parents' work was very different. My mother herded sheep and did the weaving. She mostly herded during the daytime. Our father worked on the farm, from spring until fall, when the produce was all gathered. When I was small, I remember, it was probably hard on my mother to take care of us and the sheep at the same time. Father would put us in the wagon and take us up there, where we played.

We had no store-bought toys. We never went to the store; we were always with the sheep. We made playthings from the rocks at the farm and from the different-colored beans our father grew. The beans we used for sheep and cattle and horses, and we made corrals for them out of the stones. This is how I developed my life plan, I think, from the things that I played with as a child. While I was growing up, I played with clay. Where I work now, I am teaching the students how to make pottery. I think I learned this from playing with clay as a child.

It was the same with the sand paintings. One day, my father's brother, *Nakai Tsoh* (Big Mexican), had a ceremony done for him. The medicine man left the sand painting under the bushes. I picked up these sands, and my sisters and I made some sand paintings while the sheep scattered. Our mother saw the sheep all over the place, and she sent our older brother to investigate. He scolded us and scattered the sand. When I later saw ceremonies done, I learned that they used many different kinds of sand. So when I teach my students at the school how to work with sand, I turn my old toys into reality.

This life I have is from what I observed when I was growing up. Even the weaving, my mother did not teach me. I learned by watching her carding the wool, spinning it, dyeing it, preparing the loom. I copied my mother's handiwork. She never told us how to do things; we just watched and learned from doing, even with the sheep.

Helen Claschee and Alton Nakai remained on the *Tó'ligai* side for many years after they were married. In the traditional manner, Alton Nakai traveled back and forth between his wife's hogan and the hogan of his mother, ensuring that both were properly maintained and had sufficient supplies of food, water, and firewood.

In approximately 1918, however, when Helen was in her early to midthirties, a series of events resulted in a major upheaval in her life. The 1918–19 Spanish influenza epidemic hit the Navajo with immense force, leaving few families intact. Many of Alton Nakai's relatives died at that time, and several children were orphaned. His sense of responsibility for these children and his desire to maintain the family's claims on the lands in his own community of Wide Wash led him to reestablish residency there. At about the same time, Helen's troubles with Big Gap Woman intensified, and she eventually followed her husband.

In talking about this period in her life, Helen was visibly upset. She seemed embarrassed when describing the behavior of her grandmother. She began by telling several stories about her relationship with her grandmother after she had married Alton Nakai. These stories were similar to the one she had told about how her grandmother had thrown rocks at her. She then described the specific events that had led her to uproot her family and separate herself from her kinfolk:

> Even after I had my children, I still took care of my grandmother's sheep and my uncle's sheep as well as my own. Sometimes my grandmother would come and she'd herd the sheep. But when she'd bring them back in the evening, my sheep would be earmarked so that my sheep would now belong to her instead of me.[7]
>
> One day my grandmother came to help. When I cut out my sheep at the end of the day, I only had a few sheep left. In time I expanded my herd again, but then it happened a second time. The last time that my grandmother got the herd and made the earmarks, I was upset and I just came over to the Wide Wash side with my children. And then we stayed.
>
> But they made a big fuss over at Big Gap and they said that I ran away. They said that there was no one left to herd the sheep on the *Tó'ligai* side. After a while, my grandmother sent one of my grandfathers over to me. The message was that I had to come back and take my remaining herd out. He said that there would be police witnesses, from Shiprock, to make sure that I got my own sheep and that it was all legal, proper. So I went back and just took my herd and left the other herd. I took only nine livestock, because all the others were already part of my grandmother's herd, because of the earmarks.
>
> My friends and relatives knew what kind of person my grandmother was. And so they always told me that I was doing things the right way; that I shouldn't be upset about anything. So that's how I brought my herd to the Wide Wash side. After that I lived permanently on the Wide Wash side, but my relatives still came over and visited.[8]

Once settled on the Wide Wash side, Helen's life stabilized again into the established way of life she and Alton Nakai had always shared, with Helen primarily responsible for herding the sheep and for the activities on the inside of the hogan (weaving, childcare, food production) and Alton Nakai primarily responsible for the large livestock (cattle and horses) and for activities on the outside of the hogan (farming, maintaining the corrals and fences, building shelters, trading). The new life, however, included responsibility for the care of additional children, those left orphaned by the epidemic.

Still in the prime of her childbearing years, Helen gave birth to five daughters between 1920 and 1931. Her firstborn children were at the age where they could help with the herding of the rams, but Helen remained responsible for the sheep and was also doing a considerable amount of weaving. Her need for assistance with childcare, cooking, and other responsibilities inside the hogan was met by Alton Nakai's *nálí* (or grandmother on his father's side), *Asdzáán Yazhí* (Little Woman).

Asdzáán Yazhí was related to Alton by clan and was the mother of his father's second wife. She moved in with Alton at the two-room stone hogan he had built at the farm and tended the small children while Helen and her older daughters took care of the sheep. This arrangement lasted well into the early 1930s, when Helen's last-born child had begun to get around on her own. *Asdzáán Yazhí* returned to her own family at that point, dying about two years later.

Unlike the stressful period when she had been under her grandmother's thumb, Helen was now part of a kin group that worked together harmoniously. These interactions shaped her view of the world and became part of what she stressed as important in life. Reflecting on this period in her life, Helen said:

> This family has always been responsible, with people helping one another. People need to work together with the sheep, the cattle, the land, the farm. For if people have sheep, they have land. And if they have land, they have value as people. Land is a symbol, evidence that one is responsible, a thinking human being. The larger the land, the more capable they are. The larger the land, the more independent they are, because then they have the means to do things. It frees them. People need to have this connection to something bigger than them.

Around the same time that Helen's last two children were being born, her eldest living daughter, Pale Lady *(Asdzáán Libahé),* gave birth to Helen's first grandchildren, a daughter and later a son. When Pale Lady unexpectedly died in 1934, following an accident on a horse, her husband left the two children in the care of their maternal grandparents, Helen and Alton. Eventually Helen's granddaughter went to live with another relative, while the infant grandson remained to be raised by his grandmother alongside her own children, including one almost exactly his age.

In an interview with Helen's grandson, Gilbert Todacheenie, he described what it was like growing up with his grandmother:

> My grandmother was my teacher at an early age. She had her own kids whom she looked after and taught, but she always had time for me. She always told us what was what, what we needed to do for the day, and these

kind of things. She told us what we were not to do or things that we should do, and she'd tell us how to go about being good.

We lived in a hogan near *Ts'ah Bilda'yisk'idi* (Sage-Covered Hill), right near that. All of us slept in the same hogan. Three of her daughters were at home most of the time: her oldest daughter, her second youngest, and her youngest. The youngest was about the same age as I. Two daughters attended schools. The two sons who were the oldest were rarely around. They were either working at the farm or working elsewhere. My oldest aunt herded the sheep most of the time, and my grandmother wove rugs.

My grandmother brought me up in the traditional environment. We spoke only the Navajo language, had one religion, ate Navajo food. Every member of the family had chores to perform. The girls' or women's work was cooking, cleaning the hogan, washing the family's clothing, weaving, and so on. Boys' or men's work was hauling and chopping wood, caring for the horses and cattle. Farmwork like planting, irrigation ditch repairs, irrigation, and fence mending was our work, too. Sheepherding was shared by all members. Other shared work was hoeing, harvesting, and lambing.

We had a large flock of sheep. They needed daily tending to keep them from straying and to keep the predators such as coyotes, bears, and bobcats, and sometimes wild dogs, from attacking them. During lambing in spring, we had to keep another predator away, the crows. We began our training by herding rams during the summer and fall. Eventually we graduated to herding larger flocks. I was still herding rams when I was put in school. In my early training, I used to herd the rams during the summer, from June to early November. My grandmother was usually the one who gave instructions as to what to do and what not to do.

In the early 1930s, the federal government's drastic stock reduction program severely upset the established lifestyle and economy of the Navajo people. Particularly hard hit were families who had established large herds and extensive grazing areas. Among those most deeply affected in the community of Wide Wash was the family of Helen Claschee and Alton Nakai, with an estimated herd of at least 600 sheep.

Although stock reduction was ostensibly imposed in a gradual manner, the most significant reductions came in 1940, when grazing permits were established, limiting herds in the area to a maximum of 104 "sheep units."[9] Seemingly overnight, Helen's source of mutton, wool, leather, and trade goods was dramatically slashed, leaving her family quite literally "struck with hunger."

Like other livestock owners in the community, Helen opposed the reductions. She bitterly resented the seemingly arbitrary manner in which stock reduction was imposed by the federal government and was shocked by the wanton slaughter of valued livestock. Along with several other livestock owners in the community, Alton Nakai was jailed for his refusal to cooperate, and Helen was forced not only to reduce their herds sufficiently to obtain his release but also to prove to officials that she had done so. Helen's memories of that period, some 50 years later, were among her most vivid, and they shaped her view of the world. She told me:

> During Collier's time, things were designed to hurt people.[10] The stock reduction and everything else caused people mental anguish. Just as we were getting better off, they attacked our way of life.
>
> Today we have land divisions. We have only a certain part of the land that we can use. We can't move from place to place any longer. If someone doesn't have a grazing permit, they can't even graze their sheep outside; they have to keep them in the corral.
>
> Nowadays, there are few people with sheep. After the sheep were reduced to the minimum, increases were hard to achieve. Now it is very hard to make ends meet.

Throughout the 1940s, 1950s, and 1960s, Helen Claschee and Alton Nakai managed to maintain the traditional way of life they had always led, although they were much more economically constrained due to the limitations on livestock. During this time, Helen assumed responsibility for raising several of her grandchildren, including not only her grandson, Gilbert Todacheenie, but also several granddaughters. This childcaring served a dual purpose, one immediate and often short term, and one future. As Helen explained it:

> Part of the reason for having a large family was so that there would be someone to care for you in your old age. You know that children have different kinds of thoughts; all are different. Out of all of them there may be one who will care for you. Some people have lots of children, but the children do not take care of the parents. And then there are some couples with no children. When they are old, there will be no one to help.
>
> Sometimes grandparents had a grandchild come and live with them. This wasn't a formal adoption. Sometimes this child was kind of left out in a family. Then the grandchild grew up on that side and took care of the grandparents.

In 1965 Alton Nakai and Helen Claschee were approximately 80 years of age. Although Alton Nakai's health was somewhat fragile, the pattern of their life continued as it had throughout their married life. In the summer of that year, however, along the unpaved road that linked Wide Wash to Shiprock, a tragic accident brought that era to a close. In a head-on collision, Alton Nakai was killed and Helen Claschee was severely injured, both legs broken. Both the personal loss and the need for a lengthy recovery period effectively ended that part of Helen's life that was devoted to the sheep.

Helen told me that when her husband died, her life stopped. It must have seemed that way to her, for the life that she had been living until then changed dramatically. No longer able to get around as well as she once had, because of the physical injuries she sustained in the accident, Helen became more and more dependent on her children's support. She moved between the homes of one daughter and another, sometimes living within the same household and sometimes living at least semi-independently. One of Helen's granddaughters told me what it was like having Helen live with their family during this time, describing a frail and unhappy old woman who screamed at her grandchildren and threw rocks at chickens, not unlike the behavior of Helen's own grandmother, Big Gap Woman.

As Helen's health improved, she eventually returned to living a more independent life. She continued to weave, producing a rug for the physician who had cared for her while she was in the hospital recovering from her injuries, but her eyesight and eye-hand coordination were such that the quality of the weaving was not like that of her younger years. Her hearing also began to decline.

When I interviewed Helen in 1984, she was living with her middle daughter for the summer months, having spent the winter months living with one of her other daughters. She and her granddaughter and I spent many weeks that summer traveling back roads, often interviewing for eight and 10 hours at a stretch. It was exhausting work, but exhilarating. One theme that emerged again and again was that of "good thinking" *(yá'át'ééh ntsáakéés)*. In one of our discussions, Helen talked about the kinds of things she had taught her children—and was trying to teach her grandchildren—about living a good life:

> If the young people now, who are getting educated and so on, value the life before them, nothing will go wrong. But if they don't value it, if they are not responsible for their own thinking and their own behavior, then there will not be enough to hold them together. The Navajo Nation will then die out eventually.

Each person must do this themselves. It is an individual struggle. But if there are enough with the same values, it will stay stable. There are certain people who think ahead like that. From my observation, there are some people who are very long range in their thinking, who work for the future. And there are some who are shortsighted, who are just tossed about by whatever comes along.

In my own family, I see the grandkids. Most of them don't look far enough ahead; they only see things at short range. I talk to them about good thinking. I tell them, "Take care of yourself."

To think good is to make a good living, to take care of your kids, to take care of your livestock, to build a good home, to improve your life, to share with others and cooperate. If people live by you, you don't judge them. They do their own living. You're only concerned about your life, how far you're going to go. Just the decisions, the lives, that are close to you. And if it "goes with" your neighbors, then it's all right. You should be harmonious with the people with whom you're interrelating.

Helen became quite sick the following winter, suffering a mild heart attack. Since Wide Wash is over 30 miles from the nearest hospital, she went to live in Shiprock with her youngest daughter, Anna, soon after. When I returned to the area during the summer of 1985, I tried to see her but could never seem to make contact. Late in the summer, however, I observed a revival meeting, somewhere near Teec Nos Pos. At the end of the service, as is customary, worshipers went to the front of the revival tent for the "laying on of hands." I thought I saw Helen Claschee as a participant; with her was a dark-haired woman whom I have since come to know as her youngest daughter. At the time, however, I couldn't believe that it was actually Helen whom I was seeing participate in the "laying on of hands," and I mentally dismissed it as unreal. These feelings, of course, were based on what I thought I knew about her belief system. I learned that I was wrong, for she most certainly was actively participating in the revival and perhaps had been "saved" at that very meeting.

In 1986 I visited Helen several times in the company of her grandson. Helen was still living with her youngest daughter at the time, in a small trailer on the family's land. In mid-October she finally allowed me to take a picture of her, dressing for the occasion in her best clothing and jewelry. By the time late October had rolled around, she was beginning to want to talk again about her life and about the things she had been thinking. During these few short interviews, she talked about her life since I had last interviewed her in 1984; she wanted to fill in the time between then and now. We talked at length about her conversion to Christianity, and we talked some about the old people who were now gone, the *ch'iidii* (ghosts), and about the passing of the old way of life, again with specific reference to the impact of stock reduction.

The next week Helen became very ill and was hospitalized. Helen's grandson and I spent many days visiting her. She continued to want to talk and even to be taped, but we simply visited and I didn't tape. She had developed pneumonia, and her heart was very enlarged. Finally, in early November, she died.

Shortly after her death, the entire family met to discuss the burial arrangements. Some 100 people arrived for one meeting, and the various tasks were divided among them. People contributed time and what money they could. Helen had once described her husband's family as being like ants: "As soon as one saw the view, they all got together," she said. This was what happened here. There were conflicts, however, particularly over the form that the service should take, since some preferred more traditional approaches, others wanted a Christian service—modeled after the religion of the Christian Reformed missionary who had worked in Wide Wash in the 1940s and 1950s—to take precedence, and others felt that since Helen had converted in her last years, more of an evangelical approach was appropriate. Ultimately the situation was resolved by incorporating elements of each.

GRANDMOTHERING IN A MODERN NAVAJO WORLD

Helen Claschee's approach to grandmothering had its roots in a way of life that valued continuity with the past. It was an extension and deepening of the essential role of woman in Navajo society. As such, it emphasized living in close proximity to and maintaining supportive relations with one's relatives; maintaining a lifestyle based on sheep, which was perceived as a more dependable source of livelihood than wage work; living conservatively and nonostentatiously; maintaining one's land use area; and sharing the land, along with other family resources, with one another.

The pace of life has so changed on the Navajo lands, however, that modern grandmothers face an entirely different world from Helen's. Many of today's grandmothers—including three of Helen's own daughters—received at least some education, the result not only of Collier's program to build day schools in local communities but also of the demands of veterans returning to the reservation following World War II for more and better education. Educational resources both on and off reservation were stretched to meet the demand. Beginning soon after the end of the war, the Five-Year Navajo Special Program was established. Situated in various locations off reservation, most of them in the West and Far West, this program provided older Navajo students, even if they had never before attended school, with a combined academic and vocational education. The program was geared toward preparing both men and women for wage work opportunities. On completion of the program, many of the students found work, at least initially, in communities far removed from their Navajo homeland.

A simultaneous growth in both governmental regulations and services—initially at the federal level and later at the tribal, agency, and local levels—opened on-reservation opportunities for some, and many of the people with whom I talked eventually returned to the reservation, taking jobs with the Bureau of Indian Affairs or with the Navajo Tribe. For the women, most of these jobs were as food service personnel in the schools, as nurse's aides or teacher's aides, or as maintenance personnel or housekeepers; that is, in jobs that by 1950s standards were deemed appropriate for women. All of these women have been steadily employed since their return to the reservation, and wage work has either superseded or coexisted with the former emphasis on livestock as the economic underpinning of their lives.

It is not surprising, therefore, that when this new generation of grandmothers talks about "good thinking" and "forward thinking," they have a new focus. The issue of wage work is an important one for these women, and they push their children and grandchildren in the direction of advanced education. They assume that the future is focused in the urban areas, and most of them already live there, close to their jobs, to stores, to entertainment. Their children marry—when they do—in Christian ceremonies or simply begin living together. They have less concern with clan restrictions in terms of marriage, and they assume that young people growing up on the Navajo Reservation today will begin living independent lives soon after they become legal adults at age 18. They worry, however, that there will not be sufficient employment opportunities for their children and grandchildren and are preparing themselves to accept the fact that young people are likely to move away from the reservation in order to "get ahead" in the world.

Now a grandmother herself, Helen's granddaughter, Lilly George, described the personal impact of these changes:

> During our younger days, people helped one another a lot. It was just a general practice they had. In the old days, even if a stranger came to the house, we would feed them and give them coffee. People aren't like that anymore. I think it's the trend. All over it's like that. Families would rather be responsible for their own immediate family these days, not for their relatives. This probably has something to do with the current economic

situation. People still get together for holidays and for special events. But they don't help each other like they used to. Because we have jobs, our relatives think we don't have any needs. That is not true, but that is what people think. No one feels compelled to assist others any longer.

Most people in the younger generation speak English, and they think in the English way. Kids won't spend a night in their grandparents' hogan; they are anxious to get home into the "modern world." You hear people saying that their kids are not listening to them.

Sheep are going out, and we have a lot of land disputes. When someone says, "This land is ours," others say no. Few people are farming anymore. Instead most people look to work for their livelihood. Education helped ensure that I had a good job. I see education as the way for my children as well. But jobs are hard to find on reservation, and they might have to leave to get work.

As Lilly suggests, this new generation of grandmothers struggles with the ongoing tensions between the old values and old ways and the new. Helen's daughter, Louise Nakai, discussed the ways that she and her daughters are addressing these issues in their lives:

When my maternal relatives, the women who came before me, started with the sheep and built their herd, they were thinking ahead. That was good for all concerned. If each of us do this in our own way for the younger generation, that is what is needed. But we must also teach the Navajo ways.

Diné, The People, that is what we are. Prayers are a part of that. My mother and father used prayers in all their life. I remember my mother always praying, putting the ashes in the back of the fire, and praying as she did that. She thanked the Holy People for our good life. We are getting away from all that. People are not taught. They do whatever they like.

Good thinking means teaching our children that we must know one another in the family. We must maintain harmonious relations. We must share with one another. We must be able to depend on one another.

I am already old. I won't achieve as much as my grandchildren will. I have still not reached all of my goals. I did not get much education. Both of my younger daughters stress a good education for their children. My grandchildren are the ones that are going to benefit a lot from the schools. My granddaughter says that she wants to be a doctor. Perhaps that will happen.

Many people are not teaching the Navajo language. My children speak Navajo. My children are teaching their children the Navajo language. They have problems teaching them, but they are learning. My grandchildren know that they are Navajo. That way they won't lose their identity.

SUMMARY AND CONCLUSIONS

As this story of Helen Claschee and her female relatives illustrates, Navajo grandmothers, both traditional and modern, function in a wide variety of roles. They may serve simultaneously as substitute parents, kin keepers, teachers, role models, storytellers, and transmitters of tradition. These roles are acquired quite naturally as women move through the developmental stages of their lives and are associated with their basic position as elderly women in Navajo society.

The grandmother role is shaped, however, by the unique personalities of individual women. The ideal grandmother has a real-life counterpart. Some women, such as *Asdzáán Biké,* assume the role of grandmother with grace and humor, providing those who follow with positive models. Others, like Big Gap Woman, serve primarily as examples of what not to do and how not to behave.

As differences in the teachings of these women have demonstrated, however, the *content* of the grandmothering role is a reflection of economic and social change over time. Although both traditional and modern grandmothers would agree with Helen Claschee's general statement that "to think good is to make a good living, to take care of your kids, to take care of your livestock, to build a good home, to share with others and cooperate," the specifics regarding how one should accomplish these goals would vary. Both traditional and modern grandmothers stress the importance of maintaining close family ties, for example. While traditional grandmothers sought to strengthen those bonds through an emphasis on the land and the sheep, modern grandmothers emphasize the need for a good education and steady employment, recognizing that the economic underpinning provided by the traditional way of life is an option for only a few because of a rapidly expanding population, a limited land base, and few jobs available on reservation. Although they know that the economic necessity of obtaining stable wage work is likely to result in either temporary or long-term separation of members of the kin group, modern grandmothers take a pragmatic approach in advising the young. In effect, they have been forced to adjust the perimeter of one set of goals in order to make room for another.

The roles played by grandmothers in Navajo society remain vital ones. Although the concept of the "ideal" grandmother originates in Navajo systems of belief, the life stories of real Navajo grandmothers demonstrate that reality is a merging of the ideal, the unique, and the pragmatic.

NOTES

1. The word *shimá* (my mother) is commonly used as a term of respect for *any* woman above one's own age. The more specific terms for grandmother include *masání* (old mother)—which refers specifically to one's maternal grandmother; that is, one's mother's mother, or one's mother's mother's sister—and *nálí,* which refers to one's paternal grandparent, male or female, but is also used to mean one's grandchild through the father's line. In this matrilineal system, where families also live matrilocally, a Navajo child is most likely to come into regular contact with his or her maternal grandparent. I will therefore focus on those relationships. I will also use the term *masání* throughout the chapter as a way to distinguish the role of grandmother from that of mother.

2. Literally, *kéyah* means "beneath one's feet."

3. Pseudonyms are used throughout this paper to protect as well as possible the identities of both the women and the community.

4. Since elderly Navajos rely on memories of events to establish their age, the exact date of Helen Claschee's birth is difficult to determine. Census records assign her approximate date of birth at 1889. However, based on the ages of her living children and on the relative ages of the four children no longer living, who preceded them, her first children were born just after the turn of the century. Since that would make her only 11 at the time, the 1889 date seems unreasonable. The earlier date reflects other statements made by Helen about her early years. My guess is that the actual date is somewhere in between, but closer to 1880 than to 1889.

5. "Crosscut" is a local way of referring to roads that are short routes between places. In this case, the term refers to an unpaved road that originally was just a trail and now serves as the link between the communities of Red Valley and Sanostee (Wide Wash and *Tó'ligai*).

6. This seems to be a story that Helen had heard rather than one she actually observed.

7. As a means of identification, the ears of the sheep are cut in a distinctive pattern for each owner. The new earmarks were also, of course, a not so subtle form of stealing. Given the importance of these animals to Helen, one can begin to understand how she must have felt.

8. This is a reference to the loss of *ké* Helen experienced when she moved away from her clan relatives. *K'é* is one of those key terms in Navajo with layers and layers of meaning. Essentially, it implies kinship and a sense of belonging. *K'é* is translated literally as "relatives" but the term implies much more than what is meant by relatives in English. It implies bonding, shared relationships, etc. One of the worst insults to Navajos is to tell them they act as if they had no relatives. Loss of *k'é* is a terrible blow to a family, tearing them apart, causing them to quarrel and fight among themselves, and leaving them defenseless.

9. Sheep units were a measure of the number of differing kinds of livestock one could own. One horse was the equivalent of five sheep, one cow was the equivalent of four sheep, and one goat was the equivalent of one sheep. The number of sheep units allowed per owner within a given district varied by population density and range conditions, with a high of 280

in districts 3 and 5 (Tuba City agency) and a low of 61 in district 14 (Fort Defiance agency). In district 12 of the Northern Navajo (Shiprock) agency, the district in which Wide Wash was a part, 104 sheep units were allowed per permit.

10. The only area that Helen regarded as positive during Collier's era was with respect to the farm. She said, "Collier and the BIA were promoting farm development, and the farm at Wide Wash was very productive during this period. Apricots were planted; also cherries, apples, wheat, corn, squash, watermelon, potatoes, carrots."

GIVE-AND-TAKE

Navajo Grandmothers and the Role of Craftswomen

◆

ANN LANE HEDLUND

Generally, the grandparent-grandchild alliance was described as the strongest bond in Navajo culture [apart from that of mother-child]; this was a warm association in which perpetuation of traditional teaching could be effected (Shomaker 1989:3).

   The Navajo have always been matrilineal, with women holding a position of prestige in Navajo culture. . . . Weaving helps ensure the continuation of this position for women (Roessel 1983:595).

INTRODUCTION

Many Navajo grandmothers contribute to household productivity and the economic welfare of their families through their involvement in traditional craft activities such as weaving. Also, through these craft practices and re- lated activities, grandmothers maintain and share broader cultural values, such as those of hard work, patience, humility, and traditional knowledge, with younger generations. In return, as both craftworkers and elders, these grand- mothers are frequently accorded status and recognition because of their spe- cialized knowledge and associated skills. Their craft activities reinforce social and economic relationships that might not otherwise be maintained.

   That give-and-take—the contributions made and the benefits received—by weaving grandmothers in contemporary Navajo society is discussed in this chapter. Although the patterns described here are frequently mentioned in informal ways (i.e., embedded in life histories, indirectly referred to in museum catalogs, and peripherally noted in other ethnographies), these patterns are a previously unexamined part of the larger picture of women's roles in Navajo society. Not all Navajo grandmothers are productive craftswomen, but for those who are, the craftwork provides meaning to their lives in significant ways. The experiences of those who weave—who number in the thousands if not tens of thousands on the Navajo Reservation today (Hedlund 1992:21, 23n.)—are emphasized in this study.

After a brief introduction to the roles of grandmothers in Navajo society and to the historical position of weaving among the Navajo, this chapter explores the contributory, advisory, and residual roles that weaving grandmothers may play within their households, communities, and tribe. In addition to positive aspects, role conflicts and strains for weaving grandmothers in the 1970s and 1980s are also briefly examined. For the most part, the unit of analysis for this study is the household and extended family residential group (often termed a "camp," although it is far from temporary); certain comments are also germane at the individual, community ("chapter"), and tribal levels.[1]

METHODOLOGY

This chapter is based on ethnographic field research, principally through participant observation, on the Navajo Reservation during the summers of 1978–82, 1985, and 1988, with periodic fieldwork at other times of the years, and on continuing visits with many individuals belonging to a number of Navajo extended families, at their homes and mine, over the past 12 years. The original study (Hedlund 1983) was based on data for 181 weavers in one central reservation community plus survey data from a number of other areas; since then, ethnographic information on many other weavers across the reservation has been compiled.[2] Although grandmothers were not an original focus of my research, it became clear to me during broader investigations that the behavior and values associated with weaving embody much of what grandmothers represent in Navajo society. It also became apparent that weaving plays a recognizable role in producing and maintaining a positive status for older women and helps provide a pathway to successful aging.[3] Descriptions of people and their actions have been excerpted and/or adapted from my field notes from 1978 through 1990 (Hedlund 1978–1990). Pseudonyms for individuals have been used throughout.

GRANDMOTHERS IN NAVAJO SOCIETY

Consanguineal (biological) concepts of kinship, affinal relationships (through marriage), and other behavioral parameters come into play when defining "grandmother" from the Navajo perspective. In this matrilineal society, in which descent is reckoned predominantly through the mother's line and one belongs to one's mother's clan (Aberle 1961), the mother's mother is called *shimá sání* (literally, "my old mother" or "my aged mother"), glossed in English as "my grandmother."[4] Whether or not they have biological children and grandchildren of their own, this maternal grandmother's sisters and the maternal grandfather's sisters are also called *shimá sání* and may play grandmotherly roles (as described below) within the family.[5] Other older female relatives belonging to the maternal grandmother's clan may be referred to as *shimá sání* as well. All may be considered "grandmothers" in a traditional Navajo way. In English, children often refer to their mother's mother as "my *real* grandmother" in order to distinguish her from other *shimá sání* and from the father's mother.

Father's mothers (and father's fathers) are most often referred to by the fully reciprocal term, *shinálí* (the father's parents use this term for their son's children and they in turn use it for their paternal grandparents). When speaking in English today, Navajo children will refer most often to their father's mother (or father's father) as "my *nálí*" rather than as "my grandmother." Bilingual paternal grandmothers will often switch between "my grandchild" and *"shinálí,"* depending on the context of discussion (i.e., when an English-speaking listener is present, the English form is more likely to be used, whereas with a bilingual or Navajo-speaking person, *shinálí,* the more specific referent, is more often used). Both maternal and paternal grandparents may refer to their grandchildren in English simply as "my grands."

The most significant difference between Navajo maternal and paternal grandmothers is the fact that the maternal grandmother and grandchild share the same clan and therefore a lineal descent, whereas the clans of the paternal grandmother and her grandchildren must, in this society with exogamous clan membership, almost always be different. Although a paternally linked relationship is acknowledged (one is said to be "born for" or "born into" one's father's clan), descent is not considered lineal (Witherspoon 1975:42).[6]

Considerable emphasis is placed by Navajos on the behavioral correlates of kin status that is, one must *behave* like a family member in order to be considered a proper relative. Witherspoon (1975:21) observes:

For those who follow American and European cultural beliefs, according to which "real" or "true" kinship is limited to those human beings who are blood relatives, it must be pointed out that Navajo define kinship in terms of action or behavior, not in terms of substance. . . . Kinship is discussed in terms of the acts of giving birth and sharing sustenance.

Thus "grandmothers" may be understood as those who behave as grandmothers should, whether or not they actually have biological grandchildren of their own or whether they are associated with the maternal or paternal side of the family.

The behavioral models for both *shimá sání* and *shinálí* are closely related since either may have a significant impact on the socialization of their "grandchildren," providing affection, informal discipline, food and other forms of subsistence, financial support, and even an alternate home for the children of their male and female children.[7]

The considerable range of actual relationships possible between maternal or paternal grandparents, their grandchildren, and other relatives should be emphasized. In fact, variations in individual roles and family relationships within each of these groups, although empirically untested, may indeed be greater than any between-group differences.[8] Extended households may be matrilocal or patrilocal, or residence may alternate between the two, affecting the amount of time that children spend with their grandparents. Neolocal residence, in which a nuclear or single-parent family lives apart from either set of grandparents, is increasingly common. Also, because household composition does not remain static through life, grandmothers may have varied contacts with and many different roles within their families through time.[9] Because of these varied patterns, grandmothers referred to here may belong to either the maternal or the paternal side of a family as long as they conform to the Navajo *behavioral* standards for "grandmother" status. What, then, are these ideal characteristics?

The basis for all forms of Navajo kinship, including grandmothers, is *ké*, meaning "kindness, love, cooperation, thoughtfulness, friendliness, and peacefulness" (Witherspoon 1983:524). Both parents and grandparents are expected to provide affection, discipline, instruction, and economic assistance to their children. Leighton and Kluckhohn, in the classic publication *Children of the People* (1947:102–3), note that the relationship of grandparents with their grandchildren ideally is very warm, loving, solicitous, and indulgent.

Grandmothers' roles, representing a conservative and family-oriented perspective, form the baseline for the most traditional aspects of women's roles.

Grandmothers' roles are closely linked to the behavioral expectations for all women in Navajo society regardless of age or particular status. Frisbie (1982:12) underlines several persistent standards of ideal behavior for traditional women: "dignity, strength, energy, self-sufficiency, stability, and supremacy in the hogan and the immediate kin world." From an extensive survey of ethnographies and life histories, she summarizes the "skills, behavioral traits, and personality characteristics that were valued for women in traditional times":

> Women were to be industrious, healthy, supple, strong and energetic, and good runners. Instead of being lazy, they were to be willing to work hard all their lives, in any kind of weather, for their husbands, children, and their property. They were to get married; if you lived without a man "you will be as though without arms and legs" (Dyk and Dyk 1980:480). They were to possess pleasant, good natured, friendly, wise, and generous dispositions, and they were not to be mean, quarrelsome, sassy, or physically abusive. They were to look beautiful, not ugly; thin, not real heavy or skinny; and at the time of marriage, they were to be young and virginal. They were to have patience and were not to get jealous; while being faithful themselves, they were not to demand absolute constancy from a man. They were not to run around, drink, gamble, gossip or cause trouble; rather, they were to stay home, caring for children, relatives, and visitors. They were to be honest, moral, and modest and restrained in front of men and strangers; they were to bring honor to their family, thus carving out a respected place in the community (pp. 19–20).

Traditional Navajo women are active in both domestic and wider community spheres. Domestic responsibilities, shared to varying degrees with male members of the family, include childbirth and childrearing, housekeeping, food preparation, farming, hauling supplies, animal husbandry, arts and crafts production, and involvement in ritual knowledge and performances. The documentary record for activities outside the home is not as complete, but traditional women appear to have played limited but occasionally significant roles in military and political exploits as well as in community-based social and religious events and in regional trading (Frisbie 1982).

Many of the Navajo expectations about grandmothering may be understood through the pervasive and somewhat ironic balance maintained between communal responsibility and individual autonomy. This dualism, which Witherspoon (1983:533) has termed complementary rather than contradictory, has received much discussion in the literature (Aberle 1961, 1963; Witherspoon

1975, 1983:533–35; Lamphere 1977). Grandmothers in particular demonstrate
this duality as figures of considerable experience and therefore authority while
simultaneously being somewhat removed from the nuclear family arena.

With the maturing of their own children and the decline of their parents, a
subtle and implicit increase in responsibility—"for herself, for her younger kin
and affines, for the care of her dependent parents and for the maintenance of
society"—marks those with grandmother status (Counts 1985:50). This is an
extension of the mother's roles rather than a radical departure from the ways
of earlier life. Ideal behavioral attributes of the grandmother as head of an
extended family or household include participation in the socialization of
children through discipline and instruction (often in the form of example
setting), making decisions on the scheduling and conduct of extended family
activities—trips, major expenditures, livestock events, home improvements,
religious ceremonies—and contributing to the family's economic well-being
(often through sheepholding but also with grazing permits, pension and government assistance checks, and craft sales).

Lamphere notes:

The primary kin (parents and married children) who live within shouting
distance and who are in daily cooperation, especially for livestock and
agricultural activities, and who jointly make use of the same area of land,
form a regular pattern of communication and cooperative effort. Specifi-
able patterns of authority indicate that the older couple in an extended
family residence group are the main requesters who organize herding and
cultivating activities (1977:85).

In general, the older couple is *t'áá bee bóholníih* (he is [they are] the
boss, or it's up to him [them] to decide) for most situations and is in the
position of making requests for aid of their children and spouses, especially in matters concerning livestock, fields, and transportation. The
younger couples are most often in the position of giving aid or asking for
loans or help with a ceremony (1977:84).

On the other hand, grandmothers may enjoy considerable autonomy from
the day-to-day responsibilities of childcare and household maintenance. The
concept of *t'áá bee bóholníih*—"it's up to him or her"—may be turned around
here to mean that each individual has a right to decide for himself, that no one
should have authority over another person. Grandmothers may actually relinquish what authority they once had in favor of a more distant and removed
presence in the household.

Navajo weaving itself provides opportunities for grandmothers to maintain a balance between authority and autonomy in the extended family and establishes a platform from which to participate in the household on several levels (contributory, advisory, residual) while maintaining personal independence. The responsibilities and freedoms acquired with the position of grandmother appear to be reflected through the weaving enterprise. Indeed, although not universally practiced, weaving appears to embody some of the key aspects of being a Navajo grandmother.

WEAVING AMONG THE NAVAJO

Estimates run anywhere from 12,000 (Sunset 1987:106) to 28,000 (Roessel 1983:596) adult weavers on the Navajo Reservation in the early 1980s. Although no reliable statistics are available, informal surveys and one community study have shown that a significant number of these weavers—at least half—are over 45 years of age, with many in their late fifties and sixties (Hedlund 1983:317, table 12.3). In fact, an overriding concern for traders and collectors during much of the twentieth century was that *only* older women were weaving and that with their eventual decline no one would carry on the tradition.

In contrast to this mid-twentieth-century emphasis on middle-aged and older weavers, a growing number of younger women have become interested in the craft since the 1970s. Although still clearly in the minority, these are women who have young families and who want to work at home but still earn income or who recognize weaving as a part of Navajo culture and heritage that they would like to maintain. A few have discovered that their artistic efforts may be highly rewarding both personally and financially. Skipping a generation, many of these women in their twenties and thirties now look to their grandmothers rather than their mothers for guidance in the craft.

For at least the past three centuries, Navajo weavers of the American Southwest have produced cloth by hand on their upright looms. Tools and basic techniques were initially borrowed from neighboring Pueblo peoples, probably sometime during the seventeenth century. Traditionally women's work, weaving was accomplished at home, integrated into the daily round of domestic activities. Little evidence survives concerning individual weavers' lives prior to the twentieth century, but the historical framework for the craft is well known. Well into the nineteenth century, the weaving of wool blankets and garments was maintained both for domestic use and for regional and intertribal trade. By the third quarter of that century, however, dramatic changes began taking place within the craft as Navajos faced the growing economic, social, and political upheaval of U.S. western expansion. Weavers no longer sold to native clientele;

the production of blankets and garments was rapidly replaced by the making of rugs and other decorative items geared to a commercial Anglo market. Styles and materials changed in response to the outside market's tastes (Wheat 1977, 1981; Kent 1985).

Today women weavers have maintained their dominance in production that still takes place at home. Female kin networks provide continuity in passing weaving skills on to the next generation, although educational programs outside the home are an additional source for learning to weave. Some of these craftswomen receive sizable incomes from their work, and these funds have a significant impact on individual family budgets; others are small-scale operators whose weaving contributes relatively small amounts to the household till. Very few weavers work without any monetary return for their rugs.

Like their predecessors, who borrowed Pueblo and Spanish styles and materials, weavers remain responsive to outside trends, from the selection of color schemes, design motifs, and materials to the ways woven goods are marketed and distributed. Sales strategies, formerly limited to barter and credit transactions with local trading posts, have been augmented with cash sales to craft stores, galleries, and museums. Since the 1960s boom in native crafts, weavers have enjoyed increased attention from national and international markets, although most still find it difficult to earn sufficient income from the craft alone.

Navajo weavers working in the traditional idiom are naturally associated with traditional cultural values and activities.[10] Weaving is associated with stability, self-sufficiency, and the "old ways" of subsistence, even as it is a sign of outward communication with a foreign market. Families and entire communities show pride in having members who weave, despite the fact that this sort of pride is not a conspicuously indigenous or traditional value itself.

Yet in recent decades, opportunities for varied self-expression and innovation on the traditional base have grown out of the broad spectrum of lifestyles and alternative role models available to people on the reservation. Trends have included the development of new rug styles, the incorporation of new materials, the discovery of new marketing outlets, and, most importantly, the expansion of weaving beyond a household subsistence enterprise into a recognized, albeit incipient profession. These trends have been reinforced by the arts and crafts market, always seeking elements of tradition coupled with innovation. The range of weaving practices has diversified, with the women taking a variety of approaches, from lucrative profession to barely bread-and-butter production and from highly artful enterprise to homely hobby (Hedlund 1983).

Navajo weavers contribute to traditional social and economic systems as well as interacting with outside markets. Although no longer uniformly practiced by all, weaving is still acknowledged at individual, household, community, and tribal levels as an important and useful, but not requisite, activity for women. Some girls are encouraged to learn how to weave; some women are positively sanctioned when they do. Many who do not actively practice the craft nevertheless associate it with the ideal Navajo woman's identity (Roessel 1981). I next examine whether grandmothers who are weavers make certain contributions and receive other benefits especially because of their combined status as grandmothers and weavers.

NAVAJO GRANDMOTHERS AS CRAFTSWOMEN

Grandmothers who weave have a variety of options in performing their craft, depending on their individual life circumstances, including the socioeconomics of their household, their family configuration, their health, and, of course, personal inclinations. Weaving may continue much as it did earlier when a woman's children were growing up, or it may increase or decrease. Increased production can be associated with new freedoms from raising a family, whereas reduced production may be related to physical restrictions or to activities given higher priority due to other roles of the grandmother (for instance, arranging and presiding over religious ceremonies or traveling to visit relatives).

From a study of Mesoamerican peasant communities, Press and McKool (1972, as cited in Fry 1980:4) suggest that four "prestige-generating" components may be responsible for the statuses associated with aging and may have universal validity:

(1) *Advisory:* as manifested in seeking out and obtaining advice from older people as well as the degree to which it is heeded;
(2) *Contributory:* as apparent in older people participating in and contributing to social activities;
(3) *Control:* as seen in the influence an older individual exerts over others through a monopoly over resources and supernatural sanctions;
(4) *Residual:* as evidenced in the retention of prestige through association with former statuses and competencies.

The recorded activities of Navajo grandmothers in my research range from direct craft contributions, to cooperative efforts, to teaching and serving as role models and culture bearers, to indirect support through household administration and childcare. Modifying Press and McKool's categories in accord with basic Navajo cultural propensities, I suggest that these activities correspond with three of the basic prestige-generating modes, organized here by descending degrees of direct participation:[11]

> (1) *Contributory:* direct participation and collaboration in craft production and specific contribution to the family's social and economic life;
> (2) *Advisory:* instructional and cooperative efforts in which grandmothers share their expertise in craft technology and cultural lore;
> (3) *Residual:* knowledge of craft technology, aesthetics, and lore reflecting a set of larger cultural values in which the grandmother provides a role model for cultural competence.

These approaches are detailed below and illustrated with examples from fieldwork on the Navajo Reservation.

Contributory. Weaving provides distinct opportunities for direct and valued contributions to the social and economic welfare of the extended family. The roles associated with grandmotherly status often encourage craft activities, although they are moderated by each woman's physical capabilities. For grandmothers who are still strong and active, weaving may remain the same as or increase from earlier periods of life and may operate in concert with other contributory activities. It may also become a collaborative activity between grandmother and grandchildren, contributing to socialization processes, household cohesion, and the family economy.

Showing continuity with the past, grandmothers may maintain their earlier weaving practices with little change from before. Weaving is viewed as integral to the traditional roles of a Navajo woman. No dramatic change may take place when a woman gains status as grandmother, because grandmothering can be viewed as an extension of being a mother. Weaving that was conducted while performing myriad household duties and participating in other family activities may simply continue as a natural part of a woman's daily routine. Grandmothering may have little impact on weaving either because the grandmother has entered the role gradually through relationships with her sister's children's children and others who are, in the Navajo way, also considered as grandchildren or because the grandmother is living at some distance from her children and has had little exposure to the extended family either before or after becoming a grandmother.

> Corinne, in her late forties, has woven since she was a little girl. She married when still in her teens and began having children right away. Now several of her adult daughters and one son have children about the same age as her own youngest child. As grandmother and mother, she

*Elsie Jim Wilson and grandchildren, Navajo Nation, Arizona. Photograph by
Ann Lane Hedlund, 1981.*

weaves surrounded by small children who are indistinguishable (to an
outsider) as her children or grandchildren. Several of her older daughters
often have jobs outside the home, but because she weaves on a full-time
basis, they all share household maintenance activities (cooking, cleaning,
childcare, sheep and goat tending, and so forth), balanced with their
respective jobs. If she must concentrate on a big project, her older daughters care for her children as well as their own. The sale of Corinne's rugs
provides her major source of cash income and pays for almost all of her
own household expenses, including a recent remodeling of her home and
a pickup truck and gasoline.

Grandmothers who are still vital may become more proficient than ever.
Once the family has grown up, more time may be available to concentrate on
one's own creative work and its marketing. The decrease in intense family

obligations plus the cumulative experience and maturation of a craftsperson allows some grandmothers to weave whenever and however they please. Often this leads to more lucrative production and greater contributions to household finances.

Geraldine's weaving fairly exploded after her only child grew up and started raising a family of his own. For the first time she had the time to spend planning and thinking about her work, she had some capital to expend on partially processed raw materials, and, most of all, she had the quiet to concentrate on perfecting her weaving technique. Her brother built her a weaving shed, separate from the house, where no one could disturb her looms, tools, and yarns. When her young grandchildren come to visit from their off-reservation home, she protectively locks up the shed and returns to it only after they leave.

Because many restrictions on a woman's social relationships beyond the family are removed as she grows older (Brown 1985:7), grandmothers gain freedom of movement that younger women do not enjoy. Navajos commonly tease about older women who are "travelers—always going places." Whether visiting grandchildren away at school, relatives across the reservation, or simply a trading post never visited before, they can take advantage of new opportunities both to see different rug styles and to market their own goods.

"Retirement" is the joke for Marie, a young grandmother in her fifties, whose family says she is more active now than when the kids were growing up. In addition to weaving at home, she also teaches workshops and at several schools and does museum/gallery demonstrations that take her out of state regularly. In her travels she has gathered new dyes and different commercial yarns to try. She has also found new outlets in which to sell her work.

More often than not, weavers receive cash for their work today, although credit and trade are still employed in some posts and rug rooms. Prices received for a rug generally depend on the relative technical quality of the weaving and the visual appeal of the design and may range from $10 to $200 per square foot. It is entirely up to the weaver how her earnings should be spent, but money derived from rug sales usually provides direct support for the craftwoman's household and residential group—groceries, clothing, transportation, household supplies, livestock needs, and so forth.

At fifty-five, Sarah is a relatively young grandmother, with six sons, one daughter, and four grandchildren. All but one son who is away at college live in her residence unit. Because she takes a "professional" approach to weaving, most household work is delegated to her daughter and daughters-in-law in residence while her weaving takes precedence for her. In fact, she has worked forty hours per week as a weaving demonstrator outside of the home for years. Several years ago she "retired" and gave up her hourly wage from the Park Service job so that she could catch up on her private orders at home. She is still healthy and active, able to continue a full day's work at her loom. Her income from commissioned rugs is quite high because of her reputation for fine quality of work. Because of weaving, her frame house is more elaborately furnished than most in the community, complete with a gas-operated refrigerator.

Although grandmothers are eventually free from raising their own children, they often serve as caretakers for their grandchildren while their daughters work outside the home. In rural areas where daycare means a cooperative family enterprise, grandmothers who weave are ideal candidates for "childcare specialists." Craftwork coupled with childcare is an ideal combination, both taking place at home, with flexible scheduling.

Wilma spends a great deal of her time at her loom. So do her out-of-school grandchildren, whose divorced mother commutes to work and leaves them with Grandma each day. This provides Wilma with doubly useful roles.

For a period of several months during one year Marie moved to her married son's modern frame house in town. She left her own house in the hands of several older daughters and their children. This move served a variety of purposes—she could set up a large loom with a special rug and not be concerned that her work would get soiled from her own dirt floor hogan, she could weave during the evening with the electric lights, and she could stay warm with the central heating instead of constantly tending her woodstove. In exchange, she watched her son's two smaller children, along with her own baby daughter, while the son and his wife were at work.

Grandmothers may collaborate on rugs with their grandchildren and other family members. Roles within Navajo craft production are not as rigidly defined as sometimes portrayed in the literature (the one woman/one sheep/one rug approach), and considerable latitude exists in role specialization. Many rugs are woven as collective enterprises rather than exclusive creations. One woman may take charge of the planning and may advise on the execution of a weaving project, with several relatives contributing to the spinning, dyeing, weaving, and finishing of a rug. It is natural that a grandmother, with experience and specialized knowledge, participate in such collaborations or provide auxiliary help.[12] The presence of an accomplished artisan can be influential in sustaining the high quality and monetary value of the rugs produced. Later I will describe how the name of a well-known grandmother may be used to increase the value of a rug without her direct involvement in its creation.

> As many as six or seven weavers can be found working at their respective looms under the shady ramada built in Barbara's family camp. Her daughter and granddaughter weave side by side, with her own loom a short distance away. Across the way two of her nieces (also called "daughters") work on their rugs on opposite sides of the same loom. One of her own sisters and, sometimes, another daughter also weave here. Smaller children and several puppies play nearby. The weavers take unofficial turns watching the children, while Barbara and her sister, both grandmothers, supervise the younger women's weaving and troubleshoot problems on any of the looms.

Some grandmothers contribute to the group effort by spinning yarn and doing other simple yet essential tasks (carding, skeining or winding yarn, stirring dye pots, and so forth), allowing others to excel in the more demanding activities such as designing and executing complex patterns. When younger women are employed outside the home or are going to school and simultaneously maintaining weaving projects, help from grandmothers in this way can be invaluable.

> Irene was once a very proficient weaver. Born in 1924 and rather frail now, she only weaves a small and very ordinary rug once in a while. She now belongs to a fairly large group of "occasional" weavers who do not sustain the craft over long periods. It is hard on her eyes and painful for her arthritic limbs. She does, however, supply several younger weavers with her own handspun yarn. This she does while herding sheep or while supervising her son as he cares for her cornfields. None of her own daughters weave, but Irene's role as spinner is important to other clan relatives in the community even if her own weaving has diminished. With three sons, four daughters, 19 grandchildren, and several great-

"grands," the income she derives from spinning (she is generally paid by the skein) supplements the subsistence earned from both her flocks and fields and from welfare funds. It thus provides a modicum of independence from her offspring, such that she still maintains two residences, one within the family camp and the other near her cornfields.

Sometimes weaving assistance becomes reciprocal between generations:

Rita's daughter, Ellen, first began weaving as an adult in the mid-1970s under her mother's tutelage. The mother set up the loom and at the very end undertook the difficult process of inserting the very last threads. In the intervening years Rita has lost some of her strength, and it is Ellen who now sets up their looms and who puts in the finishing threads while her mother weaves the middle portion. Mother and daughter share the proceeds from their jointly woven rugs in proportion to their contributions to the work.

Beyond basic maintenance or enhancement of rug production, grandmothers also may share responsibility for selling rugs. A grandmother may accompany her granddaughter to a trading post or other rug dealer and may enter into negotiations for a good price (although it is always acknowledged that the actual rug maker has final say on any decision to sell). Another grandmother may need assistance from a grandchild in selling a rug, often in the form of transportation or translation services.

Continued craft production is only possible as long as a woman's health is good and her back, hands, and eyes remain relatively strong. Even on an occasional basis, weaving requires physical activity that many older grandmothers cannot sustain, and those who are contributory decline in numbers as age increases. Extant weaving quality and local market tolerance for flaws in older women's work varies considerably, however. Some traders express a special fondness for the "grandma rugs," as Hubbell Trading Post's manager, Bill Malone, dubs them. Household contributions in this case may be viewed as minimal self-maintenance; that is, as at least enough for the grandmother to avoid being an overburdening financial or emotional drain on the rest of the family.

Over 75 years old and with failing eyesight, Shirley continues to weave fair-looking rugs that are still marketable. Her products are not as fine as they once were and she has slowed down considerably, but she is able to devote much more time to her craft now than when she was actively raising the family. In fact, weaving is one of the few activities she pursues these days, as she rarely leaves her residence unit. Weaving is her sole source of earned income, which is supplemented by government subsidies. Her husband died some years ago, and although she sleeps and weaves in her own hogan, usually one of her grandchildren comes to lead her to one of her two daughters' nearby houses for meals.

Even when the quality of a woman's rugs has decreased considerably, weaving may sustain her autonomy and thereby contribute to her family's well-being by keeping the aging relative happily occupied and out of harm's way.

Although over 70 and restricted with severe arthritis, Joanna has two homes—a winter home with electricity and a summer cabin in the cool mountains. She has always divided the year between them, moving the family and a few possessions—especially her weaving tools—back and forth seasonally. Now her children are grown and married, with children, jobs, and lives of their own; some live in nearby towns while others have moved out of state. Because her husband is gone and she is getting frail, her children take turns visiting and doing household chores and general maintenance for her. Her grandchildren visit but only occasionally because they go to school and have other preoccupations. Living alone, Joanna spends most of her time seated at her loom, her days punctuated by occasional visits from family members and a few remaining friends.

Advisory. Many grandmothers have considerable specialized knowledge of and experience with weaving. They teach and provide advice to both beginning and more accomplished weavers. These instructional and cooperative efforts in which grandmothers share their expertise in craft technology and in cultural lore represent a more subtle form of involvement and status gain than the contributory mechanisms just discussed. The grandmother may assume an advisory role when she is no longer physically able to sustain an active production schedule, but she is just as likely to fulfill such a role while she is still active as an extension of a sharing and role-modeling pattern set earlier in life. Advisory capacities are intermediate between and may be maintained simultaneously with contributory and residual capacities.

Because grandmothers are expert weavers and because they are available while sitting at their looms, teaching others to weave often falls to them. Many young weavers credit their grandmothers as much as their mothers with getting them started. Some have memories of going to "Grandma's sheep camp in the summer" and learning to weave there. Others remember their grandmothers coming to their home or living in their common residential unit and allowing the young girls to watch them as they wove. A number of mothers have encouraged their daughters to seek help from their more experienced grandmothers rather than from themselves.

Jenelle's mother, Jean, is a good weaver, but Jean admits that her own mother is even better—more experienced, with a wider range of styles and techniques. Jean asked Jenelle's grandmother to set up a first loom for the granddaughter and arranged for Jenelle to spend the summer with her grandmother at sheep camp.

Grandmothers or grandparents who live alone often have grandchildren come and live with them. Sometimes this occurs on a temporary basis, for instance, during the summer, when school is out, but at other times informal fosterage, or more formal adoption, occurs, in which the grandmother (or grandparents) and grandchild form a more permanent nuclear family. Shomaker (1989, 1990) has recently documented fosterage practices in three Navajo communities and observes that while earlier reports mention children who were given to grandparents to take care of chores and give aid as their elders grew older and more frail, today grandparents more commonly become foster parents to benefit the child, not themselves. Reasons for fosterage range from incompetent parenting to economic hardships. More often than not, it is a daughter rather than the grandchild who is available to help aging grandparents after the foster children (biological grandchildren) have been raised. The cultural benefits accruing from the grandparent-grandchild relationship include most notably "the validation of Navajo values and grooming of intergenerational relationships" (Shomaker 1990:28).

Sally grew up with her grandmother, while the other kids in her family were raised by her mother. She says that they had too many kids to be all together at home. At her grandparent's, there was always something to eat. Her grandmother wove big rugs very well. Sally also says that she learned everything from her grandmother by watching and imitating. Her grandmother never "taught," that is, lectured, her directly. Now Sally can make twills, two faced, and belt weaves as well as regular tapestry weaves, just as her grandmother could.

Mary's son spent as much time with his grandmother as he could during the summer. It was from her, one year when he was about eight, that he borrowed some yarns and learned to weave a small mat. His grandmother said that even though his own mother ignored his interest, she herself encouraged him. She is proud of his accomplishments, even though (or perhaps because?) it is uncommon for a Navajo man to weave.

The Navajo way of teaching is through demonstration—showing, not through lecturing, providing lessons, and making rules. Thus grandmothers often remain detached from any authoritarian or controlling position while still holding a certain amount of responsibility for weaving-socialization processes, just as they do in the other Navajo realms of childrearing and socialization (Leighton and Kluckhohn 1947).

Carol's grandmother showed her how to weave when she was a little girl. "I just sat there and watched her," she says, "Later, she helped me make a little loom and I just put the yarns into it, like she did. She wouldn't talk to me about the ways that it should be done—just show me. And then she would let me do it myself."

Not all grandmothers, of course, are effective teachers, nor are their pupils always successful learners. Young girls, used to the didactics of the modern school system, occasionally object that their grandmothers "don't know how to teach" properly and are often abrupt and unhelpful. They are, it is complained, "too old-fashioned."

Donna called her grandmother "mean" and said that she would not teach Donna how to weave. She would not explain how or why things were done a certain way. She would not set up a loom for Donna but instead expected the girl to watch her at work and to copy what she was doing. This old-fashioned way of learning was not how Donna and her schoolmates worked in their classes; they expected instruction and specific guidance. The grandmother, on the other hand, felt that if Donna couldn't watch patiently and learn to correct her own mistakes, then she wouldn't ever really understand how to weave. Teasingly, she called her "lazy." She wanted her granddaughter to learn how to weave but did not feel it was her job to direct each step.

Jenelle was eight when their grandmother set up a small loom for her when she spent the summer at her sheep camp. At the end of the summer Jenelle was not yet finished. Neither the grandmother nor the mother coerced her into completing it. After it was laid aside, the web became hopelessly tangled and was eventually discarded. Several years later, Jenelle asked her grandmother to set up another loom for her, which she did. This loom, also incomplete at summer's end, went home with Jenelle.

Only when Jenelle's mother would sit next to her and help with each weft passage would the girl weave. Because of school and other activities, Jenelle was still not finished with her small rug after two years.

Residual. Maxwell and Silverman (1970; cited in Fry 1980:4), in their cross-cultural study of 26 societies, conclude not surprisingly that "esteem of the elderly is related to the useful knowledge they control." Whether they continue to weave actively or not, grandmothers' knowledge of craft technology, aesthetics, and related lore remains a significant resource for following generations. Moreover, what makes Navajo weaving particularly special is that knowledge about the craft is often generalizable to other parts of the Navajo world and belief system. While grandchildren are taught or shown the tools, materials, and techniques of weaving, they may also be introduced to broader cultural beliefs and appropriate behavior. Through weaving, Navajo grandmothers can provide important role models to younger people and serve as resources about traditional life and thought. Once again, this knowledge often resides with a grandmother and is imparted to grandchildren whether she is actively weaving or "retired" from the craft.

To the Navajo, the concept of "making a living" refers to more than merely earning income but to *appropriate* ways of sustaining one's life.[13] Traditional values concerning subsistence activities—being active and productive, maintaining self-reliance, balancing your needs with those of others, retaining a closeness with the land, raising healthy livestock and crops—provide directions on *how* to live, not just how to acquire the wherewithal to live. "Making a living" represents an array of activities that contribute to a total way of life, including attitudes about that life. Weaving represents a productive set of tasks and thought processes on both economic and social levels and so represents the continued ability to make a "good living," or to live a good life. Based on the use of sheep's wool, it is a direct extension of raising sheep and living close to the land, both central issues in the right way to make a living.

Carolyn is a true crusader for weaving, sheep raising, and a traditional way of life. As a girl she attended Catholic schools, learned excellent English, and, in contrast, saw the value in her Navajo culture. She acknowledges contemporary changes on the reservation and because of these, although now over 65, she has attended Navajo Community College workshops and conferences on modern family welfare and health issues. Carolyn is a "revival" weaver in that she weaves less for economic reasons, according to her, than for its value as a marker of traditional Navajo life and its importance in retaining harmony and balance in the

Navajo way. She takes an interest in the old style churro sheep and keeps samplers of many of the older saddle blanket weaves—her own mini-museum, as she calls it. She takes a direct interest in the education of her numerous grandchildren and frequently has several living with her, helping around the house and corrals.

Grandmothers and other elders are expected to maintain and disseminate traditional values such as those of hard work, patience, humility, and moderation. Weaving clearly exemplifies these values, and craftswomen embody them.

During a *kinaaldá,* the puberty ceremony for young girls/women, tools from the loom are used to massage the body of the girl by an older and much esteemed woman in order to transform or "shape" the girl into a woman. These tools symbolically and literally represent aspects of traditional productivity and economic prosperity. Today they are often present in conjunction with modern symbols—car keys, cash, and other commercially manufactured valuables.

Recognizing the importance of intergenerational relationships in cultural preservation, several tribal programs in recent years have promoted grandparental contacts with children and young adults, using weaving as one of the linkages.

Wilma was hired by the tribe to weave as a demonstrator in one of the local chapter houses. She is not strong enough to weave the large, handsome rugs that she used to make, but she is sharp enough to share her knowledge and values through weaving. Just her presence in the meeting-house provides a significant image, seated at a loom in the main hall, weaving rhythmically as others move in and out, preparing meals for the preschool and elderly program participants or working on Youth Corps projects. Workers occasionally stop to chat or admire her growing rug. Wilma reminds everyone of their own grandmothers and their special cultural heritage.

Barbara reported that the dorm mothers at her BIA [Bureau of Indian Affairs] boarding school were encouraged to spend time weaving or doing other crafts when they were not otherwise occupied. They were not hired to teach students, but it was hoped that their presence would be a positive and pervasive influence on children removed from the traditional activities of their homes. Barbara remembers watching a woman at her loom whenever she returned to the dorm from classes and between meals.

In a society in which knowledge and thought are considered tantamount to action; that is, where thinking the right thoughts and singing the right songs can powerfully control the world (Witherspoon 1977), knowing how to weave and understanding the philosophical and cultural background of the craft may be just as important as being a practicing, producing weaver.

Shirley's failing eyesight prevents her from weaving rugs like those from her youth. Still, she works at her loom more often than not. Although none of her granddaughters, between the ages of four and 17, is learning to weave, they come around to watch from time to time. They are able to explain to a visitor just how she makes her rugs. Local traders consider her too old to contribute to the household economy—in their eyes she is "retired." But to her family, she still leads a productive life; she knows about weaving; she is a weaver.

Occasionally a grandmother's name on a rug's sales tag may be the only tangible contribution that she makes to the production of the rug. Certain family members have been known to use names of their well-known relatives (some quite elderly and unable to accomplish what the younger weavers could) to increase the prestige and price of a rug. Motivations for such misattributions may range from purely economic to an understanding at some level that, indeed, the grandmother was responsible for the creation of the rug even if she did not actually weave the entire piece.

Stella posed proudly for a photograph, holding one of the rugs that her daughter-in-law had woven, as though it were her own. As she got older, weaving became physically too difficult for Stella to work at for hours on end, and yet she was still known as the best weaver in the area. Stella had taught her daughter-in-law how to weave, and the style of this little rug was almost indistinguishable from her own of a few years before. And besides, from time to time when her daughter-in-law wasn't working at the loom, Stella herself did weave small sections of this rug.

The impact of a grandmother's presence, of course, often remains long after she is gone. Examples set and lessons learned last for more than a single life-time and may be passed on for several generations. Active craftswomen and noncraftswomen alike may credit their grandmothers and great-grandmothers with providing them with an appreciation for traditional ways. Weavers often acknowledge a grandmother for both the inspiration and the technical know-how to work at the loom.

Born in 1907 and raised by her grandmother (there were too many children to all stay with her mother), Bessie herself is now a grandmother to many children. She still recalls her own grandmother sitting at her loom, setting an example for how one should weave. Just as her grandmother "didn't teach me, she showed me," Bessie has never "taught" any of her granddaughters, but several have learned to weave "by watching me." Bessie weaves twills, two-faced rugs, and sash belts as well as regular tapestry rugs, just as her grandmother did.

Paula learned to weave from her older sister after their mother died, but she said the inspiration came from her grandmother. She and her sisters have a strong feeling of carrying on what the "old people" were doing. They worry that the traditions would be lost without their current efforts. Many bits of advice, warnings, and precautions about weaving came from Paula's grandfather, too. Ironically, Paula rarely follows any of the taboos that he taught her, but she remembers what she was told and hopes to teach her daughters the same things.

CONCLUSIONS

Through weaving, grandmothers' social responsibilities and cultural roles become symbolically manifest and pragmatically maintained in contemporary Navajo society. The practice of weaving represents opportunities to display and reinforce many valued aspects of culturally appropriate behavior—hard work, calm control, humility, resourcefulness, moderation. It provides a productive economic niche for many grandmothers and allows older women to continue working in their homes after other job opportunities have diminished. Many of these craftworkers also speak often of the personal satisfaction they derive from these creative activities.

Navajo grandmothers may gain or retain highly regarded status with their weaving activities through contributory, advisory, and residual roles. They participate in household economics and contribute to cultural integrity through continued craft production, through cooperative work and teaching, through role modeling, and through childcare and other localized tasks while they or others produce craft items. Knowledge and experience may be as valuable as actual production in many cases, especially where the knowledge of a traditional handmade craft has diminished with time in the general population.

The texture and details of Navajo life are highly varied from region to region, community to community, and family to family. Moreover, the culture is undergoing considerable change in response to both internal and external pressures. The preceding examples were drawn from a wide socioeconomic range of families living on the Navajo Reservation, but all have highlighted families who carry on certain traditional activities, including weaving. These families along with many others also acknowledge significant changes in their lives and those of their children. Nuclear families are increasingly separate from the extended family, especially from the older generation. Many children live apart from their grandparents and are not exposed to the traditional activities of their elders on a regular basis. Young adults, even while living on the reservation, are often involved in outside schooling and employment that take them away from their extended families and leave little time to pursue craft production.

As Navajo culture continues to change and evolve, the usefulness of traditional knowledge, and of the grandmothers' roles in embodying and transferring that knowledge, must be constantly reevaluated. On the one hand, modern Navajo society places less and less emphasis on traditional life and values, which have been replaced by an emphasis on formal education, jobs, and off-reservation priorities (housing, transportation, goods, and services). On the other hand, revitalization has occurred in the form of increased appreciation for those evanescent elements of Navajo heritage that, while perhaps no longer economically expedient, still function as social and religious markers and ethnic identifiers.

Interestingly, there is growing evidence that many young Navajo women in their twenties and thirties are learning to weave for the first time, at later ages than women from earlier generations.[14] Moving beyond a sense of weaving as an integral part of the ideal Navajo woman's roles, some of these young women perceive weaving as a means to professional status as Native American artists. This future generation of grandmothers and weavers may conceive of their roles in considerably different ways than their own grandmothers do.

Weaving represents meaningful activities for grandmothers on the Navajo Reservation today on several significant levels—economically, socially, and psychologically. Navajo weaving provides effective economic roles for older women in contemporary society, serves to establish and sustain significant intergenerational relationships, and provides avenues for the effective maintenance of grandmothers' autonomy and self-respect.

NOTES

1. An earlier, unpublished version of this chapter (Hedlund 1985) examined the craft production of both elderly Navajo weavers and Pueblo potters. This chapter is an outgrowth of that earlier presentation but focuses solely on Navajo weavers.

2. Data collected for individuals and family units include the types of rugs woven and tools and materials used; accounts of the learning, weaving, and marketing decision-making processes; demographic and biographic data; and specific explorations about weaving aesthetics and belief systems.

3. Studies of elderly people have often evolved in this manner, as Simič (1978:13) notes: "Most ethnographic sources including material on the aged are not the deliberate product of a specific problem orientation concerned directly with the question of aging, but rather the incorporation of data of gerontological interest has been the inevitable by-product of anthropology's so-called holistic approach, by which cultures are perceived in their totality as functionally integrated systems."

4. Kin terms are listed here from ego's perspective, in their first-person possessive form, generally consisting of the prefix *shi-* (my) plus the stem, in this case, *-má* (mother) plus the adjective *sání* (old). Alternatives would be to use only the stem (cf. Aberle 1961:196) or the impersonal pronoun form, *ha-* (one's). The orthography of Young and Morgan (1980:399–401) is used throughout this chapter.

5. This parallels the practice of referring to the mother's sisters as *shimá* (my mother) or as *shimá yá zhí* (my little mother). "Navajo often say, *'Ashįįhi* ('mother's clan') *ei shima adaat'e'* ('Those of my mother's clan are my mothers'). The person, as a cultural construct, of one's mother's matrilineal descent category is one's mother" (Witherspoon 1975:43).

6. The paternal clan term "born for," *báshíshchíín* ("I am born for him or it" [Lamphere 1977:87]), contrasts to the maternal clan term "born to," *nlíjí,* "I am, I belong." Witherspoon explains further: "[In addition to matrilineal descent,] Navajo culture also defines a child as a descendant of its father. All children whose fathers are members of the salt clan are put into a descent category called 'those born for the salt clan.' 'Born for' is the linguistic description of the father-child relationship according to descent reckonings. This category, however, excludes the father, and is therefore not patrilineal. . . . The affective and functional meanings that are part of this descent category are the same as those of the matrilineal descent categories. Those who are born for the same clan are not to marry, but are to be hospitable to each other and to give each other help in ceremonies" (1975:42).

7. Lamphere (1977:170) has documented for the Navajo cultural system the strength of both maternal and paternal kin ties and of local clan associations over any general clan membership.

8. A *nálí* may, in fact, come to be considered as *shimá* under certain circumstances. Witherspoon (1977:128) notes that in the case of patrilocal residence after a mother has died and the father and his children remain with his family, the children may switch from *shinálí* to *shimá* (my mother) in referring to their father's mother.

9. Lamphere (1977) has described this changing nature as part of the "development cycle" of domestic groups. For senior couples within the group, she notes, "As a couple becomes older, their position in relation to others in terms of authority and communication changes" (1977:84).

10. The term "tradition" is used here in a dynamic sense that includes notions of change and the incorporation of "foreign" ideas into indigenous ways rather than in the narrower, more conservative sense. Weaving itself is a borrowed "tradition" that has been embellished

over three centuries by Navajos in response to outside stimulus and markets. This more flexible and dynamic concept of what is considered to be contemporary "Navajoness" reflects the current cultural critique by Clifford (1988) and others.

11. Press and McKool's "control" category has been deleted, as monopolistic control is not an ideal nor a pragmatic Navajo orientation. Although it can be argued that at times Navajo individuals may gain and maintain control over others' actions, such behavior is overshadowed by the Navajo sense of individual autonomy and for the purposes of discussion may be subsumed into the other three categories.

12. It should be noted that this direction of a collaborative effort is not "control" in the sense that Brown (1985:7) suggests when she notes that elder women often gain increased authority and the right to extract labor from younger kin; in this, as in most Navajo undertakings, the individuals involved still retain their independence.

13. Terry Reynolds, now at New Mexico State University in Las Cruces, first pointed out this concept to me.

14. In contrast, most women in earlier generations learned to weave during their preteen or teenage years.

COYOTE LOOKS AT GRANDMOTHER
Puget Sound Salish Grandmothers in Myth and Message

◆

PAMELA AMOSS

INTRODUCTION

Although women learn to be grandmothers as they learn to be mothers, from experiences with the women in their own families, the models of the grandmother are encoded in cultural texts shared by the entire social group. Women measure their grandmothers and eventually themselves as grandmothers against the fictional grandmothers offered in those texts. It is in such texts that we read what a social group thinks about how grandmothers should behave and how they should be treated.

In this chapter I examine texts collected from Coast Salish Indian grandmothers in the mid-twentieth century. Because both stories recited by the grandmothers and messages they were sending to their friends are represented, I am able to compare grandmothers as presented in myth texts with grandmothers as the women raconteurs describe themselves and others in recorded messages.[1]

Myths, tales,[2] and public speeches were the preeminent cultural texts of pre-White Coast Salish society. Only vestiges of public speeches survive from the early historic period, but many stories, both myths and tales, exist.[3] Although they have their roots in the aboriginal past, by the time they were recorded, the stories, like the people who told them, had been influenced by a century or more of radical change in native life. Nevertheless, it is usually assumed that myths and tales are more conservative than other cultural texts, such as speeches. Whether that is true or not, the narrators clearly believed they were telling stories that represented the old ways. We can therefore assume that the family roles presented in the stories are comments on ideal patterns that persisted even when actual family and household structure had changed.

Most scholars who have studied the family relationships depicted in Puget Sound Salish folklore were interested in what they could infer about aboriginal or early historic culture and society (see especially Sally Snyder 1964), not in contemporary people. Because the traditional stories have not been told in communal settings for many decades, students of contemporary Indian families have considered it unlikely that the characterizations in the stories were shaping or reflecting contemporary people's attitudes to family relationships. Attempts to understand the roles of twentieth-century Coast Salish grandmothers have therefore largely ignored stories and relied on ethnography, with some attention to public speeches (Kew 1970; Amoss 1981a and 1981b). A notable exception is Bierwert (1986), who used stories in her semiotic representation of contemporary Fraser River people.

Recently it has become possible to learn from stories something about the attitudes of mid-twentieth-century grandmothers by examining a collection of stories and messages dictated by grandmothers. From 1951 to 1958 Leon Metcalf, teacher by profession but self-taught linguist and ethnographer, paid a number of visits to some half-dozen old Coast Salish Indians living on the reservations in western Washington State and made audio recordings of songs and traditional stories. During the same visits he recorded messages that the singers and storytellers wanted transmitted to friends and relatives in other Indian communities. Each message was addressed to a specific recipient, and many were responses to earlier messages.

Although copies of Metcalf's recordings were archived at the Burke Museum, a branch of the Washington State Museum at the University of Washington, for many years nothing was done with any of the recordings. Linguists who had listened to some of the tapes believed the sound quality was so poor that the material might be useless. In the late 1970s Violet Hilbert, a Skagit woman and native speaker of Puget Sound Salish, began transcribing and translating them.[4] Although Hilbert has published all of the stories in English translation (Hilbert n.d., 1980, 1985) or Lushootseed and English (1985, 1990, 1995a, 1995b), she has not published all of the messages. The messages are rich sources of information on vocabulary and grammar and rhetorical style, on the thought processes of the narrators, on Coast Salish life in the 1950s, and on the attitudes and concerns of grandmothers at that time.

The people Metcalf interviewed had little opportunity to communicate with their peers in other villages. They were very old, and some were in poor health. Few of them could read or write, and none of them had telephones in their homes. Under these circumstances, Metcalf and his tape recorder provided a welcome opportunity to contact old friends and relatives. All the stories, songs, and messages were recorded in the Lushootseed language, also known as Puget Sound Salish. Lushootseed is one of the languages of the Coast Salish branch of the Salishan family. It was spoken by people living in what is now Washington State on the eastern and southern shores of Puget Sound and along the river courses flowing from the western foothills of the Cascades to the Sound. There were two principal dialects, northern and southern. The stories and messages that are part of this study are all in the northern dialect.

Since Lushootseed speakers did not have a vehicle for writing their language until the 1970s, when Thom Hess devised a practical orthography, there was no "letter" model to guide the old people in creating the messages Metcalf recorded. There was instead the oral genre of the public speech. In the traditional culture, speeches were an important vehicle for instructing, welcoming, honoring others, and claiming prerogatives for self. People who spoke well were respected for their skill with words and were called upon to make important announcements at potlatches, funerals, and other gatherings. Although special aptitude was recognized and rewarded, to some extent every adult and every old person who claimed high-class status was competent to speak extemporaneously.

Metcalf did not speak or understand more than a few words of Lushootseed, so the narrators were not shaping their texts to please him (Hilbert 1995b:78). They did, however, know he was going to keep copies of all the tapes so that "coming generations of young people will hear it" (Hilbert 1995a:323), and they framed their messages for this unseen audience as well as for the specific addressee. This is another reason that the style of the messages is rhetorical rather than conversational and follows many of the conventions still observed by speakers at Indian gatherings, such as feasts, funerals, or other formal occasions.

Personal anecdotes are an important element frequently woven into contemporary speeches. The personal anecdotes that appear in the messages are abbreviated "true life stories" and conform to the conventions of tales distinct from the myths told by these same narrators. By the 1950s, when Metcalf was recording, Coast Salish people had also become fluent in a subtype of rhetoric—adapted from their white neighbors—the "testimony" given in church or at revival meetings. The message texts may owe some of their form, especially the repeated injunctions to "keep a good mind," to the testimony model (Hilbert 1995a:300).[5]

Metcalf recorded messages from a number of people, including three grandmothers who provided both stories and messages: Susie Sampson Peter, Martha Lamont, and Ruth Shelton. They told a total of 17 stories, of which almost half concern grandparents and just under a third concern grandmothers specifically.

GRANDMOTHERS IN THE MYTHS AND
GRANDMOTHERS IN THE MESSAGES

What were the people like who created the myths, and what kind of world did they live in? Since the myths are old stories first told many years before White contact, information on the life of the people who created them is very scarce. In fact, in addition to what little archeology tells us and what can be gleaned from the accounts of the first explorers, we infer much of what we believe about life in aboriginal society from the content of the myths themselves. To avoid this obvious circularity, I will set aside the inferences that are usually made from myth texts but will make use of other ethnographic information (Haeberlin and Gunther 1930; Smith n.d., 1940, 1949; Sally Snyder 1964; Waterman 1973; Collins 1974; Miller 1988; Miller and Snyder n.d.) and what is available from archeological (Nelson 1990) and linguistic evidence (Warren Snyder 1968; Hess 1976, 1995).

Aboriginal Coast Salish people of northern Puget Sound lived a good life of fishing, hunting, and gathering. Like most Northwest Coast people they relied primarily on anadromous fish, specifically salmon, supplemented by the chase and by a great variety of gathered foods—berries, roots, shoots, shellfish, and birds' eggs. Those on the saltwater estuaries of the major rivers had not only richer salmon harvests but also saltwater resources available year-round. Groups upstream had smaller salmon harvests and depended more on hunting. Trade and gift exchanges distributed local resources over a wider area and provided a kind of insurance against episodic local food shortages. Not surprisingly, fishing technology was quite sophisticated. Puget Sound people were also skilled woodworkers who built large communal houses of cedar planks and crafted canoes suitable for travel on rivers or sheltered salt water.

People lived in permanent villages, from which they spread out during the spring and summer months to take advantage of seasonal harvests. In the fall they returned to the winter villages. Although they had accumulated enough stored foods to see them through the winter, they continued to do some hunting, fishing, and collecting during the winter as well. The winter season was the time when the old people helped while away long dark hours by telling stories to the children and adults living together in the big communal houses.

Class distinctions were important in native thinking, although true differences in power and access to basic resources may have existed only in the largest and wealthiest villages at the mouths of rivers (Amoss 1993). Upper-class men were expected to seek wives in other villages and bring them home, but a young man could make his home with his wife's family. Kinship was reckoned bilaterally and marriage forbidden with close kin on either the mother's or the father's side.

Despite the dense populations, no centralized political authority seems to have existed beyond the village. The network of gift exchange and intermarriage preserved generally peaceful relations among the villages of a single river drainage. Although relations with more distant neighbors might not have been so friendly, all groups benefited by trade networks that disseminated certain crucial elements obtainable in only a few places, like obsidian. Stories also seem to have spread along these networks. By the time of White contact, Puget Sound people had been subjected to slave raids by Coast Salish from the Straits of Georgia and had formed some temporary alliances to resist these incursions.

In adolescence, young men and women sought spiritual helpers who would guide, protect, and empower them with the skills necessary to be competent adults. Youths who hoped to become healers or warriors had to prepare themselves more rigorously and endure longer quests. During the winter season people gathered to celebrate the gifts of their spirit guardians by singing and dancing. Although in theory anyone could encounter a strong spirit, upper-class families claimed to give their children special instruction and preparation that helped them acquire the more desirable spirit guardians. Upper-class people were expected to demonstrate their good spiritual connections by industry and careful demeanor. Failure to behave properly could plummet a well-born youth into the lower class (Suttles 1958).

With White settlement and political control, the economic foundation of native life was completely undermined and with it the plausibility structure that supported the belief system. Newly introduced Christian ideas were accepted and woven together into a new synthesis with aboriginal conceptions of how humans relate to spiritual things. One expression of the new worldview was the Indian Shaker Church, preached in the 1880s by a Coast Salish prophet, John Slocum, and his wife, Mary Slocum (Amoss 1990).

By the mid-twentieth century, Coast Salish people participated in Protestant and/or Catholic Christianity, in the Indian Shaker Church, and in the persistent tradition of honoring their individual guardian spirits. Although most Christian clergy urged them to adopt an exclusive allegiance, most Coast Salish people continued to adhere to a more catholic style of faith and practice.

In the nineteenth century Indian labor had been essential to local economic development, but by the mid-twentieth century most of the industries that had employed natives, such as logging, had declined. In the 1950s most native people were poor. On the reservations or in the surrounding rural communities there were few jobs, and Indians experienced discrimination that limited their educational and employment opportunities. Most had to be content with seasonal work. Many houses had no electricity or running water, and alcoholism had become a serious health problem. Families were large, but infant and young child mortality was high.

This was the world that Susie Sampson Peter, Martha Lamont, and Ruth Shelton lived in and the tradition they drew on—an aboriginal past filtered through more than a century of response to alien contact and domination. Who were these women who sent the messages and told the stories? What did they say about themselves as grandmothers? What did they perceive their responsibilities to be? What did they report about how other people treated them? How did the differences in their lives create their varying patterns of strengths and weaknesses in old age?

THE NARRATOR GRANDMOTHERS[6]

Susie Sampson Peter[7] lived with her son, Alphonse Sampson, and his children on the Swinomish Reservation near La Conner, Washington. A widow who had been married at least twice, she had two grown sons from her first marriage and a number of grandchildren, including a granddaughter. At the time she dictated the messages and stories, she was blind. Although she may have understood some English, she did not speak it. Both of Peter's sons were fluent and well educated in English and supported her participation in Metcalf's work. Alphonse Sampson interpreted for his mother, and his presence undoubtedly had an influence on what Peter said (Hilbert 1995a:70–71).

Peter had been raised under traditional rules. In her youth she had been identified as a bright child and taught to remember stories and family history, and she had trained to be a healer, or "Indian doctor." Later in life she embraced the Indian Shaker Church, which did not imply a rejection of her spirit helpers but rather that they as well as she would be converted together (Hilbert 1995a:xii). In her old age she used to sit repeating the myths over and over to herself so that she would not forget them. She wove Christian and traditional concepts together so that the powers of one complemented the strength of the other.

Martha Lamont[8] lived with her second husband, Levi, on the Tulalip Reservation near the town of Marysville. She had been raised speaking only Lushootseed. In the 1950s she undoubtedly understood some English, although she did not speak it. (In the 1970s, after her husband's death deprived her of her translator, she began to use English.)

Lamont had been raised in a traditional style and was secluded at her first menstruation. According to elderly women questioned in the 1950s, this custom had to be abandoned when girls were sent away to school, but Martha,

Susie Sampson Peter. Photograph by Leon Metcalf.

who never had any formal education, was trained as a proper young woman according to the old customs. It is likely that she encountered a guardian spirit during her menstrual seclusion, the time when young women—ordinarily not allowed to quest in the wilderness—were expected to receive spiritual help. She was a fine basket maker, and for that reason alone it can be assumed that native thinking would have credited her with special supernatural assistance. She had

Martha Lamont. Photograph by Leon Metcalf

Ruth Shelton. Photograph by Leon Metcalf.

been an active and vigorous young woman who was known for her skill and strength in handling canoes on the river.

In the 1950s Lamont was an adherent of the Indian Shaker Church. Although her isolation and poverty kept her from attending Shaker gatherings, she remained very devout and was said to have had a gift for curing.

The grandchildren Martha Lamont spoke of in the messages were the children of offspring from her first marriage. They did not visit often, so that Lamont and her husband, Levi, led a relatively isolated existence.

Ruth Shelton also lived at Tulalip. A widow, she made a home with her married daughter, Harriette. Shelton's husband had been a tribal leader, well known for negotiating successfully with the Indian agent. Like her husband, Shelton was literate in English. She participated actively in the Roman Catholic Church. Shelton herself came from a family with claims to upper-class status and was very conscious of her responsibilities to set an example within her own community and to represent her family well to outsiders.

Although fluent in her native language and conversant with old customs, Shelton probably had not been secluded at menarche and had not had the opportunity to acquire guardian spirits at that time. Her emphasis on Christian values in the messages she dictated suggests that she saw Christianity as a powerful supplement to, if not replacement for, the traditional sources of spiritual power. She told Leon Metcalf only one story: "Mink and Whale" (Hilbert 1985b:59–61).[9] Although it contains no references to grandparents, the moral underscores the importance of heeding the advice of elders (1995b:60).

THE MYTHS

I will focus primarily on three of the stories in which grandmothers are prominent characters. "Nobility at Utsalady" presents both the ideal loving grandmother and her antithesis, a cold rejecting one. The good grandmother was a counselor and advocate for her grandchild; the bad grandmother deserted her daughter and her grandchild. "Star Child" presents an incompetent foolish grandmother who allowed her grandson to be kidnapped. And "The Eyes of Coyote" gives us an ambiguous grandmother, on the one hand piteous, on the other, menacing.

In addition, two minor grandmother characters appear in stories told by Martha Lamont. One, in "Seal Hunting Brothers" (Hilbert 1985:73–86, 1990: 162–253), continued to long for the return of her grandsons when others had given them up as lost (Hilbert 1985:82). The other, who appears in "Coyote's Son Had Two Wives" (Hilbert 1985:66–72), responded sympathetically to Coyote's son, lost in the sky world, and directed him to Grandfather Spider, who was able to offer tangible assistance (p. 67). A helpful grandfather also appears in Peter's story "Moose" (Hilbert 1995a:244).

"Nobility at Utsalady"

Susie Sampson Peter told this story (Hilbert 1980:63–78, 1996:33–39 [English translation only]; 1990:254–381, 1995a:159–82 [translation and Lushootseed text]).[10]

A high-class woman, Magpie, her grandson, Bobcat, a diligent and successful hunter, and Bluejay, a chatterbox, lived together in a village where everyone feared a raid by enemy warriors. Bluejay talked incessantly about how she would sound the alarm if enemy warriors attacked. Magpie tried to stop Bluejay's boasting. However, when warriors really did assault the village and Bluejay frightened them off by barking like a dog, Magpie apologized to Bluejay for having scolded her.

Bobcat, although afflicted with a loathsome skin disease, magically impregnated the village Headman's daughter so that neither she nor anyone else knew who had fathered her child. When the preternaturally precocious child began to call for his father, the Headman assembled all the young men of the village except Bobcat. The child rejected them all, including the clown, Raven, who insisted he was the father. Finally, when he caught sight of Bobcat, the child announced, "My father, my father."

The Headman was disgusted that his daughter had demeaned herself by taking up with someone with a disfiguring disease. He sent his daughter off to Bobcat and ordered all the villagers to pack up and leave the couple and the infant to starve. Only two people, the young woman's youngest brother and Bobcat's grandmother, Magpie, opposed his decision. The Headman's wife, the young woman's own mother, gave her daughter not so much as a blanket to keep her child warm. When Magpie resisted leaving, Bobcat warned her to go lest she be killed by the angry Headman. Reluctantly Magpie agreed, but before leaving, she gave her granddaughter-in-law food and cooking equipment.

Bobcat and his wife and child lived alone in the deserted village. Bobcat healed himself and began killing game, which he and his wife skinned, butchered, and preserved. When the wife's youngest brother returned to see them, they gave him meat to take home and distribute to the rest of the villagers, who had fallen on hard times. Learning that Bobcat and his wife had plenty of food, the villagers returned, and the haughty Headman and his wife were reconciled to their daughter and son-in-law. When the Headman's wife tried to take her grandchild in her arms, her daughter rebuffed her bitterly, eliciting a tearful apology. Although Bobcat chided his wife for speaking harshly to her mother, he shamed his in-laws by overwhelming them with fresh meat. Day after day he hunted and killed elk that they had to butcher and carry back to the village. On the last day he announced that he would sing his power song that gave him the ability to hunt so successfully. His song began, "No one can hear my spirit power song," and claimed, "My food is my spirit power."

"Star Child"

Susie Sampson Peter also narrated "Star Child" (Hilbert n.d. 37–54, 1980:38–61, 1996:23–32 [English translation only], 1995:91–126 [translation and Lushootseed text]), a story Hilbert considers "the Lushootseed creation myth" (personal communication 1972).

Two sisters digging edible wild roots far from their village were benighted in the root patch. As they lay looking at the sky, the older girl said she wanted a white star to be her husband and a red star to be her sister's husband. They awakened to find that they were in the upper world and each had a star husband. The younger woman was content with her new spouse, but the elder was dismayed by hers and wanted to escape from her marriage. The sisters continued to go root digging in the sky world. But when they disobeyed the star husbands' orders to avoid digging the long roots that broke off underground, they opened a hole in the floor of the sky world through which they could see their earthly home below. Although she was already pregnant by her star husband, the discontented elder sister began planning her escape. With her sister's help, she made cedar rope and lowered herself back to earth.

Alone on earth, the woman sought a place to make her home and a companion to take care of the child she was soon to bear. She kicked a fallen log four times and turned it into an old woman whom she called "Grandmother" and who addressed her as "Granddaughter."

After she gave birth to a baby boy, the young mother had to go fishing daily to feed her household. Before she left home each day, the mother repeatedly cautioned Grandmother to pretend the baby was a girl lest he be kidnapped by women from upstream who were looking for males. Grandmother, however, was foolish and forgetful. When the women from upstream arrived and questioned her, she inadvertently revealed that the child was a boy, and they took the baby. When the heroine returned and found her child gone, she bitterly upbraided Grandmother and turned her back into a log. The weeping mother took her kidnapped child's diaper and washed it. While she was wringing it out, she heard it cry and realized it had become a child. Although she welcomed this second son, she continued to mourn for the one she had lost.

Raven, who was living in a village upstream, was traveling by canoe and came upon the woman and her child. He captured them both, and the woman who had rejected the star husband became a slave.

Star Child and his brother, Diaper Child, grew up separately. When he had grown up, Star Child regularly went hunting to provide for the women who had stolen and raised him. They ordered him not to go downstream after game or to retrieve lost arrows. When he disobeyed them and went far downstream, he came upon Diaper Child, now also grown, in the forest. The two exchanged life stories and soon realized they were brothers. They returned to Diaper Child's village to rescue their mother from Raven, bringing with them a canoe load of game Star Child had bagged. As the villagers gathered on the shore to welcome this shining stranger, Star Child announced that he would marry the woman who would carry the meat from the canoe into the house. It was modest little Frog who won the hand of the magnificent star youth by following her mother's advice. Raven was forced to release Diaper Child and his mother.

The brothers then returned to their father's realm, the sky world, Star Child as the moon and Diaper Child as the sun. Frog went with her husband and can still be seen on the face of the moon.

"The Eyes of Coyote"

The narrator of "The Eyes of Coyote" was Martha Lamont (Hilbert 1985:96–107, 1996:87–93 [English translation only]). It most clearly reveals the darker side of Lushootseed attitudes toward grandmothers.

Coyote was living in the same house with his daughter's family and her husband's family. Coyote tried repeatedly to steal a valuable stone ax that belonged to his in-laws and was repeatedly caught red-handed. Although the family several times accepted Coyote's transparent excuses, his daughter eventually lost patience with him and persuaded her husband and his kin to desert her father. They left him entombed in a cave of ice from which he escaped by gradually warming and enlarging a small hole. But while peering through the hole as he was enlarging it, Coyote lost both eyes to Raven, who pecked them out. Subsequently two women forced Raven to give them his prize and took the eyes away with them to a distant village, where they displayed them as curiosities.

Determined to retrieve his eyes and punish the thieves, the blinded Coyote managed to track down the women. When he arrived at their house, only their grandmother, Old Illness, who kept house for them, was at home. Coyote tried to kill her several times only to have her taunt him for his failure. Finally he sought the advice of his guardian spirits, his "little brothers," who told him that he could overcome her with nettles. Coyote beat her to death with the nettles. Then he put on her skin to assume her identity.

When the granddaughters came home, the disguised Coyote tried to prepare food for them as Old Illness would have done. Although they were puzzled by his ineptitude, the granddaughters allowed him to calm their suspicions and persuade them to take him to the gathering where they were going to display his eyes. Because Old Illness was too feeble to walk any distance, they took turns packing their supposed grandmother on their backs. In keeping with his libidinous character, Coyote attempted to copulate with each of the women as she carried him on her back. The younger threw him down in disgust. The elder, however, endured his ungrandmotherly attentions without complaint.

When they arrived, Old Illness was welcomed at the gathering and seated in a place of honor. When the eyes were brought out to roll and dance before the people, Coyote quietly called them to jump back into their sockets. Once he could see, Coyote revealed himself. He urinated on the crowd, causing a thick fog that facilitated his escape.

As Coyote went from village to village, trying to take his revenge on all the people who had made fun of him when they had watched his eyes dancing, he was tricked into trying to enter a house through the smoke hole in the roof. He dropped right into the fire, and the people held him down until he was consumed.

THE MYTH GRANDMOTHERS

Four principal grandmother characters appear in these three myths. They are first, Magpie; second, the unnamed mother of Bobcat's wife (both in Peter's "Nobility"); third, the babysitting log-become-grandmother in Peter's "Star Child"; and fourth, Old Illness in Lamont's "The Eyes of Coyote." What do these myth actors reveal about the traditional content of the grandmother role?

Magpie, whose behavior and character are most fully described, was not only the ideal grandmother but the ideal high-class woman. She rebuked Bluejay for boasting—modesty, not self-aggrandizement was the hallmark of upper-class behavior. When, however, Bluejay justified herself by driving off the raiders, Magpie generously acknowledged her error. As a grandmother, Magpie was loving, loyal, and supportive. She reacted to the Headman's decision to desert Bobcat and his wife and child by saying, "Why should I leave the young one of my grandson? Why?" The Headman insisted, "Prepare yourself and load up, Magpie!" (Hilbert 1995:166). Bobcat advised his grandmother, "Get ready and go; they will kill you!" (p. 167). Magpie reluctantly prepared to leave but set aside dried fish and clams, a cooking basket, and a boiling stone that she gave to her granddaughter-in-law, saying,

> This is to warm your breast so you can nurse your child. Here is something to use when you boil a little food. This rock that I keep brushed clean, I put it on the fire. This is what you will put your sliced fish in and your sun-dried fish and smoke-dried fish. This is for your soup that you will eat to keep your breast warmed. It is not my wish to leave you folks, to leave my grandchild. . . .

The narrator explains that Magpie was weeping as she spoke because Bobcat was the child of her sister's son, and both the sister and her son were dead (Hilbert 1995a:167).

In addition to underscoring the loyalty a good grandmother felt to her kin, this incident also makes the point that the status of grandmother can be ascribed through collateral as well as lineal descendants.[11] Since the narrator points out that Magpie and Bobcat's other relatives are all dead, I further interpret it to say that despite the rhetorical deference paid to age, older people without strong families to support them would have been disregarded; hence Bobcat's warning to his grandmother that she must obey the Headman.

In sharp contrast to Magpie stands the wife of the Headman, the mother of Bobcat's wife and grandmother of their infant. Her character is sketched in two incidents. The narrator tells us that when she and her husband sent their daughter out of their house, this grandmother did not give the young woman so much as one blanket to keep herself and the infant warm (Hilbert 1995a:166). The implication is clear that although she, like Magpie, was power-less to countermand her husband's decision, the Headman's wife might have surreptitiously given her daughter some food and supplies to help her and the infant survive, as Magpie did. The storyteller subsequently suggested, however, that even this cold woman may have been redeemable. In the final episode, when the despised Bobcat has been revealed as a powerful hunter, we are told that the villagers were glad to see him because they were hungry. Bobcat's mother-in-law attempted to take her grandchild in her arms, indicat-ing that for her, food was less important than the chance to be reconciled with her grandchild and his parents. When her daughter upbraided her merci-lessly, "Would you now take the child of him covered with sores?" the mother replied,

You berate your poor mother who made a mistake. I made a mistake when we left you and we have been ashamed to come (1995a:178).

The other two grandmother characters, the bungling babysitter from "Star Child" and Old Illness from "The Eyes of Coyote," represent a very different perspective on grandmothers and old age. Magpie and the Headman's wife, though presented as opposites, the good and the bad grandmother, were alike in that both chose how to play the grandmother role. The one was rewarded by her grandson's love and respect, the other punished by her daughter's scorn. Old Illness and the incompetent babysitter, however, could not help being what they were, dependent figures. The babysitter's mind had failed; she could not remember even something vital to protecting her grandson from being kidnapped (Hilbert 1995a:98). Old Illness, despite her power to cause fatal sickness (possibly smallpox) and the respect with which she was greeted at the public gathering, was so decrepit that she had to be carried if she was to leave her house. Both clearly stand for the social burden that frail old age imposes on the adult generation. The resentment felt by competent adults, fully engaged with procuring food and providing shelter for themselves and their children, is expressed in the fates of these frail grandmothers—the befuddled babysitter was turned back into a rotten log by her angry daughter (Hilbert 1995a:98), and Old Illness was murdered by Coyote (Hilbert 1996:90).[12]

The stories express resentment against the burdensome old, but they also warn against acting on that resentment. Old Illness, who is the only one of these four grandmothers who had any real power—the power to cause sickness—mirrors the Coast Salish view, persisting at the end of the twentieth century, that the young should treat the elderly with care and consideration out of enlightened self-interest if for no better reason. Spiritual power accumulates with age, and even an old person who shows no outward signs of supernatural favor probably has the power to retaliate against those who harm him or her (Amoss 1981a:231).

Even Coyote, though a powerful trickster-transformer figure, needed help to learn how to overcome Old Illness. Furthermore, he and other characters who injured the elderly were punished. Coyote succeeded in murdering Old Illness, but at the end of the story he himself was cruelly executed. (Meanwhile Old Illness's dutiful granddaughters, who were the real exploiters of his purloined eyes, seem to have evaded his revenge.) Star Child's mother turned the incompetent grandmother back into a log but then herself suffered the indignity of being enslaved by Raven. Although Peter implies that it was the heroine's hubris in rejecting her star husband that merited such disgrace (Hilbert 1995a: 100), another narrator of the Star Child story explained that people must die because the myth woman turned the grandmother back into a rotten log (Hilbert n.d.:7). The lesson is that younger people who support their debilitated elders can expect their spiritual protection, while those who reject the useless old will be punished for it.

GRANDMOTHERS IN THE MESSAGES

What did Susie Sampson Peter, Martha Lamont, and Ruth Shelton say about themselves that illuminated their situations as grandmothers?

All three repined the loss of older relatives and peers. Peter says,

Where are my cousins, who were here, at Tulalip? There's not one alive. . . .
No, those who were living among their in-laws are no more. Where are

those who were the children of Sihwath? They were living there; they went among their in-laws to live. And they are no more (Hilbert 1995a: 322).

All three clearly saw themselves as part of a chain of Indian people reaching back into the past and forward into the future. As Peter says,

Just as my mind ponders . . . our ancestors are no more. Those of the Skagit River are no more. The Nooksack are no more, where your ancestors came from. The Samish are no more. There's not one still walking around (Hilbert 1995a:322).

They expressed a sense of personal responsibility to pass on what they knew and a deep sorrow that they were unable to teach their grandchildren because none of the grandchildren spoke the old language. Again Peter says,

Yes, there are now only a few, now only us who are Indian. All our children, grandchildren speak a strange tongue. Maybe there is one that hears the language that belonged to the Indian. No one hears the words that used to be spoken by the elders. No one, no one understands now (Hilbert 1995a:323).

Shelton responds,

It is as you have said. There are children growing up, not knowing the language of their first people (Hilbert 1995a:328).

Specific references to the grandmother role fell into three categories. First, the grandmothers reported that their children and grandchildren took care of them or visited them.

Second, the grandmothers described how the aged should be treated and were treated in the days of their youth. Susie Sampson Peter in a message to Ruth Shelton said:

They see an old person and they wrap [him or her] in a blanket, so, they say, their own breaths will be extended, that their days may be added to, because they had compassion on this unfortunate one, just as I am now.

She went on to say that whereas she was well cared for, "My son takes care of me, he takes pity on me and his children do also," not everyone of her age was so fortunate:

There are those others who do not do for their mother the way your younger cousin, my son, does (Metcalf MS, Susie Sampson Peter to Ruth Shelton, 7/18/58).

Third, the grandmothers explained how they felt about their own grandchildren. Martha Lamont told Susie Sampson Peter that Martha's "one little grandson" had a child. "It's good for me, it gives me something to care about" (Hilbert 1995a:319). They also noted that becoming a grandmother changes one's focus from children to grandchildren.

In a message to Susie Sampson Peter, Ruth Shelton said,

My mother, your aunt, and your grandmother used to say, "Children become less important and it's your grandchildren you like best" (Metcalf MS, Ruth Shelton to Susie Sampson Peter, 7/31/53).

Whether they were speaking of themselves as grandmothers or commenting on their lives more generally, all three women emphasized the difficulties and trials they faced. Not surprisingly, all three complained of loneliness and debility. Susie Sampson Peter was blind. Ruth Shelton described in some detail an illness from which she had recovered. And all of them mentioned kinfolk who did not visit. They reminded each other of the strength that came to them from their faith in God. Basically, however, they presented themselves not only as powerless to influence events but also very much under the control of others.

CONCLUSIONS

The lament that the good old days are gone and the younger generation is on its way to cultural perdition has a familiar ring. One might be tempted to dismiss the plaints of these old women as nothing more than the common, perhaps pancultural, tendency of old people to glorify the past at the expense of the present. But in this case, all the external evidence suggests that these women were right to mourn the loss of parts of their heritage.

Their fear that the old language was being lost was well founded. In 1950 their grandchildren were not learning the old language. Almost 50 years later, in the late 1990s, only a few of the great-grandchildren generation are trying to learn the old language. Given their view of the inseparability of language and culture, to our narrator grandmothers loss of language meant a loss of culture. Even Ruth Shelton, the only one of the three with a good command of

English, did not believe that the native tradition could be adequately transmitted through the medium of English. She says,

> Because our language was a high language, and this English is different. When one talks, it seems the words jab the listener. And that which was ours was not like that (Hilbert 1995a:330).

For Indian people of that generation, and to some extent for their children as well, the Indian language, like Indian teachings, was an oral tradition. To them it was inconceivable that it could be rendered, like English, in writing. Having someone read a text in one of the orthographies and produce comprehensible Indian words is still a minor miracle to most of the older speakers of the language. For the grandmothers, then, the loss of the oral transmission of language and customs within the family and community signaled the death of the traditions. In the sense that oral traditions have their own structure and style not found in the tales and texts of literate societies, the grandmothers were right: They were the last to carry the old ways of speaking and thinking, and their myths and messages recorded on tape are its final legacy. Susie Sampson Peter said that these recordings would reach those "children to come" who would hear their words and, somehow, receive their teachings (Hilbert 1995a: 328). Presumably they saw the recordings as the only opportunity for them to carry out their duty to pass on what they had learned.

Since the death of the last of these three grandmothers in the late 1960s, Coast Salish Indian people, like other Indians and other American minority groups, have begun self-consciously preserving and perpetuating their own traditions. As I have reported elsewhere (Amoss 1981a, 1981b, 1987), this changed attitude has conferred new prestige and influence on the current generation of elders, the children of the message grandmothers. For example, in the 1980s Ruth Shelton's daughter, Harriette Shelton Dover, was generally acknowledged as Tulalip tribal historian. She and one of her peers had also orchestrated the revival of the long abandoned First Salmon Ceremony on the Tulalip Reservation in the mid-1970s.

The rituals, albeit in changed forms and with new functions, survive and grow, but the language is passing into a specialized liturgical code restricted to ceremonial contexts. Ironically, some of the great-grandchildren of the narrators were among those struggling to regain their language. In the 1970s and 1980s they attended Hilbert's language classes in the alien environment of the University of Washington. In the 1990s they participated in the few tribal language programs that had survived the loss of federal funding.

How does the picture of grandmothers presented in the myths compare with the self-portraits of the grandmothers who told them? The conventional view of aboriginal social organization and cultural values gleaned from the ethnographic record shows the oldest people of both sexes managing economic and political affairs and emphasizes the deference paid to the old. This idealized picture of the cultural tradition leads one to expect that elders in myths would be powerful. The stories indeed show that the wisdom of the grandmothers was honored and that people who ignored their counsels or mistreated them came to grief, but they do not show us grandmothers who exercised real power over people or events. In this collection of stories and messages, the old people with the power to control and coerce were grandfathers, not grandmothers. It is worth noting that in "Nobility" it was the Headman, not his wife, who took the initiative in deserting his daughter and grandchild, and it was he who prevented the weeping Magpie from staying to help her grandson. In the full collection of 17 stories, four other grandfathers appear and all of them are powerful people, but unlike the Headman of "Nobility," all the others made astute use of their supernatural powers to benefit their grandchildren. In "Moose" the cunning advice offered by a fictive grandfather helps the hero, Moose, escape from his enemies (Hilbert 1995a:244). In "The Seal Hunting Brothers" (Hilbert 1985:75) the grandfather believed his grandson had been mistreated by his brothers-in-law. The old man took revenge by casting a spell on the brothers-in-law, causing them to be carried out to sea to perish. There is a clear contrast between him and the grandmother of the lost brothers, who could only weep for her grandsons (p. 82).[13]

The three women who told these myths portraying loving grandmothers with little power to help their grandchildren were themselves all dependent on their relatives for support. Their children were also relatively poor and powerless people. Martha Lamont was living with her second husband, but they also were poor. What information we have on Coast Salish life in the 1950s indicates that the narrators were, if anything, somewhat better off than many of their age mates because they did have caring kin or a spouse. But they had no power to control their younger relatives. They had lost the autonomy they had enjoyed as young women, when they still had the opportunity to leave an intolerable situation. They were dependent on their relatives or spouse for transportation as well as sustenance. That they portrayed themselves as powerless is not surprising, nor is it remarkable that they should have chosen to tell stories about grandmothers who were also powerless.

At first, the common theme of the stories and messages seems bleak. Powerless grandmothers tell stories about equally powerless grandmothers. Closer scrutiny, however, reveals that both the narrators and at least one of their myth surrogates had found ways to circumvent their incapacity, to achieve by indirect means when direct means were denied them. Magpie of "Nobility" could not protect and nurture her grandson and great-grandchild, but she managed to provide her granddaughter-in-law with both food and the means to cook it. Not only would what she left them feed Bobcat and his wife, but it would make it possible for the young woman to feed the infant. Magpie twice instructed her grandson's wife to "warm your breast."

References to women's breasts are rare in Lushootseed myths but when they occur always denote maternal-child bonding and connote the process of making a human being out of an infant. The emphasis the narrator placed on the *cooking* of food—the boiling stone, the cooking basket—is further evidence that Magpie was binding her grandchildren to a cultural tradition. Furthermore, her urging the younger woman to warm her breast to feed the infant shows that she was empowering the grandchild generation to provide for their children and for the generations that would succeed them. The loving care with which the narrator described the food Magpie left and the boiling stone "kept well brushed" is a powerful statement of the grandmother's role in transmitting not just food but cultural traditions that, taken in with mother's milk, would sustain the coming generations.

Like Magpie, our grandmother narrators were unable to endow their descendants directly. They were blocked from teaching their grandchildren the cultural traditions. Like Magpie, they took advantage of the indirect means available to them. Metcalf and his tape recorder were the means. By entrusting to him and his machine their stores of cultural riches, they hoped to nourish their grandchildren and great-grandchildren.

NOTES

1. This chapter is the first phase of a project analyzing the cultural content and style of the messages in the Metcalf collection. I thank my adopted sister, Violet Taqwsheblu Hilbert, for permission to use her transcriptions and translations of the stories and the messages recorded by Leon Metcalf. I also thank her for her unfailing support, encouragement, and advice. It goes without saying that although she should be given credit for nurturing whatever is of value in this chapter, she bears no responsibility for my failures of fact or interpretation.

2. I use the term "myth" in its more general sense; that is, an explanatory story about the origins of a people, their customs, or their natural world. "Myth" is distinguished from "tale" on the basis that the former is set in the "myth age," or time before the world and its inhabitants—human and animal—took their present forms, and the latter is set in the past but after the "change" or transformation of the world to conditions as the people experienced them before the arrival of the Europeans.

3. Hilbert and her collaborators, Thom Hess (1995), Crisca Bierwert (1996), Dawn Bates, and Jay Miller, continue to refine their translations and interpretations of Lushootseed story texts from ethnographic, literary, and linguistic perspectives. Former students of Hilbert's, notably Toby Langen (1989), have also been developing parallel approaches to some of the same material.

4. Hilbert has published the stories in English translations (Hilbert n.d., 1980, 1985, 1996) and in text and translation (1985, 1995a, 1995b). The 1995a publication includes a selection of the messages. She has also made copies of her manuscript transcriptions and translations available to me. When citing stories, I have, if possible, cited the most recent publication that includes both the translation and the Lushootseed text. In the case of the one story for which no Lushootseed text has yet been published, "The Eyes of Coyote," I cite the most recent published translation. Where I have quoted from messages not yet published, I have cited the manuscript.

5. The relationship between Coast Salish oral styles and forms and the cultural texts of their rural non-Indian neighbors remains to be studied.

6. A biography of Susie Sampson Peter appears in Hilbert 1995a and of Ruth Shelton in Hilbert 1995b. Hilbert and Hess include personal recollections of Martha Lamont in Bierwert (1996).

7. Dr. Toby Langen (personal communication 1982) kindly shared some of what she had learned about Peter from her interviews with Leon Metcalf.

8. Dr. Thom Hess, who employed Martha Lamont as a linguistic consultant in the 1960s, kindly provided information about her.

9. There is some doubt that Lushootseed myths and tales had titles in the usual sense. The same story appears under different names, and rather different stories can have the same name. In this chapter I use the titles that Hilbert has adopted for her publications.

10. Peter told Leon Metcalf "Nobility" first in 1951 and then again in 1954 (Langen 1988). Violet Hilbert transcribed and translated both versions and has published the shorter one in Huboo (1980:62–78). Longer versions appear in Hilbert 1990 and 1995a. Quotations are from Hilbert 1995a.

11. In precontact and historical Coast Salish society, the theoretically important distinction between "old woman" and "grandmother" was largely irrelevant, since any woman of the grandmother generation, whether she had lineal grandchildren or not, would have had collaterals, e.g., siblings' children's children, who called her "grandmother" and treated her accordingly (see also Kew 1970).

12. In their stories the Coast Salish often expressed hostility to characters or situations by holding them up to ridicule. So, pitiful though Old Illness and the forgetful babysitter may have been, the narrators and their audiences found a grim humor in their fates. The audiences would also have laughed at Old Illness's ambivalent responses to the sexual innuendos in Coyote's threats. Though this text is somewhat vague, other versions by other narrators are quite explicit (Snyder 1964:364). Even funnier would have been the spectacle of Coyote disguised as Old Illness being carried piggyback, trying to copulate with each granddaughter in turn. Part of what was funny was Coyote, always famous for his voracious and indiscriminate sexual appetites. But in addition, the idea of such inappropriate lust

being expressed by someone disguised as a grandmother was funny because it resonated with other stories by other narrators in which the grandmother herself sought unusual and ridiculous sexual outlets (see "Wren and His Grandmother" in Snyder 1964:363).

13. Not all grandmothers who appeared in stories collected from other narrators in the 1950s were powerless. Sally Snyder recorded stories about grandmothers who exercised real power (Snyder 1964:356).

DISCONTINUITIES IN THE STATUSES OF PUGET SOUND GRANDMOTHERS

◆

BRUCE G. MILLER

One would expect that contemporary forces of change and modernization might diminish the status and reduce the role of Indian grandmothers of the tribal communities in western Washington State, as has happened with neighboring White grandmothers. The consequences of change are not uniform for all grandmothers, however, and the Indian grandmothers cannot adequately be considered as a single group. Surprisingly, some of the economic and political changes that have lowered the status of White elders and made their lives difficult have produced a rise in the status of some Puget Sound Indian grandmothers. A second group of Indian grandmothers have faced these changed circumstances without the advantages possessed by either their predecessors of the contact period or those experiencing the unexpected rise in status, and their circumstances and statuses within their own communities parallel those of neighboring Whites. Unlike Amoss, whose work in this volume focused on the 1950s, I concentrate on the 1980s and 1990s.

POLITICAL LIFE

An important indication of the increased status of the first group of grandmothers, the "elite," is their new political role. In recent years a significant number of grandmothers have held formal political positions through election to the tribal councils of the several tribes of the Puget Sound. In the 12 federally recognized tribes of the northern Puget Sound, western Washington, 41 percent of council seats have been held by women since 1961, a glaring contrast to earlier periods (Miller 1992). In precontact times, aboriginal women only infrequently took public leadership roles (Mitchell and Franklin 1984), and in the contact period male leadership was reinforced by Whites. Although not all of the women elected to tribal councils are grandmothers, many are. At Upper Skagit, for example, 47 percent of council seats have been occupied by females since formal recognition by the federal government in 1974, half of whom were grandmothers.

In this chapter I will suggest explanations for the unusual position of grandmother politicians in these Indian communities. Rather than living passive lives, as they are often depicted (Bataille and Sands 1984),[1] these grandmothers have actively sought out their new political authority and today enjoy high status due to a culturally acknowledged contribution and through the control of important resources. I argue that the grandmother role itself contributes to the ability of these women to participate in tribal political life in that aspects of the grandmother role are conceptually linked to leadership. As Amoss notes, understanding the Coast Salish grandmother role requires separating out the power, prestige, and affection accorded them. My findings are based on intensive interviews with 15 politically influential grandmothers from nine Puget Sound tribes (1985–86) and a two-year study (1986–88) of the Upper Skagit community, a northern Puget Sound tribe with five political grandmothers.

The situations facing these 10 tribes are not identical, and this variation influences the grandmother's role in complex ways. Several tribes were recently (1970s) federally acknowledged, whereas others are more established and experienced in dealing with the various levels of American government. Generally the similarities are more important, however. The tribes are all small, each with 3,000 or fewer members, and from an area characterized by considerable cultural uniformity and intertribal social interchange in both the pre- and post-White contact periods. The tribes all face serious problems of health, housing, and unemployment and are similarly positioned from neighboring cities. All are administered under the same BIA agency, the Puget Sound Agency, and all have been, at various times, joined in regional political ventures, such as Small Tribes of Western Washington. All the communities are classified linguistically as Coast Salish, although English is the predominant language of everyday life.

In addition, members of these tribes have all actively sought change in the last 20 years, years that have been characterized by significant political and cultural activity. Old rights have been restored, including rights to half the salmon catch, the settlement of generations-old land claim cases, and the reestablishment of federal recognition of tribes. In addition, new reservations and tribal enterprises have been established, tribal centers and HUD housing projects built, and old religious practices reinvigorated. This revitalization has been stimulated in part by federal policies, such as the policy of supporting tribal sovereignty and the federal War on Poverty (Miller 1990), but has also resulted from the influence and knowledge of elders, who provided continuity through the difficult decades from the 1930s through the 1960s.

These decades posed many problems for Indian communities, including in some instances the gradual decline in participation in traditional religious life[2] and a dispersal of population as many people left regions long inhabited by their ancestors in order to find work. Elements of social organization, such as the system of kinship and the practice of sororate, weakened or changed, and belief systems changed, too, as new religious and secular practices entered the lives of Indian people.

First I will describe several of the influences on the lives of the first set of grandmothers, especially in regard to their new political opportunities. Then my focus will shift to those in the opposite situation, who are politically powerless and whose status is diminished in their communities in comparison to the precontact period. Other grandmothers' statuses lie somewhere in between these two, and their circumstances are not at issue here. Data from Upper Skagit are used to provide a close look at the circumstances of Puget Sound grandmothers.

POLITICAL WOMEN AS GRANDMOTHERS

My consideration of these political grandmothers has two analytically distinct components: the first concerns them as elders and as grandmothers, and the second concerns them more broadly as women. Women occupy the status and play the role of grandmothers by virtue of their relationship to other tribal members, particularly family members, and they are either the most senior members of their families or have grandchildren, who in the case of political grandmothers are usually adults.[3] The women's social position includes the nearly automatic statuses ideally resulting from their stage in the life cycle (i.e., the recipient of respect for "white-haired" people) as well as statuses that cannot be accorded simply by virtue of life cycle, particularly political office, and that by definition exclude others.

One way to view the status of elders, including grandmothers, is to argue that the "position of the aged is expressed in terms of how much the old contribute to resources of the group, balanced by the cost they exact, compounded by the degree of control over valued resources" (Amoss and Harrell 1981a:2). This model for assessing status is useful because it takes into account contributions that grandmothers make, including contributions to the political preservation of their tribes as well as contributions to the preservation and adaptation of the traditional practices of their people, and also control of resources, including financial, cultural, and informational resources.

Amoss (1981a) found that Coast Salish elders today enjoy rank comparable to that of old people in their precontact society. The nature of the contribution they make and the resources they control, however, have changed from knowledge of localized resources and skills, such as food procurement, boat-building, and ritual knowledge, to the present emphasis on knowledge of ritual and the external world. In the postcontact period, and until quite recently, factors such as the introduction of wage labor, Christianity, and the rejection of some traditional practices diminished the potential contribution of the elders, removing their control over important knowledge and material resources. Elders, even the more influential ones, were unable to compete successfully for power as a group, and their status diminished. Since the 1970s, however, elders have again come to control an important resource and are viewed as making a very significant contribution (Amoss 1981a:237).[4] The significance of ethnic identity and the political and economic stakes associated with tribal membership have risen sharply, and the cultural knowledge of the elders is regarded as essential to validate and guide the present cultural and social practices.

The recent emphasis in the United States on the allocation of resources on the basis of membership in ethnic groups is partly responsible for the increase in salience of membership in such groups (Clifton 1989).[5] In Washington State, 50 percent of the salmon catch is allocated to Indian fishers under the "Boldt decision" of 1974, and this has contributed to the status of elders in several ways. One of the less obvious ways is their influence over membership rolls. Since membership in a tribe gives fishing rights, these rights have become much more significant since the Boldt decision. Elders have played an important role in determining eligibility for tribal membership, and their knowledge of the past allows them some control over a critical political process. Today most of the Puget Sound tribes formally incorporate elders or bodies of elders into their systems of determining membership under provisions of tribal constitutions and codes.[6] Control of membership lists takes on special importance for the tribes, such as the Upper Skagit, which have become federally acknowledged and received settlement for land claims. In addition, rights to family fishing sites are controlled by elders.

During the formative years of the political careers of many of the present political grandmothers, generally the 1940s to the 1960s, elders provided their communities with informal political and ethnic continuity as well as continuity of cultural practices. There is a payoff for today's elders: those who have ritual knowledge and control (i.e., knowledge of Indian names, shamanistic abilities, or influence over the process of initiation into dancing societies) are in demand and are valued in their communities. Often women provided this continuity during the period when, as one political grandmother put it, "Many tribal members thought being Indian was not a good thing."

POLITICAL GRANDMOTHERS AS WOMEN

The second of the two components of political grandmothers concerns them as women. In the pre- and immediate postcontact periods the political role of women in the region was nonformalized and nonrigid, allowing some latitude for exceptional women. For example, Smith (1940:48) wrote about the Nisqually and Puyallup people of Puget Sound: "Women, although they might obtain prestige as women, were excluded from the public operations of authority, a discrimination against them for sex differences alone, which is almost unique in the society." Women were able to exert influence through other, generally nonpolitical avenues, depending largely on their own capacity. Chiñas, in discussing the Isthmus Zapotec (1973:93), contrasted formal public roles that are recognized by all adult members of society with nonformal public roles, which are not clearly perceived or rigidly defined by all adult members of society; this description fits the political grandmothers I am discussing.

In the period from the mid-nineteenth century to the present, political roles of elite women that were previously informal underwent a shift to a more public and formal role in which women act as council members. This development occurred in phases. Collins noted among the Upper Skagit that after the establishment of formal chief positions, as required by U.S. policy following the Point Elliott Treaty of 1855, the office continued in the family of the prior chief. In one case an exceptionally forceful, vigorous woman served as chief, and her granddaughter was considered as a possible successor (Collins 1974: 37). Women also served as headmen. This was a kinship-based position, however, and not "political" in the sense that it did not entail direct control or influence over nonfamily members (Collins 1980:112). In another case, a woman assumed the role of village head following her husband's death because of the importance of her deceased father.

Several factors influence the political role of the grandmothers today. First is an emphasis by the grandmothers on continuity in women's roles. These present-day women state that the continuities in their own roles are more significant than the changes, and the majority of them described the continuity of women's roles as central to their own personal civic-minded activities. That the new formal nature of their roles is less important to them than the ongoing elements can perhaps be explained by the need to emphasize tradition and continuity to legitimize both their own roles (as women officeholders) and that of the tribal political system itself, and by a cultural emphasis on modesty as appropriate traits of leaders and also of women. In any case, female officeholders frequently attempt to direct attention away from their own political role by asserting that women have indirectly always run the tribe anyhow.

Second, these political grandmothers uniformly believe that their own political interests have grown out of their traditional female concern for their families, their informal role as teachers, and, in some instances, a sense that a political position is an appropriate inherited role for members of their family. Some reported learning this social role as children, often by being taken to council meetings and other social and political gatherings, and by the instruction and example of their grandparents. Others had no such preparation for their present role. Many enhanced their ability to expand this role by gradually obtaining the training necessary to meet the new demands facing their tribes. These skills include bookkeeping, grant writing, and administration.

The traditional teacher role reported by political grandmothers has also taken on a new political meaning in some cases. These grandmothers serve as mentors to children and grandchildren and even to young people of ability not in their own kin network. Several prominent young leaders reported participation in such relationships, as have the mentors themselves. The nature of this relationship was described by one middle-aged woman as "placing a coin in my hand" (a metaphor derived from the practices of the winter ceremonials), thereby creating an obligation on her part to speak publicly in tribal affairs and to contribute to the community through mentoring the next generation of leaders.

The grandmother's new political role has occurred despite historical processes that have, for the most part, tended to work against the status of Coast Salish women (Donaldson 1985, Wright 1981, Mitchell and Franklin 1984). The introduction of White political values reinforced the association between leadership and men and also isolated the formal male leadership from the sort of reciprocal give-and-take of prereservation times that empowered women politically to some degree. The changed political economy diminished the significance of female production and their control of domestic and trade goods. The ability of these women to cope with these and many other changes and to provide a sense of cultural continuity during times of diminished and dispersed population helped shape the political role today of those women who actually hold formal office.

GRANDMOTHERS IN UPPER SKAGIT SOCIETY

Grandmothers in the Contact Period

My own data from Upper Skagit and the data of others who have worked in the immediate vicinity allow a closer look at both the social forces influencing grandmothers and the contemporary roles of these grandmothers. My examination of the lives of Skagit grandmothers relies heavily on Snyder (1964) and Amoss (1981a), who provide the most detail concerning the elderly during the early contact period to the present day in the Puget Sound. Snyder based her view of the elderly on her own work with Skagit elders starting in the early 1950s and on an analysis of the content of myths told during the time of her fieldwork. Amoss gained insight from her fieldwork with the Nooksack, neighbors to the Upper Skagit, and the writings of earlier anthropologists who worked in the region, none of whom made the status of the elderly or of women a special concern. I focus here on those aspects of the grandmother role that contribute to understanding the present-day political grandmothers and their opposite, the low-status grandmothers.

Although it is unclear what the precontact period may have been like, by the late nineteenth century women were heavily constrained throughout most of their lives by male relatives and by ideals of female modesty. Consequently the years from middle age to death, the postmenopausal or grandmother years, were a release for many women, and both Snyder (1964) and Amoss (1978) emphasized the broad range of behavior permitted to women in these years:

> The net result for . . . older women is that there is a broader range of types. . . . I would deduce that this range is a faithful reflection of the breadth of activity that was permitted older women who took advantage of the status that came with age (Snyder 1964:355).

Furthermore, "Characterizations of older women in supportive roles anticipate the liberties that society expected them to take sometimes" (p. 365).

Amoss noted, "Many of the taboos that applied to people in their youth and maturity were waived for the elderly" (Amoss 1981a:323). Both Snyder and Amoss also described the inclination of the elderly to work until unable to do so for physical reasons and the increase of authority and power associated with aging. Snyder took note of the increased power of elderly women in the household, and Amoss, following Haeberlin and Gunther (1930), held that leadership was in the hands of old people, especially members of wealthy and influential families. These happy aspects of old age even included the obligation of younger family members to cheerfully care for ill and feeble old people (Collins 1974:231). In the aboriginal period, as today, not everyone was a member of a wealthy and influential family, and for these people, the picture was considerably different. Even for the elderly of important families, old age was associated with blindness, the decline and loss of spirit powers, psychosis, and the disgust felt by younger people about them:

> Other older women in the literature are cast in parts that arouse pity, derision, or revulsion. Stories reveal unusual sentiment . . . over the bereft feeling experienced by the aged who face death and whose contemporaries are few. The women of those stories are said to live a solitary existence, a statement that does not conform to social reality, but is a dramatic way to show that the elderly really suffer psychological isolation. In story 58 an old woman in her need for a human relationship creates Pitch Boy to be her grandson. Because he will melt in heat she must fetch him before daybreak, the time that he fishes in the chill of the early morning. But one morning as he calls her to come, she fails to waken, and he perishes in the sunshine (Snyder 1964:357).

Old women are depicted in Skagit myth by several figures. These include the Basket Ogress who represents older women such as mothers-in-law who might inflict harm on strangers to their village or house and the foolish and incestuous grandmother of Wren. Grizzly Bear (an old woman in some of the stories in which she appears) embodies several traits thought to be characteristic of disagreeable old women. Grizzly Bear is a psychotic who serves feces to her family (Snyder 1964:357, 362, 366).

Status in old age was influenced by the relations between generations, between men and women, and between members of different social classes. In each case, the ambiguity in these relationships was reflected in the mythology and in difficulties in actual social relations. Particularly problematic, for example, was the relationship between elderly influential women freed to play a "man's" political role and a lower-class male in a role subservient to her. Less troublesome was the status of elderly women who were not able to assume the important positions potentially available to them.

The use of political influence and the attainment of power was only one aspect of the grandmother role, however. Grandmothers were thought of as succoring and permissive, and they had a special relationship with grandchildren as they grew out of the infant stage to became toddlers (Collins 1974). The toddlers grew apart from their busy mothers and closer to their grandmothers, who were the most influential persons in the toddler's life until the age of five or six, when the toddlers entered childhood and became subject to strict discipline and socialization into conformity (Snyder 1964). The grandmother-grandchild bond remained an especially close one throughout life, and Snyder (p. 356) noted tales of grandmothers', rather than grandfathers', acts of supernatural assistance to younger relatives. The ideal grandmother was wise and kind and gave advice at important times such as marriage. Furthermore, in the Upper Skagit kinship system the grandchild relationship included a broad range of younger people, including the offspring of the children of the grandparents' brothers, sisters, and cousins. Grandparents frequently reared children in the event of the death of a parent.

Present-Day Grandmothers

Grandmothers today, as before, vary in their circumstances and many continue to provide significant support to family members. Grandparents, especially grandmothers, continue to raise the offspring of their own children (they are perhaps less apt to raise a brother's or sister's grandchild than were their predecessors in the contact period, although this still occurs) in the event of a death or incapacitation and to participate in the upbringing of the children whose parents are not incapacitated. Grandmothers still are expected to be wise and kind to younger people in a variety of circumstances.

Upper Skagit grandmothers exhort family members in private residences to respect traditional values and practices, and they also bring their concerns to the larger body of tribal members at informal gatherings, funerals, winter ceremonials, feasts, and other events by the use of prayer, speeches, and giveaways. At both private and public gatherings, the moral basis for the legitimacy of the grandmothers' "teachings" is derived in part from age and experience but also from kinship ties and biological links to the audience. These kinship ties are commonly made explicit through recitations of genealogy or through commentary about the interrelatedness of the tribal members. Grandmothers in effect extend the metaphor of kin relations to all of tribal social relations and employ the notion that they are addressing family members in order to give significance to their messages. Grandmotherhood, in this sense, is made literal, and grandmothers do not depict themselves simply as ubiquitous elders when assuming their role as advice givers.

Grandmothers attempt to instruct family members in the subtleties of genealogy by such means as laying out dining utensils to represent family members, thereby graphically demonstrating the kin connections, and by speaking out against romantic liaisons between those whose kinship connections can be recalled. Some make or purchase objects of value, such as blankets and shawls, with the intention of providing them to grandchildren who take a traditional name, become initiates in the winter ceremonials, or are involved in other ceremonials.

Grandmothers, until they become feeble, are visible and active. Upper Skagit life histories show that women maintain an avid interest in community events in the years after they attain elder status, which officially comes at 55. This activity is less characteristic of men, who frequently withdraw from active participation in public affairs of the community. For example, tribal election data show that in the 58-and-over age group, women vote at a rate higher than the average for all eligible voters. Women in this age group make up 9.1 percent of the population and cast 10.6 percent of the votes, a rate of voting 16 percent above the tribal average. On the other hand, male voters in the 58-and-over category constitute 9.4 percent of the population and cast 7.4 percent of the vote, or 21 percent below the tribal average and 32 percent below women of the same age group (Miller 1989:226).

GRANDMOTHERS AND FAMILY NETWORKS

The status and role of grandmothers, especially the political grandmothers, must be understood in light of their contribution to and place within their family network. In both the contact and early historic periods, corporate families formed around sibling sets. Families fished together, supported one another in ceremonial life, and lived and moved together. Family life is structured similarly today, and it is within this family network system that the political grandmothers thrive. Many of these grandmothers are "heads of families"; that is, they play the appropriate leadership role within the family that draws them the support of family members at election time. These grandmothers are able to play this role because of their control of important resources that contribute to the lives of the family members. Collins described such a social structure during a period when such groups were still coresident in plank houses:

> The oldest active man or woman in each generation of brothers and sisters and cousins was the head of the generation. He or she did not casually give orders but did make requests or suggestions which the younger members of the generation could follow (1974:111).

Mooney (1976) regarded what she called "interhousehold economic assistance networks" as central to present-day Coast Salish life. These networks, in her view, are based on an ethic of "Indian collectivism," a term she borrowed from Jorgensen (1972). She found that reciprocity and assistance occurred primarily within these networks, which approximate what the Upper Skagits

Marilyn Williams, Upper Skagit Tribe, Sedro Woolley, Washington. Photograph by Bruce G. Miller, 1998.

call "families." Collectivism is still at the heart of the family ideology of the Upper Skagit: families at Upper Skagit are important economic units, forming fishing cooperatives, sometimes pooling resources, and practicing an inter-generational interdependence in the care of children and infirm elders.

The Upper Skagit family networks are not permanent, although tribal members often speak of them as such. Instead family networks cycle in a manner similar to households or other ephemeral social units, and the phase in the family cycle is critically important to the ability of grandmothers to have a public political role and indeed to the grandmother role generally. In the period of formation of the family network, politically adept people, often a group of siblings with significant resources, create a following, starting with their spouses and offspring. The members of the family network ordinarily engage in generalized reciprocity in daily life, and the leaders gradually attract other relatives who affiliate themselves on a regular basis. As the offspring of the family head or heads mature and have children themselves, family net-works grow and leaders are able to exert influence within the tribe. A mature family, one with three generations of voting adults, is at the height of its influence within the tribe and has a critical mass of family members to suc-cessfully support the family leaders in tribal elections. The leaders provide family members with timely information concerning tribal affairs, access to jobs and training, and a family voice on the tribal council. It is during this mature phase that family networks are most likely to place members on the tribal council. Eventually these families fission, some collapsing into politically powerless isolate households and others recoalescing under new leadership. Routine reciprocity between members breaks down, the social distance be-tween the youngest generation of members produces irritation, competition increases between family members on the family fishing grounds, and some members quit actively participating in tribal life.

Tribal data show clearly the importance of the phase in family cycling, and the resultant family size, in the tribal elections. Simply put, the large, mature families succeed in electing members and small, noncorporate, or fissioned families do so with difficulty. Voting for family members is a first priority for the great majority of Upper Skagits from large corporate families, and in some cases, families can elect members without the votes of other, nonfamily tribal members. The three largest families, in the years 1975–87 (following the cre-ation of a new constitution and system of governance under the terms of the Indian Reorganization Act), have placed 13 family members on the council for a total of 65.5 years, and all other councilors total 14, with 31.5 years of service. Analysis of head-to-head competition for the council shows that male and female candidates from large families defeated other candidates 80 percent of the time (Miller 1989). Those candidates who do defeat large-family candidates are generally not small-family candidates but rather a separate category of "technocrats"; that is, women (and rarely men) with technical training and tribal administrative posts, who draw the votes of those who oppose the candidates of large families. These technocrats are also sometimes grandmothers, although they are considerably younger on average than the "traditional" family candidates when they first are elected to the council.

Upper Skagit data show (Miller 1989) that council women have significantly higher and more stable incomes than do tribal members as a whole, who are characterized by low income and high unemployment. Data gathered by Robbins (1984) show that over half of Upper Skagits were employed 16 weeks or less in 1983, and my own data show a tribal employment rate of 55 percent. Half of all households were earning $10,000 or less in 1983 (Robbins 1984), and tribal data show a median household income of $8,500 in 1984.

Estimates of the "survival costs" for Upper Skagits make clear the difficulties most families face, particularly those living off reservation and with expensive housing payments. A household of two adults and two children living in a two-room residence can receive $578 from the State Department of Human and Health Services and $195 in food stamps for a total income of $773. A "basic survival cost" (excluding diapers, dental or medical costs, clothing, or transportation) of $1,054 leaves this hypothetical household approximately $281 short each month (Roach 1987). Many Upper Skagit families live close to the edge of poverty or in poverty, and others could fall into this category with a little bad luck. The 1980 U.S. Census reported that 29.8 percent of Indians, Eskimos, and Aleuts in Skagit County fell below 125 percent of the poverty line, and problems of undercounts among the less stable households suggest this figure is higher.

Meanwhile, the sources of income for Upper Skagit men have diminished and employment opportunities for women have increased. Rix (1987:54, 113) described the segregation of the American labor force into men's jobs (heavy and highly skilled industrial jobs, professional and management positions) and women's jobs (service and sales) and noted that between 1980 and 1985, 6.9 million new jobs were created in the female-dominated sector and a half-million jobs were lost in the male-dominated sector of manufacturing, mining, construction, and transport. This trend describes the Skagit County situation, and the two main sources of male employment, logging and agricultural work, significantly diminished in the 1980s (Roberts 1987).

These financial difficulties make the stable and relatively large income of family heads all the more important. Family leaders provide help in keeping cars running, houses heated, and children clothed in addition to the steady supply of information concerning tribal and outside affairs.

Service on the council can be viewed as an extension of the tradition of women's, and especially grandmothers', concern for their families. Interview data at Upper Skagit (Miller 1989) show that the most widely admired female traits are caring for the family (100 percent of the randomly selected interview population rated this as important) and jobholding (100 percent), another form of service to the family. Women were also admired for knowledge of tradition (71 percent). Men, on the other hand, were most admired for a jocular, outgoing personality (66 percent), and caring for the family is not so universally expected of men (55 percent). No one reported that an ideal woman should be outgoing and jocular. Most significantly, men were not admired for the traits most admired in political leaders—impartiality, calm, and reserve. These traits are strongly associated with the ideal grandmother, drawing a clear conceptual link between politics and femininity, especially grandmotherhood. Impartiality, calm, and reserve are also traditional markers of membership in the upper class, a circumstance that reinforces the tie to authority. This link between female qualities and leadership is further strengthened at Upper Skagit, as in other Coast Salish communities, in that women are expected to handle family finances and to intervene with bureaucracies on behalf of the household or family. The ability to deal with bureaucracies (such as the BIA, the Indian Health Service, courts, and county and state government) is the second most frequently mentioned quality of leadership. The present-day link between political capacity, femininity, and grandmotherhood is sufficiently great that one Upper Skagit man claimed that Upper Skagit women are better suited to political life because of the impartiality needed to handle children and to direct family affairs. Men, on the other hand, were described as too committed to amicable relations with other men to succeed in political life.[7]

Interview data show that political grandmothers further fulfill the core element of the traditional female role, that is, concern for the family, in the issues they take up while on council. For male councilors the overriding concern is fishing in its many facets (including the size of the harvest, enhancement and enforcement of regulations, and negotiations with other governments with interests in the fisheries). Men secondarily express concern for the development of tribal industries. Women councilors, on the other hand, have specialized in social issues such as health, education, alcoholism, and the reservation culture. Female councilors, including the grandmothers, protect family members through public action (in addition to their work for their families) as was characteristic of earlier periods.[8]

In effect, women have benefited politically from their ability to embody and even define the traits regarded as significant in political leaders. Women, especially those who are sociologically and biologically grandmothers, have assumed positions of significance within the family networks and have converted this into political authority.

OTHER GRANDMOTHERS

The situation is rather different for today's grandmothers who do not control important resources, do not have an important specific contribution to make to the community, and do not have a wide network of kin relying on their advice and resources. Data from interviews and participant observation show these grandmothers do not share in this increased status, and their statuses and roles approximate that of neighboring White elderly who are thought to have lost status with the rapid social changes associated with modernization.

A significant difference between Whites and Indians is said to be the pan-Indian tradition of respect for elders. This respectfulness shows up in various ways, such as the tone of public announcements concerning the elderly, the establishment of service programs for the elderly, and the mourning over dead elders. Many elders themselves observed that "all the elders are gone" and lamented the loss of cultural and historical knowledge possessed by the elders of their younger days. This respect for elders is not enough to significantly alter the living conditions for many grandmothers. The traditional respect for elders seems to be most pronounced for those with important resources and authority.

At Upper Skagit, grandmothers who are not central figures in family networks and indeed are not members of such a corporate group may be structurally isolated from community members and community resources. They have fewer kin who will assist them and fewer kin to lend assistance to, thereby depriving them of participation in much of the process of resocialization into community life. The isolation of these grandmothers shows up clearly in relation to tribal fishing, an activity of great importance to Coast Salish "fishing people."

Fishing is an important concern of both men and women, whether they personally fish or not. The nature of the social groupings that have emerged in response to the demands of fishing heavily constrains and structures the lives of tribal members and influences the position of individuals within the community, including grandmothers. Fishing is important because of its centrality in defining the social identity of tribal members; moreover, fishing today symbolizes tribal members' resistance to White encroachment on their lives (Robbins 1980).

Salmon is both a core resource and a core cultural symbol, as it had been aboriginally. One elderly woman said:

Fishing income is essential to my household and as a direct source of food. I smoke and can a lot of salmon every year. Fishing is particularly important to older people. The most important thing about fishing is the income it provides. It is part of our heritage. It seems to come naturally to Tribal members. Fishing gives me a good, free feeling, a thrill (Robbins 1980:76).

Fishing requires interfamily cooperation, however, and this is the aspect of fishing of concern here. Thirty-five of 54 on-reservation families fish intensively, and 18 of these families have formed into three large multifamily cooperatives (the family networks described earlier) in order to succeed under difficult circumstances. These cooperatives represent about 70 percent of the fishing households (Robbins 1980:61). While no one is excluded from fishing or from having fish, the costs of undertaking fishing are high enough to eliminate families without enough money, or help, from fishing. Furthermore, competition for fish is great, both with non-Indian fishers and members of other tribes. The fish runs themselves are no longer as productive as they once were, despite efforts at conservation and enhancement.

In addition, the likelihood of one's fishing is related to the age of the household head. In households with a head over 50 years old, only 27 percent fish commercially, 20 percent subsistence fish only, and 53 percent do not fish (Robbins 1980:19). In comparison, with household heads between 20 and 29 years old, 59 percent fish commercially, and for households with a head 30 to 49 years old, 53 percent fish commercially and only 18 percent do not fish at all. Households that do not fish are generally at the beginning or end stage of the household cycle (conjugal pairs or single-person households), a circumstance that works against elders not closely tied in with younger relatives. Because fishing sites are held as a form of property, the failure of elders to fish or to be part of a fishing cooperative suggests that they are probably not in possession of a fishing site, cannot pass on rights to a site, and cannot assume a central position in a family network.

Fishing, then, provides money and reinforces the tribal identity and the identity of individual members. Ability to fish successfully provides status and recognition within the community and also reinforces the importance of kin ties because of the significance of interaction between members of the fishing cooperatives. Access to this important symbol and resource is not universal, however, and some grandmothers are nonparticipants in the system. This nonaccess negatively affects their ability to create and maintain high status in the ways I have suggested: through the control of significant resources, both material and symbolic; through the contribution of resources; and through their location at the center of a large kin network where their advice will be important. They differ in these ways from the elite grandmothers.

Ceremonial life is another significant element of the community, and knowledge of traditional practice is another important resource. Ceremonial practice is particularly important because it serves as a useful ethnic boundary marker, showing tribal members to be distinct both from members of other tribes and from neighboring Whites. Disputes over proper ceremonial practice sometimes occur between members of different tribes, and the common interests of fellow tribesmen are reinforced by these disputes. Ceremonial life is also important because of its relation to the achievement of personal standing in the community. As was the case with fishing, some grandmothers are unable to take advantage of the link between age and ceremonial importance. Amoss wrote:

> Both Shakerism and spirit dancing exalt knowledge of the old ways, something only older people possess. (Not all old people, however, have such knowledge.) (Amoss 1981a:239–40).

Lack of knowledge hinders these grandmothers, as does the expense and time involved in active participation in religious life. A naming ceremony, for example, may cost $2,000 to $4,000. The successful conducting of ceremonies contributes to the position within the community of all family members, and as Snyder noted, the status of elders may be increased with the actions of their descendants. Grandmothers who are not members of the corporate families are not likely to benefit from the ceremonial actions of their younger kin.

Finally, the nonelite set of grandmothers does not have significant personal accomplishments from their own youth and maturity to draw on for status within the community. The social costs for these elders outweigh their contribution to the community and significance of their resources.

In short, the significant routes to prestige in the community are effectively blocked from many grandmothers. This was true both in the early postcontact period and today, although why this is so has changed somewhat. The position within society of these grandmothers is hindered by their lack of special knowledge of important religious practices, by their inability to fish themselves or to participate in family fishing, by the structure of their family, and even by the status of their family members. These grandmothers resemble the sort of structurally isolated women who were depicted in the story of Pitch Boy, and they are largely outside the social and cultural forces that draw some grandmothers to center stage. They are frequently unable to fulfill the grand-mother's role of caring for the family, giving kind advice, or even contributing to the raising of family members.[9]

CONCLUSION

The present period, particularly from the early 1970s to today, has seen an increase in the status of elders in general and of some women in particular. These categories of "elders" and "women" overlap in the personage of political grandmothers, who have high status and hold formal political office. The status of elders may now equal that of precontact elders, and the status of political women surpasses that of their precontact ancestors in that while both groups possessed some political power, today specific formal authority is held by a significantly large number of grandmothers. The grandmothers' present political authority reflects in part a change in the nature of the political system generally but is nevertheless a new aspect of an old role.

Indian grandmothers in the Puget Sound provide an interesting example of diversity of response within a single population to a changing environment. Some grandmothers have increased their status through knowledge of both traditional practices and skills in the present-day world. Others have found their status diminished. While I have focused here on grandmothers actively engaged in politics, there are others who enjoy high status in the society but have not transformed this into political position.

Considerable ambiguity surrounded the status of grandmothers at the time of contact. Some women exercised political influence because of their own accomplishments (such as the acquisition of spirit helpers), because of their own personal attributes, and through the status of male and female relatives. These accomplishments gave authority over men, who apparently accepted this state of affairs with some resentment. Other grandmothers were not so lucky but nonetheless generally continued to be included within a web of kinship. Although this is difficult to determine, and some women of the early contact period were undoubtedly structurally isolated and many more may have felt psychologically alone, social institutions such as the sororate, systems of food distribution, and residence in multiple-family structures likely kept most within the social universe.

After contact and the establishment of reservations, the status of women diminished under the new economic and political conditions. With the estab-lishment of formal councils, men held for themselves what political authority was left to the tribal people, and agents of the federal government held much of the rest. Much later, when federal policy again acknowledged tribal sovereignty and permitted the distribution of resources on the basis of ethnicity, the value of elders was increased as reservation communities looked to them for expertise in interpreting the past for younger generations. Meanwhile local economic conditions favored the participation of women, rather than men, in wage work, giving women new and significant economic clout in their families and communities.

A select group of grandmothers transformed this opportunity into real political authority of a sort that the elected representatives of the tribe did not have in an earlier, less autonomous period. Although the operations of local politics vary among the northern Puget Sound tribes and the particulars are different than for the Upper Skagit case described here, the results have been the same for the elite women. Some ambiguity remains even for these present-day political grandmothers, and one powerful and skillful grandmother, mindful of this, said, "Really, men should run tribal governments."[10]

While one group of women enjoys high prestige and authority, another set of grandmothers exists, who are without many of the structural supports of the contact period and who consequently lead isolated lives. Current conditions make this difficult to avoid. For example, federal regulations forbid the employment of relatives in the at-home care of grandparents, and some grandchildren do not help grandparents without receiving small cash payments. In addition, these grandmothers are removed from the control of resources or knowledge that would increase their status and integrate them within their own communities.

These processes in Puget Sound appear to be occurring elsewhere as well. One of the clearest expositions of this trend is the account of the life of a distinguished contemporary Haida woman, Florence Edenshaw Davidson (Blackman 1992),[11] who came unexpectedly to occupy a significant place in her community as an elder and symbolically as a grandmother recognized for her knowledge of traditional practice. The Puget Sound material and Haida example point to the relevance of historically situating the concept of "grandmother" and of looking carefully at the specifics of their changing contributions to their communities in addition to examining conceptions of "grandmother" that emerge from traditional narratives.

NOTES

1. Bataille and Sands's book *American Indian Women: Telling Their Lives* (1984) examines the genre of autobiography to bring Indian women's lives and modes of expression into sharper focus. Green (1979, 1988) and Berkhofer (1978) provide accounts of the processes

whereby narrow and misleading media representations of Indians, including "passive women," were developed. Green reports that "the Indian woman is between a rock and a hard place. Like that of her male counterpart, her image is freighted with such ambivalence that she has little room to move. He, however, has many more modes in which to participate, though he is still severely handicapped by the prevailing stereotypes." Green argues that two primary images of Indian women, the Princess and Squaw, prevail. The Squaw is a "depersonalized object of scornful convenience. . . . She is powerless" (1979:713).

2. The primary religious traditions are the Seowin, or winter spirit dancing, and the Shaker Church, which grew up among Coast Salish peoples of Washington State, Oregon, and the lower mainland of British Columbia beginning in the late nineteenth century. Both religions are still practiced today, along with Pentecostalism and other practices. Jilek (1982) has documented the contemporary growth of spirit dancing. There was no winter spirit dancing house at Upper Skagit for a 40-year period between the early 1940s and 1980s. In addition, the frequency of important cultural practices with religious overtones, such as namings (in which significant ancestral names are given to community members), had declined since the early contact period but revived impressively in the 1980s. Cultural teachings and valued family knowledge, or "advice," however, never disappeared.

3. The grandmothers depend on family voters to support their candidacies and often must wait until the family is large enough to vote them into office—a circumstance associated with the coming of adulthood of grandchildren.

4. Amoss writes, "The early history of Coast Salish acculturation thus supports the assumption that rapid social change displaces the old. But the situation in the 1970s presents a striking contrast: contemporary elders have somehow managed to secure an esteemed place in society. This change cannot be explained by claiming that Indian society is now stable. . . . Rather, Indians now see value in affirming their unique position within American society, an enterprise to which old people not only contribute but to which they are essential" (1981a:237).

5. A series of important issues having to do with how people construct their identity, claim membership, and gain access to the resources available to members of groups are related to the one I raise here. Clifton (1989) somewhat cynically noted, "Since . . . the ascendancy of minority rights and acceptance of ethnic distinctiveness as a popular ethic, Indians have been significant beneficiaries of increased tolerance and many programs promoting cultural persistence, political separatism, and—supposedly—the enhancement of their situation." Clifton's work demonstrates that the manipulation of Indian identity by individuals for personal and political purposes is not new. Demographer Jeffrey Passel noted a 70 percent increase of people reporting themselves as Indian on U.S. census forms between 1980 and 1990 (*Philadelphia Inquirer* 1991). Disputes between federally recognized tribes and those without official sanction are perhaps the most significant and visible of the contemporary manifestations of the issues of resource control, tribal membership, and personal identity (*New York Times* 1992).

6. My study (1995) of the constitutions and codes of eight tribes of Puget Sound shows that six of the eight incorporate elders into the process of deciding on membership claims. This is arranged in various ways, and the Puget Sound tribes do not rely on highly for-

malized councils of elders but rather make provisions for the testimony of elders in the court as interpreters of custom or provide for elders' seats on the membership committees. In the Upper Skagit case, the elders who sit on the membership committee are ordinarily women, including grandmothers.

7. Amoss points to the importance of cultural texts as a determinant of behavior among Puget Sound Salish and argues, "In cultural texts . . . we can read what a social group thinks about how grandmothers should behave and how they should be treated." Amoss's study concerns the 1950s. Mine largely focuses on a later period and relies on individuals' reports of how they perceive cultural values and, in effect, how they interpret and internalize cultural texts.

Cruikshank (1990), in making a point related to the one made by Amoss, has underscored the importance of looking beyond "Western economic and social explanations" in understanding the perceived adaptability of Tlingit/Athapaskan women of the Yukon. She notes that women appear "more practical," "more adaptable," and "more flexible" in coping with postcontact change than men and better suited to working within Western institutions. Cruikshank argues that explanations of such differences in gender expectation must give weight "to indigenous models embedded . . . in stories" (p. 345). Narrative models are said to influence both men and women, and men in positions of political and economic influence often are those who have left home for training and returned, the modern equivalent of a spiritual quest. "Successful male protagonists [in these stories] return with what appears to an outsider to be spiritual knowledge; successful female protagonists seem more often to return by demonstrating their learned, shared, practical abilities" (p. 344). But Cruikshank emphasizes that the narrator "would see nothing inherently more 'practical' in such a woman's behavior than in the entirely practical male vision quest that . . . could result in a mutually supportive relationship between hunters and game" (p. 344). In short, expectations of women overlap more easily with the demands of contemporary life and Western institutions. Politically successful women have been able to stay within the community, raise a family, and hold a regular job. Men's activities, however, are not devalued.

My impression is that, as with the case Cruikshank describes, there are culturally underwritten ideas of appropriate male and female life courses that influence behavior in at least some Coast Salish households and communities. The way people speak of and value male and female experiences and contributions clearly affects the manner in which people choose to live. This is so even though in both regions, women's knowledge and experience overlaps more fully with the expectations of the modern world. In both areas there is, to use Cruikshank's terminology, "greater consistency between narrative models and normative expectations for women's roles than there is for men's roles" (p. 345). But although men's knowledge, experiences, and behavior are of the kind that are frequently devalued in the mainstream society, they are not necessarily thought to be of lesser value within the community.

There are important differences between the peoples of the two regions (Puget Sound and the Yukon) as well. There is no significant difference, however, in the mobility of Puget Sound men and women, and girls do not remain in school longer than boys (Miller 1989), both factors thought to be significant in understanding differences between the sexes in employment and training.

8. It is important to note that not all women share the same interests, and several Puget Sound political women have specialized in treaty-related fishing issues.

9. The issue of the relationship of elders to younger family and community members is concisely addressed in two recent books dealing with Coast Salish communities of Puget Sound. Guilmet and Whited (1989) note that in the Puyallup community many youth regard elders as an unending supply of money and that some elders give away their possessions to the young until they are destitute and homeless.

A book published by the Swinomish Tribal Mental Health Program (1991) reflects the viewpoints of a team of women, all grandmothers, who are regarded as "natural helpers" and who have been employed by the multitribal mental health system. The women describe the significance of the extended family (what I refer to as family networks) in providing emotional, financial, and ceremonial support to members. They argue that the mental health needs of the young and old are bound together complementarily. Elders teach "advice" (family sacred knowledge and proper behavior) to youth and experience gratification and a sense of purpose by doing so. Mental health problems arise when elders experience a gap between their expectations of respect and their own circumstances. The women report a trend of a gradual loss of respect for older people by youth. This view is not in disagreement with the argument presented here, however, because the Swinomish mental health team members note the opposite trend as well, of heightened respect for and interest in the views of some elders.

Finally, Amoss interprets Skagit narratives told by grandmothers in the 1950s to indicate that difficulties for some old people are not new: "Despite the rhetorical deference paid to age, older people without strong families to support them would have been disregarded." Amoss also points to the importance grandmothers place on the passing on of knowledge and to the evident sorrow of the storytellers of the 1950s because of the inability of the younger people to speak Lushootseed.

10. Elsewhere I describe localized variation in ideologies of gender and the implications for politics (Miller 1992).

11. Davidson somewhat unexpectedly gained a significant position in her community in her later years, and "to her own people . . . she has become a fragile link to the past, a veritable cultural treasure" (Blackman 1992:153) during a period in which people want to affirm their cultural identity. The interesting twist in Davidson's case is that although she was the daughter of a noted carver and community leader, she did not learn much Haida oral tradition as a young person. Later she learned her husband's songs and other traditional knowledge. Part of Davidson's story is her ability to mediate between her community and the outside world; she is well known for her work with academic researchers, and this role reinforces her position within her own community as a legitimizer of cultural practice. Interestingly, Davidson has become the "universal grandmother" (1981:xxi) known widely as "Nani," Haida for "grandmother."

BEING A GRANDMOTHER
IN THE TEWA WORLD[1]

◈

SUE-ELLEN JACOBS

INTRODUCTION

In this chapter, I provide a brief description of what approximately 25 percent of women of various ages at San Juan Pueblo have told me about being a grandmother and observations I have recorded concerning use of kinship terms and other kin-based behaviors. In my attempts to understand the range of grandmotherhood, I use the concept of "grandmother" to denote both an achieved and an ascribed status: achieved by living long enough to raise a child healthy enough to have a child; ascribed by custom when a child of a child is born. One cannot change these biological facts. One *can* choose whether or not to engage in behaviors expected of this life stage.[2] This study is based on analysis of oral history materials I have collected, reading of Doris Duke archival materials, formal interviews with a range of tribal members, and informal discussions and participant observation with over 300 members of a Tewa[3] extended family with whom I have worked annually for various lengths of times over the course of 23 years.[4] The full extended family represents approximately one half of the Tewa who live at San Juan Pueblo.[5]

CULTURAL CONTEXT

The Tewa of San Juan Pueblo, New Mexico, are bilateral,[6] with dual organization consisting of two moieties[7]: Winter and Summer. In everyday language, people refer to the "side" they are born into, marry into, or are initiated into.

Whether by birth, marriage, or initiation, all Tewa are either on the Winter or Summer side; they count, fulfill, recount, and transmit their ceremonial and everyday life obligations accordingly. Moiety membership is sometimes inherited through the mother, although it is usually inherited through the father. Moiety membership for females may not be fixed for life: women who marry outside their side customarily join their husband's side. When this happens, children belong to the side of both their father and mother. If the mother does not join the father's side, the children belong to their mother's side. In the process of fulfilling their many roles vis-à-vis children, grandmothers must keep in mind the side to which each of their grandchildren belong and carry out (especially) socialization and other childrearing activities accordingly.[8]

Formerly subsistence farmers, for the past 50 to 60 years most Tewa families have depended on wages received for work, on or off the reservation, to meet basic needs. Members of extended families consisting of three to four generations used to live in the same household or, if not under the same roof, in close proximity to one another, their residential units divided by walls in the classic "apartment" type of dwellings characteristic of the Pueblos until recently.[9] Modern homes tend to be more widely dispersed, built for and occupied by either nuclear or simple-extended families.[10]

In everyday life, great emphasis is placed on family structure and organization.[11] Childrearing is a common topic in everyday conversation and influences the organization of household as well as extra domestic work. From the birth of their own children to the ends of their lives, women (and most men) will be engaged in childrearing, along with other work and responsibilities. Thus, if one is to discuss grandmothers in this part of the Tewa world, one is drawn to focus on the work and roles women play in childrearing.

BIOLOGICAL AND CULTURAL CRITERIA AND LINGUISTIC MARKERS

If they have children and live long enough, most women at San Juan Pueblo achieve the status of grandmother. It is a biological, social, and ordinary eventuality of most women's lives. The English term "grandmother" used in the Tewa context denotes a kinship relationship and connotes the roles women play in the social reproduction of their extended families. The term is also used respectfully when addressing unrelated older women in the community.[12] The comparable English term of respect for old men is "grandfather." "Grandmother" is not synonymous with female elder. The Tewa term for "grandmother" is *sa³yâa;* the term for "grandfather" is *thehtay.* When asked for the Tewa term for "elder," several people have said it is *kwiyó.* When asked what this word means in

English, they have said "old person." This is the same word used for "old woman" and "wife" (see table below). Red Clay Basket[13] (whom you will meet in subsequent paragraphs) said that *kwiyó* is used for old women and men and "for a lady, old or young, but if you really want to talk about an old man, you can say *kwiyó sedo*"[14] (an old woman's husband), which is also the term for old age.[15]

Older Tewa women also occupy the role of tribal elder, but to consider Tewa women as elders as opposed to grandmothers requires a wider context for analysis. The status of grandmother is assigned when one's children have children; I have known grandmothers as young as 36, and for some women the chronological age at which this occurred has been as young as 32. Elders are all over 50. The status of knowledgeable or respected elder is achieved by practicing traditions and sharing cultural knowledge and skills. Thus, although many Tewa grandmothers also achieve the status of elder, grandmother is not automatically synonymous with female elder.

Roles women elders play in community organization include but are not limited to being responsible for preparing and carrying out aspects of sodality (or "clan") and other tribal affairs they or their husbands and fathers engage in and serving on advisory committees set up by the tribal council, the senior citizen program, and other community programs. Until one has achieved the status of old person, one is considered green *(p'oeseewi?)*, or unripened, meaning that person does not know enough about traditions, language, and life in general to be involved in community decision making. Notwithstanding the fact that for most older women the categories overlap, the focus of this chapter is grandmotherhood, not elderhood.

At San Juan Pueblo, grandmothers are addressed and referred to as *T'saeyah* (older spelling), *Sayah* (colloquial spelling), or *Sa'yâa*.[16] Sometimes children refer to specific grandmothers and great-grandmothers by adding the first names or nicknames of these individuals to the term *Sa'yâa* (e.g., *Sayah* Rita). The *San Juan Pueblo Tewa Dictionary* gives the following terms:

Tewa	English
yíyá[17]	mother
sa'yâa[18]	grandmother
pahpáa sa'yâa	great-grandmother
yíyá kwiyó[19]	great-great-grandmother
kú'gûu sa'yâa	great-great-great-grandmother
kwiyó	old woman, wife
sa'yá'ay	grandchild of a grandmother
kó'ôe, nána[20]	aunt

Esther Martinez, bilingual educator (and compiler and editor of the *San Juan Pueblo Tewa Dictionary*) at San Juan Pueblo, says that most children use the word *sa ʾyâa* for all their grandmothers, even though a child may know the terms that differentiate degrees of grandmotherhood. I have observed that children who otherwise speak no Tewa most often address and refer to their grandparents using the Tewa terms *sa ʾyâa* and *thehtay* (grandfather). A woman elder may be addressed by any of the respect terms *yíyá* (mother), *sa ʾyâa* (grandmother), *yíyá kwiyó* (literally "mother old woman" or "mother wife"), or *kó ʾôe* (aunt).

The age range for grandmothers referred to in this chapter is 36 to 85. The average age at which women first acquire the status of grandmother in this community appears to be 40, or at the beginning of the final decade of a woman's biological reproductive cycle—the age that marks the onset of what is now called middle age. Many factors contribute to how they respond to this new status, but grandmothers whom I have come to know have all told me they were very happy when their "first grandchild came along." They say that each subsequent grandchild has "added to [their] happiness." They also say that sometimes these children have also added to their workload and consequently are "a mixed blessing."

SOME ROLES OF FOUR TEWA GRANDMOTHERS[21]

Red Clay Basket was born in 1900 and died in 1990. At her death she was an elder and a grandmother. Her grandmother taught her how to cook and sew; how to identify and collect raw materials for and the techniques involved in making pottery; how to process the harvest of corn, squash, wheat, and other produce grown in the family fields; and how to identify and use various wild roots, berries, and leaves for cooking and medicine. These skills and knowledge were important for Red Clay Basket's future roles as wife of Sun Moving (who was later to become a sodality head), mother of five children, foster mother of six additional children (whom she raised after her sister died), grandmother of 22, great-grandmother of 27, and great-great-grandmother of four.

After marriage and the birth of her first several children, Red Clay Basket periodically worked for wages as a housekeeper at the Los Alamos Scientific Laboratory, and she regularly made and sold pottery. The family depended in part on her cash income to meet expenses of daily living. In the 1980s she and her grandchildren benefited from her earlier years of employment at Los Alamos through the social security checks she and Sun Moving received.

Over the course of 14 years, I observed Red Clay Basket in her interactions with most of her grandchildren, great-grandchildren, and one great-great-grandchild. She said, "I have raised all my grandchildren," as a way of announcing that she had taken a major role in their early childrearing. Her daughters, some of her nieces and nephews whom she took into her home when their mother died, and some of her grandchildren also say "she raised all my children." The activities that I have observed include those that some scholars now refer to as "childminding" (referred to as "babysitting" by Red Clay Basket). That is, children are left with their grandmother (or great-grandmother) for feeding and general care while the mother is engaged in work for wages. Sometimes the parents of the child paid Red Clay Basket a fee for babysitting. Now, as part of a relatively new program, a child's parents may apply to the tribe for childcare subsidies that will be paid directly to the caretaker. In order to qualify as a recipient of the tribal funds, caretakers must have homes that meet federally defined minimal requirements of health and safety. Some older homes do not meet these requirements. In one instance I noted that the denial of subsidy did not stop a mother from leaving her son with his great-grandmother for care; Red Clay Basket was just paid less by the child's mother than she would have been by the tribal program.

Irrespective of the externally defined regulations on home safety standards for subsidized childcare, everyone understands that part of the responsibility of child caregivers (babysitters or childminders) is to protect children from harm. Women who grew up in the older religious traditions explain that harm can come from spirit as well as from living forces. It is relatively easy to see and prevent harm from living forces, but spirit forces are not so easily seen. They might come on even a gentle breeze and enter infants or young children if they are not properly protected. An infant or young child in Red Clay Basket's care was never left unattended. If for one reason or another she had to leave the child asleep and alone in a room, she placed a protective sacred object on the blanket covering the sleeping child. At home the children's parents did not always take these precautions. When I asked the parents why not, I was told that they "didn't believe in those superstitious things." Yet when the children became ill, for example, had digestive problems or a cold or needed other health care, the parents often sought Red Clay Basket's advice before (and sometimes after) going to the health clinic.

Red Clay Basket was well known for her curing abilities. Sick children and infants were brought to her not only from San Juan but from other Pueblos, too. Most frequently, however, it was her relatives who came to her for cures. If she decided that the solution to the health problem was beyond her knowledge and capabilities, in addition to the preliminary treatment she provided, she recommended that the child be taken to the medicine man; otherwise she undertook full curing, which usually required four separate sessions.

Red Clay Basket employed a range of healing practices. She used herbs, roots, ash, salt, soda, and other sources of medicine for a variety of adult and child afflictions. For example, she was often asked to help with the care of an infant's drying umbilical cord. Using dust from the vigas (exposed round roof beams) in the kitchen, ash from the woodstove, and salt and powder from crushed pottery sherds (if available), she made a poultice and applied it to the umbilicus, which was then covered with an abdominal binding cloth. The mother or both parents of the infant were instructed not to remove the covering for four days.

Parents of infants and young children called on Red Clay Basket's traditional knowledge for other purposes, too. For example, she performed the naming ceremony for many of her great-grandchildren, one great-great-grandchild, and some of her grandchildren. In previous times the "naming mother"[22] (customarily an elder who is a member of one of the parents' extended families) would perform the ceremony at dawn on the fourth day following birth. Most births now take place in hospitals. If all goes well, the mother and infant leave the hospital in time for the ceremony to take place on the fourth day; however, when this is not possible, the naming ceremony is performed at the earliest convenient time after the child is brought home to the Pueblo.

Children and grandchildren depended on Red Clay Basket for advice and support in matters related to the performance of traditional ceremonials. She loaned garments and jewelry from her store of these for her relatives' participation in ceremonies. On the day of these ceremonies she often dressed her granddaughters and great-granddaughters and explained to them attitudes they should have about the ceremony. She sometimes also described the experiences she had when she took part in ceremonies in years past. Since most ceremonies also involve dance and song, she sometimes showed the young women how the steps go and/or how the song used to be sung.

Children and grandchildren also called on Red Clay Basket for economic support. Most of the time she loaned money to those who asked, but she warned them sternly that she must be repaid by a certain date or they would not be given further loans. Sometimes she referred to herself as "the family banker." At other times she provided work for the young people and paid them an agreed-on sum.

Red Clay Basket stopped working on pottery in about 1982. Prior to that time, she had taught her techniques to her daughters and some of her granddaughters. Two daughters became potters; no granddaughters have become potters. I observed Red Clay Basket's grandchildren and great-grandchildren of both sexes forming pottery pieces while in their *sa'yâa*'s care. When their pottery pieces were finished, they were included among the pottery bowls, plates, and other items she either took to the Santa Fe Indian Market or sold to the traders who used to come to the house to buy pottery and carvings from Red Clay Basket and Sun Moving. The money was then given to the children.

One daughter and several granddaughters have worked as domestics in Los Alamos. Now most granddaughters have full-time employment commensurate with their level of education. Most of those who have children used to leave them in the care of their mothers or with Red Clay Basket until they were old enough for school. The school-age grandchildren used to come on the school bus to Red Clay Basket's house after school was over each weekday, where they had a snack, did some homework or watched TV (but usually would go outside to play), and waited for their parents to come home from work.

Rita (pseudonym; born 1935, died 1997), Red Clay Basket's youngest daughter, first became a grandmother at age 36 and had six grandchildren. She held "baby showers" for her daughter and daughters-in-law, held feasts following the Catholic baptism of each grandchild and following the First Holy Communion of her first grandchild, and engaged in other activities that would ensure weekly contact with her grandchildren. Working full time at the Los Alamos Scientific Laboratory during the week and with an unmarried school-age child still at home with her and her husband, she did not serve as a "childminder" for her children's children, but she provided financial and social support for them on a regular basis and her oldest granddaughter (now 12) occasionally spent the weekend with her.

Agnes (pseudonym; born 1926), in her late fifties, is Red Clay Basket's daughter-in-law. When Agnes's husband retired from industry in the Midwest at age 55, she resigned her job as a special education teacher and they moved back to the reservation with four of their 10 children. In the Midwest, Agnes had taken full responsibility for "raising" her first grandchild, who was incorporated into Agnes's home as a daughter. Subsequent children of children were incorporated as grandchildren. When Agnes and her husband moved West, all of these grandchildren stayed in the Midwest with their biological parents.

After settling into life in New Mexico, Agnes's husband began farming his parents' fields and both he and Agnes became active in community affairs. They are members of the senior citizen program advisory committee, serve on several church committees, and participate in tribal affairs. Agnes also began work as tribal librarian, writing and administering grants for the development of a community lending library. The family's main source of income is her husband's retirement money, Agnes's income from work as tribal librarian, and contributions to household expenses (food and utilities) made by the employed children who live at home. Over the past two years, Agnes's husband's farming has been yielding larger quantities of high-quality produce, stimulating an increased demand for it among local people. An expanded harvest requires a related increase in *processing* the harvest—a task that largely falls to Agnes, dramatically increasing her household chores during this season.

In a recent year, two new grandchildren were added to the family. Agnes held "baby showers" for each daughter and then provided feasts to celebrate each infant's baptism. The mother of one lived with Agnes and her husband. She found it desirable to take a job when her child was about six months old. Agnes became her "childminder" while also working part time at the library, writing grants, processing the harvest, serving on committees, and managing her household. Her husband could be called on to "watch" the baby when she needed to leave their home for grocery shopping, paying bills, opening the library for a limited number of hours, and other activities that took her away from the house. Agnes and her husband also assumed major responsibility for taking care of Red Clay Basket and Sun Moving, who lived in a separate but nearby home.

Elsie (pseudonym; born 1936), in her mid-fifties, is Red Clay Basket's other living daughter. Her husband worked full time until he died in 1995. Elsie managed their home, where they raised a son and daughter. Of their three grandchildren, the first grandchild is being raised by their son's child's mother's mother. Their daughter and her husband work full-time. The daughter's children (a girl and a boy) were left with Elsie for care during their infancy. Over the years, the granddaughter has spent an increasing amount of time with her grandparents. Elsie has crippling arthritis and has become increasingly dependent on her granddaughter, who, by the age of about seven, had learned to cook, clean house, and help her grandmother with the laundry. Now at age nine, the granddaughter rarely sleeps at her parents' home, but occasionally she used to spend the day with her mother's mother's mother (i.e., her great-grandmother, Red Clay Basket), who taught her how to make pottery when she was about four years old. Elsie and her husband provide their granddaughter with clothes, school supplies, toys, trips to the zoo in Albuquerque and other outings, and many other economic, social, and affective benefits. As with the other grandparents mentioned, a great deal of love is felt for and extended to this granddaughter and her brother.

All four grandmothers have described their feelings of love for their grandchildren, but Red Clay Basket used to warn that "it is dangerous to pet them too much" because "life is hard, and they have to learn their lessons for when

Reyecita M. Aquino and her great-granddaughter, Tina Louise Cata. San Juan Pueblo, New Mexico. Photograph © 1982 by Sue-Ellen Jacobs.

you are gone, when they are on their own." Still, she admitted to having favorites among her grandchildren, those she "wished to please," and to these grandchildren she gave extra attention in the form of actual time and conversations as well as money, clothing, jewelry, and other material goods.

CHANGING ROLES OF GRANDMOTHERS
THROUGH THE GENERATIONS

To be a grandmother in the Tewa world basically means that one has had children and lived long enough to participate in the social reproduction of one's children's children. A brief overview of some childrearing activities of four grandmothers within one segment of a large extended family aids in understanding a range of behaviors of culturally and physically caring for the next generation that ensures the community's survival. The grandmothers accomplish this by providing the following to children and grandchildren:

1. Informal teaching of basic skills and knowledge;
2. Collaboration with parents in childrearing through daily care for limited to extended amounts of time;
3. Ceremonial clothes, jewelry, and knowledge;
4. Care of sick infants and children;
5. Cash and material support in the form of loans, gifts, and wages;
6. Sponsoring or conducting the fourth-day naming ceremony;
7. Provision of new parents who live within their households (or who live neolocally);
8. "Showers" before and baptism feasts after the birth of a child as rites of recognition and incorporation to which family and friends are invited;
9. Love;
10. Other activities as needed for meeting family, moiety, and community responsibilities (e.g., helping with cooking for feast days and baking bread, pies, and cookies for weddings, feasts, and other events).

Being a grandmother in the Tewa world may mean doing all of these things for one's children and children's children and on down the generations—added of course to the work they do and responsibilities they hold for their own households and the community at large. When grandmotherhood includes direct involvement in childcare, for some women it means an increase in an already heavy workload, as in Agnes's situation during harvest season; for others (as with Elsie, Rita, and Red Clay Basket) it has meant developing friendships across the generations as well as (for Elsie and Red Clay Basket) resuming desirable primary care of young people in one's middle to later years.

Through their second-, third-, and fourth-generation childrearing activities, most Tewa grandmothers have participated in the perpetuation and mainte-nance of their community's traditional values and customs. They have also helped their own children improve their economic condition by providing daycare so that their grandchildren's parents could both work full-time. Cul-tural, social, and biological advantages seem to accrue to all generations in a family and to the whole community under these circumstances. But as in other communities where emphasis has shifted to single-family households and wage labor economies, changes affecting the traditional socialization processes that have occurred over the generations may make this observation very conditional. These changes have to do with several things: first, an overall increase in life expectancy for members of the community, and second, an increase in secured wage labor by women, with retirement coming some 20 to 30 years (i.e., at age 62 to 65) after an individual achieves the biological and cultural status of grandmother. Indeed, it is beginning to be clear that if one is going to depend on relatives for childcare, one must hope for a great-grandmother, because she is the one most likely to be freed from the workforce and able (if she is willing) to make an investment in the rearing of her children's children's children.[23]

At the time of the first writing of this chapter (1985), Red Clay Basket was 85 years old. In her generation, women first became grandmothers in their mid- to late thirties. Most women did not work off the reservation but worked in the domestic sphere of the Pueblo, making pottery, tending to gardens, processing the harvests, and other tasks that allowed them to care for children while they did other work, including spending large parts of each day preparing and cooking food for all household members. They may have worked off the reservation sporadically, and when they did, they left their children in the care of their mothers (if they were still alive) or other kin. People lived in close proximity to one another and shared in childrearing. With the birth of her first great-grandchild at about age 55, Red Clay Basket began her involvement in rearing the third generation of her descendants. Her oldest daughter, Ellen (pseudonym; born 1922, died 1969), helped with the rearing of this child and then with other grandchildren as they came along. Agnes, in her mid-fifties, had no great-grandchildren. She has engaged in childrearing with over half of her grandchildren but not as intensively as Red Clay Basket did in raising her grandchildren. Rita was not a childminder for any of her children, while Elsie has taken a major role in rearing her daughter's children. Gloria (pseudonym; born 1924, died 1976), Red Clay Basket's other daughter, had no children but assumed large financial and other responsibilities for Rita's sons. The diverse patterns found in the childrearing roles of these six women can be considered characteristic of those found throughout the reservation.

SUMMARY AND CONCLUSIONS

In the Tewa world, as in many other places, grandmotherhood is defined biologically, but it is also defined culturally. Old women are addressed respectfully as *sa'yâa,* or "grandmother," irrespective of biological relatedness. When a woman becomes a grandmother, her status changes. *She* decides whether or not her familial and community roles will change at that time or later. Thus becoming a grandmother is at first a biological event, occurring when a child of a child is born, then culturally and socially constructed. Perceived biological change is another basis for becoming a grandmother, but in a fully sociocultural fashion (i.e., no biological link is required): a woman ages and, whether she has grandchildren or not, when she is perceived to be "old," she will be called *sa ʾyâa* (grandmother) or *kwiyó* (mother old woman)—highly respectful terms used for old women who are and are not related.[24]

Since grandmotherhood is a status defined at the outset in relationship to childbearing, it is not surprising that the expected associated roles include participation of grandmothers in rearing of their grandchildren. However, changes in work and living arrangements at San Juan Pueblo are leading to changes in role performance. Previously grandmothers could care for grandchildren while doing their work, freeing mothers to have more children and to concentrate on nurturing youngest children in turn. In Red Clay Basket's younger years, there were more extended family households than now and childrearing tended to be a collective endeavor, with grandmothers taking a major role in socialization of their grandchildren. Now there are fewer grandmothers available for childrearing, as more mothers and grandmothers work off the reservation until the social security and union retirement age of 62 to 65 (or younger if they have civil service jobs). This leaves the care of many young children to daycare centers, professional babysitters, and other nonkin who are paid to mind small children during the day; others may be cared for by their great-grandmothers.

The Tewa definition of grandmothers includes an expectation of significant socialization of grandchildren, which contemporary grandmothers strive to meet. Some grandmothers experience conflict because their roles as household managers require them to provide all the domestic services (such as processing the harvest, in Agnes's case) once performed by younger adult women, who now must contribute to *their* household economies by wage labor outside the home, often off the reservation. Those who cannot meet the socialization expectations themselves may provide monetary or other support for grandchildren, or they may encourage their children to avail themselves of the help their mothers can provide (i.e., the great-grandmothers become the primary childminders). Thus it appears that with extended longevity, there has developed a specific "great-grandmother role" devoted to childminding as well as informal instruction in traditional culture (e.g., language, stories, pottery making, cooking, and ceremonial matters). Many grandmothers now specialize in household management, tribal affairs, *and* full-time employment, while most mothers are expected to bear children and spend most of their working day in wage labor.[25] Being a grandmother in the Tewa world is now much more complex (and involves less direct participation in the lives of grandchildren) than it used to be, but the status is one aspired to by all the women I know at San Juan Pueblo.

EPILOGUE 1998

With the passage of the years since this material was first presented, death of a number of the elders has resulted in their offspring assuming the roles necessary for inculcating Tewa cultural values in succeeding generations. But more than this, their passing has left gaping holes in the transmission process.

Fissioning within the family began within hours of the passing of Red Clay Basket. Arguments about her intentions regarding the transmittal of property had begun during the last two years of Sun Moving's life but reached scandalous proportions within the months following her death. In the 20 years I had known her, Red Clay Basket had always made it clear that she expected her property to be divided among specific children and grandchildren. Her only son, Agnes's husband, was not happy with the arrangements his mother had made with the tribal attorney to ensure that neither she nor Sun Moving died intestate. Their son arranged to have their wills changed so that he would inherit everything except property that was already registered by the tribe in ownership of three grandchildren (two sons of Rita and a daughter of Elsie) and a few hay patches and a garden plot. The house in which both Red Clay Basket and Sun Moving lived most of their married lives and where they both died had been promised to Rita's youngest child, a daughter. But when the will was read, the house had been bequeathed to Red Clay Basket and Sun Moving's only son.

Soon "Only Son" settled his newly married son in the house. He also began "stretching" placement of farm machinery, hay stacks, automobiles, and other personal possessions into space that was registered as Rita's property and into Rita's youngest son's property. Bitter, public conflict between them arose on more than one occasion. At one point Rita was knocked down by the son of "Only Son," who was living in the deceased elders' home. On another occasion daughters of "Only Son" engaged Rita's daughters and one of her sons in a brawl. Tribal police officers, the tribal judge, family, and community elders were called to mediate but with little long-term resolution of the property dispute. Court appearances with resulting restraining orders were issued to all parties involved more than four times. Finally the real estate manager for the tribe delivered the official tribal council opinion on land rights, and all parties were told to respect this ruling by staying off the others' property. To secure her visual and physical space, Rita's youngest daughter had an eight-foot-high wooden fence built between her home and her grandparents' home, now occupied by another newly married child of "Only Son." But by this time Rita was dying, and the resolution of the horrific problems involving the "betrayal" by her "beloved only brother" was a hollow victory. The toll of the seven years of intense family conflict was heavy.

In January 1997, just four months after the birth of her first great-grand-child, Rita died from the vicious malignant cancer that had reduced her weight to 67 pounds in the course of about 18 months. Until the last month of her life, she had struggled through the troubles on behalf of her children. At her deathbed, her middle daughter told her:

> Mom, just let go. We are all okay. We all have our own houses now. We all have jobs. We're just fine. We'll be okay.

Rita's response, her last word before her last breath was drawn, was a "No."

There is no doubt in anyone's mind that Rita loved all of her grandchildren and was very happy when her oldest son's only daughter made her a great-grandmother. But throughout the 26 years I knew her, Rita convinced me that in addition to the maternal and domestic roles she carried out so skillfully, she also loved her own life—her job(s); land, cattle, and the high country; beautiful clothes and jewelry; and giving sumptuous feasts and parties for family and friends. She was exceptionally outgoing and a dedicated Tewa citizen (participating in various yearly Tewa ceremonials until her health began to decline and regularly attending Catholic mass). Throughout the Española Valley and in Los Alamos, she had many friends. The Catholic Church at San Juan Pueblo could not accommodate all of the several hundred people who came to her funeral. Dozens attended her one-year anniversary ceremony in January 1998, held in her eldest son's home—the home she and her husband lived in while raising four of their children and into retirement.

"Eldest Son" returned to this home when he and his first wife were divorced and helped his mother care for the younger children still at home. His daughter, the granddaughter who used to come spend weekends with her grandmother, is the one who gave Rita her only great-grandchild while she was still living. Rita's brother ("Only Son") conducted her one-year anniversary service, bringing some closure to the years of turmoil as well as facilitating Rita's passage to her next spiritual stage. The cousins have begun to reconcile their strained relationship—this process being facilitated by other elders in this large extended family as well as by tribal officials, but also through the process of aging that they have been experiencing during the past eight years.

Because their mother preferred not to be a "babysitter" for their children, Rita's children found support for their supplemental childrearing needs from their mother's sister, Elsie, and her husband. Practically speaking, Elsie has assumed the job her mother, Red Clay Basket, had by feeding and watching the children before they go to school and when they get home from school. She helps her grandniece and nephew with preparation for school events and teaches the children cultural values through conversation and informal instruction. In addition, Elsie continued corearing (with her daughter) her youngest granddaughter through high school. Elsie's engagement with her granddaughter continues, along with "babysitting" her first great-grandson, born two months before her husband, the baby's great-grandfather, died.

When Elsie's granddaughter became a mother, her daughter, Louise, became a grandmother for the first time. Louise and her husband George have become loving and doting grandparents, putting their hopes and desires for their grandson ahead of many other dreams and needs. Louise told me shortly after her grandson was born:

Nothing else matters, no troubles at work, nowhere. Nothing is the same since we got him.

They share active participation in "babysitting" with the baby's father's mother and father (his paternal grandparents), but reluctantly. Unlike the father's parents, Louise and George (and the baby's mother) are active in Tewa ceremonial and cultural life. They "dress up" for public events, both Tewa and English are spoken in the home and to the baby, Tewa spiritual and religious materials are evident, and now that he is two and a half years old (and walking and talking with vigor), the grandson is being introduced to ceremonial dance steps. He is being socialized to become a participant in traditional Tewa culture by his maternal grandparents, his maternal great-grandmother, and his mother (who has retained membership in her parents' moiety).

I have lost touch with Agnes (wife of "Only Son") and her family but am told that in spite of ill health, she maintains her grandmotherly duties to the grandchildren who live in New Mexico.

From my vantage point, it seems hard to be a woman in this Tewa culture. Mothers are the owners of their homes and have the right to pass them on to their children. Mothers are very attached to their sons and work diligently to keep them close to home. Daughters are expected to find husbands and get their own homes where they will raise their children. It seems particularly hard for daughters-in-law to feel comfortable in the homes of their husbands' mothers or even close by, as was the case for Agnes. There are many instances of intense competition between mothers and daughters-in-law for the attention of the mothers' sons, and there are equally intense competitions between grandparents (especially grandmothers) for giving attention to grandchildren. A daughter may be encouraged to defer to her husband's parents to ensure that their grandchildren get paternal as well as maternal filial attention. In a number of families, I have observed that it is important that the father of the child engage his parents in the process of providing his child's mother with her own home. Consequently, no matter how hard it may hurt to have to relinquish time with a grandchild, the maternal grandparents will do so to facilitate the investment in their daughter by the in-laws.[26] This is especially important in families where there are both sons and daughters, because the parents will ultimately have to make sacrifices on behalf of the mother(s) of their son(s)' children.

Because of the uncertainty that all of her daughters would gain other support for obtaining their own homes, Rita worked hard to ensure that each daughter, married or not, had a home before she left this world. "Only Son" once told me that as the senior male left in his family line, he was worried about getting all of his children housed satisfactorily. Even with the new wills leaving most of his parents' property to him, he did not have enough holdings to pass something on to his sons and daughters. Since his wife is from another Pueblo, his children depend on his tactical benevolence to inherit property, although they can qualify for their own property once married. His "stretching" into Rita's property was clearly an attempt to improve his children's situation. In the midst of a round of conflict, Rita once told me,

> I feel sorry for my brother, with all those children to take care of while he is still in this world. In a way, I don't blame him, but he has to look elsewhere because I have my own kids to think about.

For now matters are settled.

It is especially humbling to me to have reached a point in my life where I can look back over the past 28 years of relationships at San Juan Pueblo and realize that I have a view of six generations. There are so many people I miss, people the younger ones never knew and only hear about in stories various adults tell. As with other adult members of the family, I visit the departed ones at the graveyard at least once a year when I am there, reflecting on our times together, what I have learned, and what I still owe them for their gifts of knowledge and love.

There are new friends, new generation members, and more expected. Over the years I have tried to assume some of the responsibilities expected of someone my age who stands in kinship relationship to many people in this community. Part of my grandparenting responsibility is to see that aspects of the culture are transmitted appropriately. For example, stories that were given to me by elders in the 1970s have been returned to family and wider community members through the production of an interactive multimedia CD-ROM and audio CD and cassette versions of those stories (no further distribution is allowed without permission of the tribal council). Additional works are in progress. The cycle of cultural transmission is still maintained verbally in most households, with grandparents and great-grandparents talking with their grandchildren and sharing (in the ways described above) those resources necessary to secure a new cultural future. In a kinship-based community, it is the job of everyone to care for and appropriately socialize the children, and it is still true that grandparents (and great-grandparents) assume a large measure of these duties.

ACKNOWLEDGMENTS

This chapter is based on ethnohistorical research begun in 1970, formal interviewing, and participant observation begun in 1972. Research funds have been primarily out of my own pocket, supplemented by small grants from the Doris Duke Foundation (1972), the Melville and Elizabeth Jacobs Research Fund (1976, 1977), and the Graduate School Research Fund at the University of Washington (1978, 1979). Two reading versions of this chapter were presented at the symposia organized and chaired by Marjorie Schweitzer (organizer 1985, 1986).

I am grateful to the following people for comments and suggestions on this chapter: the late Alfonso Ortiz, Frances Quintana, Marianne Gullestad, members of the Seattle Women Anthropologists Group (Charlene J. Allison, Pamela Amoss, Joann Bromberg, Ronna Brown, Debra Boyer, Julie Ann Duncan, Lydia Kotchek, and Sonja Solland), Marjorie Schweitzer, Joan Weibel-Orlando, my friends and colleagues at San Juan Pueblo, and two anonymous reviewers.

For their careful reading of several versions of "Epilogue 1998" and for their permission to publish this version, my heartfelt thanks go to Rita's daughters. I am also grateful to Sally O'Neill and Serena Mauer, two students in my graduate feminist theory seminar, for their comments and advice and to Marjorie Schweitzer for patiently working through the dilemmas faced in making both parts of the chapter presentable.

NOTES

1. With the exception of the epilogue and minor changes in the main text, this chapter first appeared in the *American Indian Culture and Research Journal* 19:2(1995:67–83) and is republished here with permission of the journal and the regents of the University of California. Members of both Elsie's and Rita's family agreed to publishing the contents of "Epilogue 1998." (See note 4 for further information on permissions.)

2. This is an aspect of grandparenthood discussed by others who have studied life cycling cross-culturally; namely, that not all grandparents are willing or able to fulfill societal expectations. For example, Joan Weibel-Orlando (1990:109–25) reports a similar finding from her research with South Dakota reservation and Los Angeles urban Siouan grandparents; however, her overall schemata of five grandparenting styles ("distanced grandparent," "ceremonial grandparent," "fictive grandparent," "custodial grandparent," and "cultural conservator grandparent") are not categories of persons found at San Juan Pueblo. Perhaps the five styles she reports *are* as clearly demarcated in the communities where she has lived, and her generalizations may fit other Indian societies as well. However, for this Pueblo world, in the practice of everyday life, sociocultural roles are seldom so easily categorized or clearly differentiated. At San Juan Pueblo, people may assume full cultural expectations for being grandmothers when it first happens to them, or they may wait until they have achieved "elder" status before meeting all objectives. Weibel-Orlando's discussion provides an interesting parallel, though somewhat contrasting, point of view.

3. "Tewa" refers to the six linguistically related yet autonomous Rio Grande Indian Pueblos located in north-central New Mexico and their ancestors. It also refers to the language of the native peoples who reside in those Pueblos, and as with the terms "Navajo," "Apache," "Cherokee," or "American" it also refers to tribal or national identity and should therefore always be capitalized.

4. Members of the family, including the four grandmothers described and most of their female kin, have read this chapter and given permission for its publication.

5. This estimation takes into account all lineal and collateral consanguineal (blood) and affinal (in-law) relations. Senior family members estimated that "over a thousand of our relatives" attended a party honoring the oldest community elder on the occasion of his hundredth birthday. The 1986 total Tewa residential figures were projected by a tribal official to be "around 1,850," while the total tribal enrollment was projected to be "around 2,500" (that means about 650 enrolled tribal members do not live on the reservation).

6. The term "bilateral" refers to the fact that people determine their kinship relationships through both their mother and their father.

7. The term "moiety" refers to the division of a society into two lineal kinship parts (or "sides"), each having specified responsibility for community social, political, economic, and religious organizations and functions. In the Tewa world, Winter people are responsible for these matters from approximately the autumnal equinox to the spring equinox, while people on the Summer side have these responsibilities from approximately the spring equinox to the autumnal equinox. The above is a gross simplification of a very complex social order; for detailed information see Ortiz (1969).

8. For details on differences between Winter and Summer people, their everyday and ceremonial obligations, and seasonal rounds, see Alfonso Ortiz (1969).

9. These complex housing structures, which were found throughout the American Southwest at the time of the Spanish arrival in 1540, have been retained in only a few locales. Old Taos Pueblo is probably the best known, as it is open to the public (for a fee) and often appears in tourist promotional photographs from New Mexico.

10. The adjective "simple" is the term anthropologists and other social scientists use to refer to small extended families that usually consist of one grandparental generation, one set of parents, and these parents' children. Anyone who has grown up in or resides as a teenager or an adult in such a household knows that they are by no means "simple" in terms of interpersonal relations, economics, and other aspects of managing everyday life.

11. This is noted in several ways: (1) in conversations people frequently discuss aspects of affinal (or in-law) and consanguineal (or blood) relationships and reciprocal obligations and privileges associated with these, and (2) in my observations I note that people talk about and organize their work patterns in ways that allow them to meet familial responsibilities; e.g., taking off from work to bake bread, prepare the house, purchase the "giveaway" or "basket" items, and attend to additional matters associated with special family or village feasts and other events.

12. Older women and men are sometimes also referred to as "senior citizens," a practice that came into being in the late 1970s as a result of the establishment of the tribal senior citizen program.

13. The names "Red Clay Basket" and "Sun Moving" are the ones approved for use by the elders before their deaths in 1990 and 1989 respectively. For this and subsequent publications they preferred that I use the English translations of their Tewa names rather than initials for their English/Spanish names as we had done in an earlier publication. It is inappropriate to use people's Tewa names without their explicit permission to do so. Other personal names that appear are pseudonyms I chose; these were subsequently approved (humorously) by the individuals to whom they refer.

14. The quote is from my 1986 field notes. The use of an inclusive unmarked term for old person and woman is similar to Alfonso Ortiz's observation that *sa²yâaing* is inclusive of grandparents and grandmothers (personal communication 1986). At the request of the anonymous Tewa reviewer of this chapter, I asked a San Juan Pueblo native speaker and linguist, Blue Water, about current usage of *kwiyó* at San Juan Pueblo. She replied that *kwiyó* is still used as a formal term of respect when addressing certain elders, can mean "old person," but is now rarely used in everyday conversational settings (personal communication 1995).

15. Esther Martinez (1983).

16. This spelling is found in the *San Juan Pueblo Tewa Dictionary* (Martinez 1983), which is based on Summer Institute of Linguistics phonetics. In letters and notes I have seen written to grandmothers, I have never seen either the older spelling or the dictionary spelling; it has always been *Sayah*.

17. Also used as a term of respect.

18. Also used as a term of respect.

19. Also used as a term of respect.

20. Also used as a term of respect, and "[i]n school children address teachers and resource people as *kóʔôeʼ* (Martinez 1983:66).

21. This chapter was first written as a draft almost 15 years ago. At that time the elders referred to in this and other publications were still able to respond to writings about them. They and their family members gave permission to publish materials submitted to them for this kind of approval. Red Clay Basket and Sun Moving were among the last elders who retained strict Tewa traditions within their home while simultaneously enjoying improved material conditions (from indoor plumbing in 1970 to acquisition of their first telephone and first television in 1978 and a double hot plate for cooking instead of "always having to use our winter wood," among others). Emphasis on Red Clay Basket in this chapter reflects the emphasis in the family for my research to be on that generation whose members are now all deceased (1993). The biographies I am writing about these elders are done with the hope that their grandchildren and subsequent generations will appreciate the elders' lives and the changes they experienced. This chapter reflects a biographical focus on Red Clay Basket because she epitomizes her generation's style of grandmothering. Her daughters and daughter-in-law are briefly sketched as representatives of modern Tewa grandmothers. The emphasis on change is deliberately contrastive. This is the material that in 1988 we all agreed addressed the issues of "being a grandmother in the Tewa world."

22. This is the English term used for the woman elder who will give the child its first Tewa name. For details on the traditional naming ceremony, see Ortiz (1969:30–31).

23. I am particularly indebted to Pamela Amoss for deducing this from information I presented in an early draft of this chapter.

24. In 1984 some children who had called me *kóʔôe* (aunt) for as long as I had known them began tentatively addressing me as *saʔyâa* (grandmother). It had been a year since I had seen them and my hair was grayer; my face, neck, and hands more wrinkled. They experimented with addressing me this way for several weeks, then resumed calling me *kóʔôe*—I am not sure why. I have noticed that *kóʔôe* is sometimes used for addressing both old and young women irrespective of biological relatedness.

25. I am particularly indebted to Pamela Amoss for deducing this from information I presented in an early draft of this chapter.

26. The ideal postmarital residence rule is still sequential: a newly married couple lives with the husband's mother for a while so the wife can learn the environment in which her husband was raised; then they live with the wife's mother at childbirth; then neolocally. This pattern is not always followed. When possible, the couple will set up their own household but generally in proximity to the husband's parents.

THE TWO ASPECTS OF
HOPI GRANDMOTHERHOOD

<>

ALICE SCHLEGEL

Many elderly Hopis were born into a home that contained a grandmother. In earlier times, young husbands generally moved in with their wives and her parents, and the children were born in the house belonging to the mother's mother. Even those children whose parents had a house of their own were in constant contact with this grandmother, for a daughter's house, if separate, was usually attached or adjacent to her mother's house. The matrilocal sentiment is still strong, even in this day of preferred nuclear-family residence, and mothers and adult daughters move back and forth freely between their dwellings. Because of this frequent and close association, grandmothers are an important part of the social world of the Hopi child.

The Hopi grandmother, whether maternal or paternal, is called *so'o*. All the women of her generation within her clan are also addressed by that term. Thus the Hopi child has a multitude of grandmothers, those from the mother's clan of which the child is a member as well as those from the father's matrilineal clan. Both the maternal and the paternal grandmothers are benevolent toward their grandchildren and can be counted on to give them little delicacies and to sing songs and tell stories, as grandmothers do worldwide.

Nevertheless, the same woman who was the indulgent grandmother to her daughters' children acted rather differently toward the children of her sons. As a paternal grandmother, the father's clanswomen did not fit the Western concept of the ideal grandmother quite so neatly. This is most evident in the way she acted toward her sons' sons. As a woman of his father's clan, the paternal grandmother fit into a category of people who have what anthropologists call a "joking relationship" with a boy and man. To these grandsons, the father's clanswomen made quite explicit, but joking, verbal sexual advances, publicly taunting their husbands with being less desirable than their little sweethearts, their grandsons. In exploring the reasons for this difference, we must understand both the Hopi system of kinship terminology, which sets the parameters for kinship behavior, and the traditional Hopi view of gender as a pervasive element in nature and society.

GRANDMOTHERS IN HOPI KINSHIP

A Hopi village consisted of a number of clans, with each clan's members claiming descent from a pool of common ancestresses. All fellow members of one's clan were considered to be kin, ineligible for marriage. Members of the father's clan were all kin as well and likewise could not be married. The importance of the father's clan is indicated by the way Hopis speak about it: this is the clan that they were "born for," and all children of a clan's male members are "children" of that clan.

The Hopi system of kinship terms is of the standard Crow type (Eggan 1950). In common with many kinship systems throughout the world, this type avoids the establishment of collateral lines by classifying collateral kin (aunts, uncles, and cousins) with lineal kin (grandparents, parents, siblings, children, and grandchildren). Thus, unlike a bilateral system such as our own, one does not have collateral relatives of different degrees of relationship from oneself, such as first cousins, first cousins once removed, second cousins, and so forth. Rather, these genealogically more remote relatives are classified with the closer ones. In common with some other kinship systems, mother's sisters and all the women of the mother's clan of her generation are called by the same term for mother, and their children are called by terms for brothers and sisters. Likewise, father's brothers and all the men of the father's clan of his generation are called by the term for father, and their children are also called brothers and sisters. That eliminates half of the sources for the establishment of collateral lines, the maternal "aunts" and the paternal "uncles" in English kin terminology.

The distinguishing feature of the Crow system is its treatment of the parents' siblings and clan mates who are of the opposite sex of the parent. We do not need to go into the question of the mother's brothers, who Hopis, when speaking English, refer to as "uncle." (For a straightforward explanation of the logic of the Crow system, see Keesing 1975.) The father's sisters,

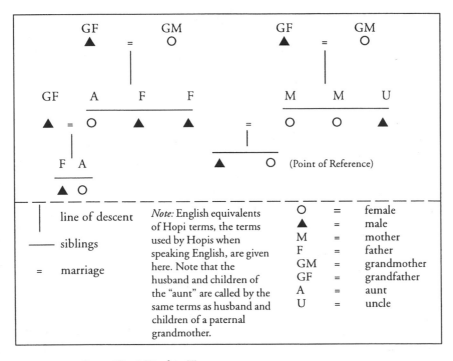

FIGURE 2   *Some Hopi Kinship Terms*

and all other women of the father's clan except for paternal grandmothers, however, are important because they are very much like the paternal grandmothers. Although they are called by a distinctive term *(kya'a)*, their husbands are called by the term for "grandfather." Their children are called by the terms one uses for the children of one's paternal grandmother, that is, "father" and "aunt." Thus, all the women of the father's clan, of all generations, become a kind of grandmother (see fig. 2). Most of the joking I referred to earlier is between a boy and his *kya'a*s, although a paternal *so'o* will sometimes join in.

The point of this excursion into Crow terminology is to show that the issue of the Hopi "grandmother" is not so simple—it depends on what kind of grandmother you are talking about. There is the maternal grandmother, *so'o*. There is the paternal grandmother, also called *so'o* but quite different from her maternal counterpart, as we have seen. In addition, there is the father's sister, *kya'a*, a kind of paternal grandmother even though she has her own kin term. It is to the behavior of these grandmother types that we now turn.

EXPECTED BEHAVIOR OF HOPI GRANDMOTHERS

The *so'o* who is a mother's mother conforms most to our idealized image of how grandmothers should behave. She is nurturant and benevolent, interceding for her daughter's children when necessary and looking out for their interests. A favorite legendary grandmother figure is Spider Woman (*kookyangw-so'-wuuti*, or "spider-old-woman"), often called Spider Grandmother. Although the type of grandmother is not specified, various Hopi informants, when asked to make a choice, have identified her as a mother's mother. Spider Grandmother is particularly benevolent to her young grandsons, the War Twins. These mischievous lads get into all kinds of scrapes, from which their clever grandmother extricates them. She helps them in many ways, hiding them when in trouble or whispering magical spells, with which they can overcome their enemies, into their ears.

Another favorite image of the grandmother is the kindly old lady who intercedes with the frightening ogre figures who come knocking on the door, threatening to steal away the naughty child. This drama, enacted to punish and scare rebellious youngsters into obedience, consists of one or more actors in costumes that include large mouths and big teeth. They announce that they have come for so-and-so, whom they plan to eat. The parents plead for the child, but in vain. Only when the grandmother intervenes will they accept the food offered as a substitute and go away.

This interceding grandmother is almost certain to be the maternal *so'o,* because, at least in earlier times, she was a member of the same household as the child and its parents. The Hopi practiced matrilocal residence, the daughter's husband moving in with her and her parents. Thus the grandmother with whom the child had the closest contact, and the one who had the greatest opportunity to behave benevolently, is its mother's mother.

The maternal grandmother is important from the very beginning of the child's life. The infant is delivered in her home, and she takes care of the mother during the period of seclusion following the birth: 40 days for a firstborn, 20 days for subsequent births. On the walls of the lying-in room, the grandmother paints the four lines of cornmeal on each wall that represents the spiritual "house" within which the child is safe. This "house" shelters the newborn against harm at the hands of witches. The cornmeal from which it is constructed is holy food, made from the sacred plant that will nourish the child's body and give it spiritual life in the years to come. This sacred substance is prepared by women, who use it both in mundane cooking and in the spiritual "feeding" of sacred objects. The grandmother's act of "house construction" is the child's introduction to the spiritual activities of women.

Anabelle Nequatewa and her two grandchildren. Photograph by Helga Teiwes, 1991. Arizona State Museum, University of Arizona.

When the period of seclusion is over, the grandmother accompanies her daughter and the new child to the edge of the village at dawn, where they present the infant to the sun. This is the first of the two rituals that transform an individual into a Hopi. (The second, in which paternal grandmothers have a central part, will be discussed below.)

The birth of a daughter's child brings particular joy to a Hopi woman. This child belongs to her in a way that a son's child cannot, for a daughter's child perpetuates her clan. It carries on the contribution she makes to her clan through bearing life.

As an older woman living in the household or a frequent visitor, the maternal *so'o* does many of the things the mother does for her child. When she makes piki, a wafer-thin cornmeal bread, the little ones hang around to beg for a piece fresh off the griddle. She sings to the restless baby or toddler; a favorite lullaby is simply the repetition of *puva,* the word for "sleep," droned on and on to a sweet melody.

As children get older, the boys' activities take them farther afield, but the girls stay close to home and play with their little friends in the streets just in front of the family houses. The grandmother may show them how to play with bone dolls, using the knuckle bones of animals that she has carefully kept until she has assembled a family: a large bone for the father, a medium-size one for the mother, and smaller ones for the children, with yet others to represent the family's small herd of sheep. In their homestead of stones used to delineate the house and sheep corral, these bone dolls move about the setting of their imagined lives, held in grandmother's fingers while she tells a story about the family she has created. Her young listeners eagerly pick up this enjoyable pastime.

The affection of the grandmother does not end with childhood. In my observation, present-day grandmothers are often more indulgent to their adolescent grandchildren than are mothers, whose patience is frequently tried by their adolescent daughters (see Schlegel 1973). It is common for teenage girls to turn to their grandmothers to teach them such traditional skills as pottery making or basket weaving, especially when mothers are busy with their tasks or, today, at paid jobs.

The fact that the Hopi are matrilineal and formerly matrilocal causes a very close identification between mother and daughter throughout their lives. They are together from the moment of the younger one's birth, and the older one will live out her final years in the care of her now grown daughter. The closeness continues into the third generation when the daughter has her own daughter; the grandmother-granddaughter relationship is but an extension of the mother-daughter one. As is common in much of the world, the grandmother has a bit less authority over the child and responsibility for it than the mother does, and she is likely to be somewhat more indulgent, as during the years of early childhood when mothers can be exhausted by their curious and energetic, but not yet competent, offspring. Here the grandmother, who has some leisure time as she turns more of the household management over to her daughter, can spell the mother in the childcare tasks. Mothers can get short-tempered when they are busy and the child is demanding; grandmothers seldom do.

At the marriage of her grandchild, the maternal *so'o* takes her place with the other women of her clan in giving or receiving a groom. The Hopi conceive of the transfer of person upon marriage as the loss or gain of a young man, not a young woman. As receivers, the bride's maternal grandmothers along with other women of her household and clan are expected to make the groom feel welcome when he marries their granddaughter. When their daughter's son marries, the grandmothers join the other women of the household and clan in showing respect to his bride. At a wedding feast, given by the groom's mother, the women of the bride's clan compliment everything and express great happiness that their young clanswoman has found such a fine husband.

This is quite a contrast to the attitude of the groom's paternal grandmothers and the *kya'as* (henceforth referred to as "aunts"), who treat the wedding of their grandson as an affront and punish his female relatives for taking away their little sweetheart and marrying him to another woman (see fig. 3). They do this through the much loved institution of the mud fight, without which no traditional wedding is complete.

I witnessed such a mud fight in 1971, on Second Mesa. We had just finished eating at the groom's mother's house when a child rushed in, calling, "They're coming, they're coming." We hurried out to see a line of singing matrons, carrying pails of mud and wearing mittens over their ears, marching with determination toward the house. When I asked about the mittens, I was told that the bride belonged to the Fox clan and therefore they were mocking foxes. Indeed, one had a bedraggled fox tail pinned to the back of her dress. The songs they sang were humorous expressions of their anger at the groom's mothers and sisters and made veiled allusions to the bride's past.

The mud was quickly put to use. When the mud fighters entered the area in front of the house, where family and guests were gathered, they grabbed all the mothers and uncles of the groom they could find and smeared them with mud. One uncle clambered up to the roof of a shed, pulling the ladder up after him. (In another case, an uncle who tried to escape was cornered by three determined women and had pieces of his hair snipped off.) Men who dare hang

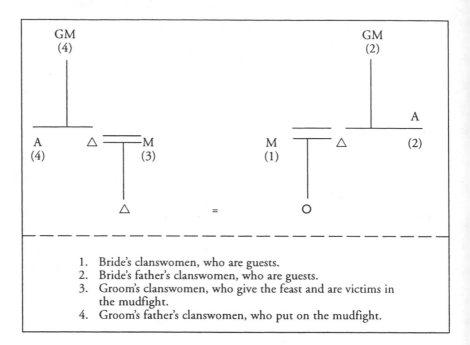

1. Bride's clanswomen, who are guests.
2. Bride's father's clanswomen, who are guests.
3. Groom's clanswomen, who give the feast and are victims in the mudfight.
4. Groom's father's clanswomen, who put on the mudfight.

FIGURE 3   *Grandmothers at the Wedding Feast*

around a mud fight—which is really a women's affair—may be singled out and end up plastered with mud from head to toe. Nobody should be left out: an aunt approached a giggling old woman, confined to a wheelchair, and gently daubed small streaks of mud on her forehead and cheeks so that she, too, could participate. All of this was accompanied by much laughter and joking. When it was all over, the "fighting" women retired to have a much needed bath and shampoo.

The paternal grandmothers, slinging mud and proclaiming their jealousy over their grandson, have more in common with the aunts than with the kindly, gentle mother's mother, and this is how the Hopi view them. Both aunts and paternal grandmothers pretend to be in love with their young grandson (who is called "grandchild" by both categories of women) and make protestations of affection to him, especially when he is a child. The younger aunts, embarrassed by sexual innuendo, might be less vociferous, but the older aunts and grandmothers take much pleasure in bawdy joking, particularly at the expense of their husbands. They make remarks like, "Hurry up and grow up so that I can get rid of this no-good old man and marry you." The husbands, for their part, pretend to be furiously jealous of their wives' wayward affection.

This joking is very much enjoyed by men when they get older, and then they compliment their aunts and grandmothers and praise them to other men. Women also get much pleasure from the attentions of their "grandsons." There is a jokingly flirtatious relationship between "grandsons" and "aunts" of the same generation, and even the most ill-favored woman has these obligatory admirers. When the child is small, however, this joking, particularly its sexual aspect, is not well understood, and the little boy can be confused and somewhat frightened by the remarks of the adult women.

The joking reaches its most extreme form when it involves the grandfathers, the husbands of grandmothers and aunts, in their pretended jealousy of the boy. One way to express this, used in earlier times, was to threaten to castrate the child. To a boy between the ages of about four to eight, this was utterly terrifying.

Don Talayesva, in *Sun Chief* (Simmons 1942), related his own fright at the pretended attack, and other old men have given me similar accounts. Don's experience was terrible: a "grandfather" threw him on the ground, held him down, and pretended to cut Don's penis with the blunt edge of the knife. Everyone, except Don, was much amused by these goings-on. Don's mother comforted him and reassured him that the grandfathers did not mean it.

When boys grew older, they could avenge themselves on the grandfathers who were particularly mean to them as children by playing hostile tricks on them. The older men were supposed to take this in good humor, accepting it as part of the cultural joking complex. Throughout life, grandsons and grandfathers (the husbands of aunts and paternal grandmothers) are supposed to express jealousy toward one another. While this is good-natured, it can in fact color the relationship. When I asked one man what he would do if his best friend ever married one of his aunts, he said, "I would be mad." He would have had a difficult time balancing the warmth and intimacy of his friendship with this man with the competitive tension inherent in the grandson-grandfather relationship, no matter how humorous that is supposed to be.

The rough joking that Don was subjected to seems to have ended, but old men remember it and may tease each other by threatening to call in the grandfathers and sharpen the knives.

The sexuality of paternal grandmothers and aunts, that is, women of the father's clan, is apparent in another treatment of the child. This is during the second of the two rituals mentioned above that transform the new infant into a Hopi. When the newborn child is ready to come out of seclusion, its mother and her female clan relatives give a naming feast to which they invite the women of the father's clan. These are the women who give the child its names, all associated in some way with the paternal clan; for example, if the father belongs to the Butterfly clan, the names will include references to butterflies, flowers, summer, and so forth. The mother later decides which of the several names will be the accepted one. While each of the paternal clanswomen is bestowing a name, she gently rubs the baby on her bare thighs. This is to ensure the child's later fertility.

WHY SEXUAL JOKING?

An explanation of the very different behavior of the two kinds of grandmothers (and aunts) requires an understanding of the Hopi view of gender as a cosmic principle. In Hopi cosmology, there are masculine and feminine principles according to which natural objects and forces can be classified. The earth and its most symbolically significant product, corn, are referred to metaphorically as "our mother." The earth, like a woman, is a repository of life, but life must be activated by masculine forces such as sun, rain, and lightning in nature and male sexual energy in the human world. This balance between the life-containing and the life-activating forces is attached, I believe, to the two clans that a person claims. The mother's clan, which is one's own, is the source of one's life and future well-being. The father's clan provided the sexual energy to beget him or her, and this clan has a special guardianship over his or her sexuality and reproductivity.

To grasp the meaning of a Hopi paternal grandmother's behavior, it is not enough to know that she is a father's mother who loves and cares about her grandchild. Her actions are shaped by the social and cultural features of Hopi life. First, she is classified with the father's sister through the logic of the Crow kinship terminology, and therefore much of her behavior can be accounted for as appropriate to an older woman of the father's clan. Second, the character of this behavior, emphasizing sexuality, is embedded in the Hopi conception of the natural and social universe and the proper roles of humans in it. The male side of nature provides the spark that activates life in the female side (Schlegel 1989). The women of the father's clan—the paternal grandmothers and aunts— give this gift of sexuality to the boy or girl infant. Later, their sexual banter will reinforce this crucial aspect of the individual's life. The father's clanswomen nurture the sexuality that enables the reproductiveness provided by the mother and her clanswomen to come into fruition. Together the women of the two sides ensure that the child will fulfill his or her life-giving potential as an adult.

CHANGES OVER TIME

Good accounts of Hopi culture exist for only a little over a hundred years. New economic activities were introduced in the late nineteenth century, changes in the political structure of the villages came somewhat later, and the transformation from a tribal to a class-based modern society has been completed within the last 50 years. These changes had momentous effects on Hopi family life. Among these changes was a shift in household composition: by the 1930s the extended or stem-family household had given way to the nuclear-family household, although daughters continued to prefer living close to their mothers if there was room to build there.

Separate households somewhat attenuated the contact between grandmothers and grandchildren, although the sentiment on both sides continues to be strong to this day. Perhaps more important than a separation of households in some cases were the new opportunities for wage work open to women, beginning in the 1890s when construction crews needed cooks and the new reservation boarding schools employed women as cooks, seamstresses, and matrons. By 1910, out of a population of about 2,000, 16 women were wage workers (compared to 247 men), and the numbers increased over time. Many of these were no doubt unmarried women, but some may have been women past childbearing. Mature widows, in their late thirties and older, were employed, as probably were other older women whose families needed supplemental income. The Hopi prefer that mothers of young children remain at home, so it is likely that employed married women were older. (Information on female employment comes from Schlegel 1988.)

These older women could well have been grandmothers. We have spoken of grandmothers as if they were old women, which is the Hopi stereotype as well as our own. However, many grandmothers were women in their forties and fifties, at the peak of their social power and activity as heads of households, active ritual participants, and decision makers within their clans. In the home of the young grandmother, it might actually be her mother, the child's great-grandmother, who acted as a traditional grandmother.

Only the occasional grandmother would have been employed steadily outside the home. More common was home-based handicraft, the making of pottery and baskets for sale in the tourist market. Older women with fewer domestic responsibilities had more time for these crafts than younger ones.

While Hopis express the preference for women to remain at home with young children, in more recent years young women, like young women in the larger society, are often employed. Unlike many of their mothers, these younger women have high school educations and are frequently in white-collar, technical, or semiprofessional employment. Some have attended college and work as teachers, nurses, or other professionals. Grandmother is usually the babysitter.

CONCLUSION

Of the two types of grandmothers' behavior—one emphasizing care, protection, instruction, and gentle authority, the other including bawdy jokes and direct sexual allusions—the former is what most Hopis think of as typically grandmotherly. The actions of the paternal grandmother blend in with those of the aunts, and thus they are thought of as more auntlike than grandmotherly. The term *so'o* brings to mind a cheerful old woman always ready to provide good things to eat or to give wise counsel. The Hopi image of the old woman is a favorable one, a person who can take pride in her descendants and does her utmost to make them happy. "Old woman" and "grandmother" are virtual equivalents in Hopi thinking: *so'wuuti* is the Hopi term for "old woman."

This picture is the cultural ideal and the norm. However, circumstances can cause deviations. First, high maternal mortality of the Hopi at the turn of the century and earlier meant that many households did not have a grandmother living in the house. By the time her daughter was bearing children, the older woman might well be dead. There were, of course, other maternal *so'os* through the clan, and the child was welcome in their homes, but it was not quite the same. Maternal mortality and other causes of death claimed the lives of mothers as well. A child might be brought up by its grandmother acting as surrogate mother. This grandmother, responsible for more household tasks than the woman with a grown daughter in the house, might find herself hard-pressed to give her grandchild the same amount of "grandmotherly" attention as could her more fortunate coeval.

Along with the deviations of circumstance go individual variations in conformity to the cultural ideal. Not every old woman is cheerful or kindhearted or wise; an old woman, like anyone else, can be greedy, stupid, mean-spirited, or cruel. Nevertheless, the Hopis with whom I have spoken have fond memories of their grandmothers, and the grandmothers whom I have observed follow the ideal closely. The traditional family structure, in which the old woman was assured of care and security and leisure time as her daughter assumed much of the household responsibility, was conducive to the grandmotherly behavior the Hopi expected. Women took pride in their grandchildren and pleasure in correcting and instructing them, and if all went well, they had the time to play with them and to forge the bonds of love that made the grandmother-grandchild tie so close.

While household structure has changed considerably, favoring the nuclear-family residence, a grandmother is still important in the child's life. She may be living near to, rather than within, the house of the child and its parents, but a few yards is little barrier to contact. The busy mother still turns her children over to the grandmother for care, even more so now that many women are employed outside the home. Will today's generation of employed women be willing to give up their jobs when they become grandmothers to become housewives and childminders? That is something only time will tell.

OTOE-MISSOURIA GRANDMOTHERS
Linking Past, Present, and Future

◈

MARJORIE M. SCHWEITZER

> *The elders pass away year by year. . . . These precious people represent an era, a way of life, that the young will never know and the tribe mourns this loss. But the elders do not mourn for themselves. It is not their way, not what they have been taught. To the young people, they can be overheard to say, "Look ahead. Get ready now. This is the way it is supposed to be."*[1]

INTRODUCTION

Otoe-Missouria grandmothers born between 1895 and 1925 have seen many changes in the way of life that once formed the basis of their parents' and grandparents' lives. They are aware of elements of Otoe-Missouria culture that are no longer practiced, and these women cherish that heritage. But throughout their lives, they have understood that they live in a world much different from that of their forebears.

During the time span of the grandmothers' lives (for many a period of almost 100 years), elements of White culture have become more and more pervasive in the lives of the Otoes. Features of non-Indian culture, such as formal schooling, Christianity, wage work, and military service in the U.S. armed forces, have been juxtaposed next to and interwoven with continuing traditional Otoe patterns such as extended family networks, the sharing of material and spiritual resources with family and tribal members, participation in intergenerational activities, a common cultural heritage, and knowledge of history, rituals, ceremonies, and skills.[2]

Change was forced on the Otoes by historical circumstances beyond their control. By incorporating many of those changes into their lives and interweaving them with old ways, the Otoes have maintained continuity in social relationships and a worldview that continues to distinguish them from other people. The result is a strong and continued sense of Otoe identity, albeit an identity blended with attributes of the dominant society. Basic to maintaining an Otoe consciousness is their ability to adapt.

The grandmothers have been active agents in that process of adaptation. In talking about the years when they were girls and young women, they viewed many changes of their lives as unavoidable. Although they did not wish to see their Otoe ways disappear, they were often eager to try new skills and ways of doing things. Their attitudes toward change continued to be important during adulthood and grandmotherhood. As *culture brokers* between traditional Otoe ways and non-Indian culture, they have successfully achieved an interface between the old and the new.[3] As *role models,* they have taught several genera-tions of children and grandchildren how to live in a changed and changing Otoe world.

Rather than look backward to times that were gone forever, they set their sights on the future. This *gift of accommodation* identifies and illuminates their position in history.

THE RESEARCH

I began my research with the Otoe-Missouria in 1974. I was interested in the cultural dimensions of aging in an Indian community in the latter part of the twentieth century. Since my primary research focus is culture history, I found the lives of older women especially compelling from the point of view of culture change and identity. The material presented here is based on partici-pant observation, interviews, life history data, archival material on the culture history of the Otoe people, videotapes, and photographs.[4]

THE HISTORICAL AND CULTURAL BACKGROUND

The Otoe-Missouria[5] are a branch of Southern Siouan speakers who lived on the prairies of Nebraska along the Platte River in the 1800s. They hunted bison and grew corn, squash, and beans in the river valleys. Patrilineally related families lived in large earth lodges in permanent villages and, when hunting the bison, occupied tipis in smaller family groups. Both men and women cultivated the gardens, but the greatest share of the horticultural work fell to the women. Men were hunters, but women cut and dried the bison meat, distributed it, and prepared the hides.

Men owned their personal possessions, such as clothes and hunting gear. Women owned the tipis and all of the things associated with them, as well as the produce from the garden. Women were secure because of their direct contribution to the economy and their property rights (Whitman 1937:xi, 1–6), but their roles were not limited to economic production. They held positions of respect and power and performed essential life-cycle ceremonies.

Clans controlled the selection of marriage partners (clan exogamy), the performance of rituals, such as the naming ceremony, and taboos. Certain tasks that affected the entire tribe were carried out by particular clans, and only clan members were privileged to hear clan origin stories and learn clan customs (Whitman 1937:18, 50).[6]

Otoe society was stratified into three main groups that cross-cut the clans. The leaders of each clan, along with their families, ranked the highest. Warriors and priests in charge of rituals and their families formed the second-ranked group. Commoners were the poor families of each clan. It was not easy for a person to move from one rank to another, as privileged families jealously guarded tangible and intangible hereditary attributes accruing from their ranked positions.

Efforts to Christianize the Otoes began in the 1830s with a Baptist mission. Other dramatic changes in lifestyle occurred when the Otoes signed away the last of their dwindling hunting grounds and were moved to a reservation on the Nebraska-Kansas border in 1854. Later, as part of President Grant's "peace policy," the reservation came under the supervision of the Society of Friends. Although the Quakers did not gain converts, acculturation continued (Milner 1982:117).

In 1881, bowing to increasing demands for land by White settlers, the Otoe-Missouria people moved to a reservation in north-central Indian Territory. The mothers, fathers, and grandparents of today's elder grandmothers were among the Otoes who first camped on the banks of Red Rock Creek. They built earth lodges, and later frame houses, on the rolling prairies near the creeks. The pastureland and wooded riverbanks were reminiscent of the homeland they had left.

The Otoes have sunk roots deep into the land they now claim as their home. Although the thoughts of the elders sometimes stray northward, their lives are irrevocably tied to the events that have taken place in Indian Territory and Oklahoma. The redbrick schoolhouse with its laundry building and rusty old windmill are visible reminders of cherished memories. Ancestors and other relatives are buried on the hill in the tribal cemetery or in one of the several family burial grounds that are scattered over the old reservation. They hold their yearly gathering at the campground and dance arena near Red Rock Creek. These places, now part of a collective history and tribal memory, are enduring symbols of contemporary Otoe identity.

THE GRANDMOTHERS

The elder grandmothers[7] were born on homestead allotments created when the Indian Territory reservation was partitioned in the 1890s.[8] Their early years were characterized first by immersion in Otoe language and traditions and, after reaching school age, in White culture.

As little girls, the grandmothers attended the Otoe boarding school, White rural public schools, a denominational school, and, later, government boarding schools such as Chilocco Indian School. In addition to English and the basic skills of reading, writing, and arithmetic, the girls learned the "domestic arts and sciences"—sewing, cooking, canning, washing, and ironing (laundry). They became adherents of the Christian religion either at home by instruction from their parents who were already Christianized or through missionaries from Christian churches.

Growing up in Indian Territory and Oklahoma, the grandmothers developed a strong attachment to the land. A deep-seated sense of place sprang from the days when, as little girls, they roamed the countryside on their ponies, swam in Red Rock Creek, went to school, and attended ceremonies.

They married and raised their families in the Otoe community and have remained there all of their lives, except for brief visits to distant relatives or job-related sojourns in other cities. Only in later years did they move into the small town of Red Rock or to the tribal housing project near the dance ground. Some remained on the farm their entire lives.

CULTURAL PERSISTENCE AND CULTURE CHANGE

The Culture Brokers—Learning New Ways

Traditionally Otoe children watched, listened to, and imitated adults to learn the skills they needed to survive. They were expected to be keen observers of their world around them. Stories and legends told around the winter hearth by grandparents explained in easy-to-understand images the bases of Otoe beliefs, the origins of the clans, how to respect the animals, and how to treat others around them.

Learning in White schools, especially in government boarding schools, was different. It was not necessarily, however, a negative experience. While questionable aspects of boarding school experiences—suppression of native languages; regimentation in dress, hairstyle, and behavior; inadequate and narrow academic training; insensitive teachers and corporal punishment—are amply documented and thoroughly criticized, the domestic skills that formed the basis of the girls' education fit well into the expected family roles of women (Lomawaima 1994; Trennert 1982; U.S. Department of Education 1980). These skills complemented and reinforced the positions that Otoe women traditionally occupied—homemakers and mothers who prepared meals, made clothes, took care of the home, and had primary responsibility for raising children.

Many Otoe grandmothers have positive memories about boarding school and the skills they learned. Fannie, as an 85-year-old grandmother, viewed school as the most important thing she had ever done:

Seems like everything I know now I learned there. I'm glad I went to school. Just like back in the old days, if I'd just went to stay by my old folks, well, I never would know what I know today. I learned lots by going to school. Try to take part in anything came along. I always thought, even today, I wish lotta these young children could go.[9]

Lizzie sees her days at school as the "happiest in her life":

I was the first Indian to go to day school at the district school. I was almost seven. I walked both ways. They used to call me "Little Pocahontas." I didn't know who Pocahontas was then.

I remember that first day of school my dad said, "You're going to school today. . . ." He handed me my dinner bucket and a primer. You had to have your own primer in those days.[10]

On the one hand, there is no doubt that Indian boarding schools reinforced and in some cases fostered Indian identity (McBeth 1983). Particularly important were the friendships formed with Indians from other tribes. These friendships continued after graduation and are especially evident at intertribal gatherings and in Indian politics. Graduates of Chilocco Indian School, for example, gather each year to renew friendships and proudly celebrate their school years.

On the other hand, continuing to learn more about specific aspects of Otoe culture was difficult for those away at boarding school. The years away from family and tribe resulted in a less intimate knowledge of historical events, people, and practices, as Fannie acknowledges:

I was away to school all along. . . . That's how come I don't know a lot of things that had been taking place.

Although it was difficult for girls to learn tribal lore or details of ceremonies when they were away at school, they continued to learn the more subtle aspects of Otoe behavior and attitudes as they interacted with their families and friends at public and private gatherings.

The grandmothers were exposed early to the teachings of the Christian religion, sometimes before reaching school age. Fannie describes her introduction this way:

> I always remember my mother and father, before we ever went to school, when we were about three or four years old, said, "Come on, children, let's talk." Papa would say that in Indian. . . . That's how my mother and father raised us—Christian ways, in a Christian home.

One of the schools that Lizzie Harper attended was a Catholic boarding school. She converted to Catholicism and even considered becoming a nun. An Irish "sister" had promised Lizzie she would take her to Ireland, but Lizzie's father did not want her to go. Her twin sister had died in infancy, and she was the only daughter still living. She has remained a faithful follower of the Catholic religion all of her life.[11]

The Otoe people have been followers of the Native American Church since acquiring peyote in the 1890s (LaBarre 1969:167). Whitman (1937:127) estimated that nearly all Otoes were followers of the "peyote road." Participation in peyote meetings is still widespread. Women do not conduct meetings, but their involvement and their duties associated with it are considered essential to the proper performance of the ceremony.

Joe Bassett speaks for himself and his wife, Genevieve (one of the grandmothers), when he says:

> We have been members of the Church ever since we were married. Our parents were members. The beliefs and rituals have been very important to us.[12]

Lizzie Harper finds no contradiction of her Catholic faith when she argues in favor of the religious use of peyote:

> I believe in it. I have great confidence and good faith in the peyote. A lot of good testimonies. People come from everywhere to get doctored by the peyote. They would go out of the tipi well and keep well.[13]

Traditional Otoe religious beliefs penetrated the fabric of everyday life, directing secular events as well as sacred ceremonies. Today Otoes are reluctant to discuss traditional sacred ceremonies that they continue to perform or have revived in recent years. But elements of native Otoe religion are in evidence at public gatherings. "Smoking off the mourners" with burning cedar shavings; praying toward the four directions; sending a message to *Wakanda,* the Great Spirit, through the ceremonial use of tobacco or through the drum; and words spoken at such times are features of native Otoe beliefs that are part of the contemporary Otoe worldview.

It can be argued that Christian religions and the educational system forced on the tribe have been instrumental in eliminating important elements of native culture. One can also argue that these institutions have been forces of accommodation for Otoes in the twentieth century. Schools, with the teaching of language and other skills, have been crucial in preparing Otoes for economic survival in a world vastly different from that of their bison-hunting ancestors.

Religion remains a complex but sustaining element in the lives of Otoes and is based on aspects of native religion, participation in an Indian Christian church with a focus on the Bible and the teachings of Jesus Christ, and the sacred use of peyote and its prescribed lifestyle. It is not unusual for tribal members to be participants in all three traditions. Religion in its various forms has helped Otoes cope with sometimes difficult conditions and loss of family members and friends.[14]

The grandmothers welcomed the new ways that school offered them, and they urge young people to get an education, to stay in school. They see education as necessary to succeed in both the Indian and the non-Indian worlds, and they believe it is good to accept the future.

At very young ages they developed a deep sense of spirituality, enriched with elements from a variety of sources. They have been persistent in passing on their strong faith as proper guides to behavior and beliefs for their children and grandchildren to follow.

The Enculturators—Rearing the Young

Becoming a grandmother is a cultural ideal in Otoe society; babies are welcome and women are proud to be grandmothers. Being a grandmother normally entails caring for grandchildren on a part-time basis.

Who is a grandmother and how many grandmothers an individual may have are in part determined by the Otoe kinship system, a version of the Omaha type that merges several categories of relatives. For example, father's brother is merged with father and mother's sister is merged with mother (Whitman 1937:43).[15] Likewise, grandmother's sister merges with grandmother and grandfather's brother with grandfather.

The significance of this pattern lies in the designation of a woman as grandmother to the grandchildren of her sister whether or not she has grand-children of her own.

Typical of Otoe women in the past, grandmothers, however, are sometimes called upon to set aside their grandmother roles and become instead surrogate mothers. They may become "mother" to a deceased daughter's children, as-sume total responsibility for a handicapped grandchild to relieve the parents of his care, or adopt a child born out of wedlock or because the parents work, are divorced, or are periodically absent from home.

Social problems such as alcoholism or unemployment may create situations that a parent finds difficult to overcome. A single mother may not be able to stay at home with her baby (or children) because she must work full-time or, if she does not work, may not have adequate resources to provide food and health care.

Keeping temporary and long-term childcare within the family (and the tribe) is seen as a positive option in Otoe society today. One of the mechanisms to promote childrearing is the practice of adoption. Older women may adopt grandchildren for any of the reasons listed above or they may adopt outside of the immediate family. When parents lose a son and adopt another family's child to take his place, they create a new grandparent-grandchild relationship. In traditional Otoe culture, women who adopted children or grandchildren were expected to treat them better than their own. Today individuals in these relationships expect to interact in the same manner as lineal and classificatory relatives would.

The participation of grandmothers in childcare today stems from the same needs as in historical times with "practical issues of division of labor," creat-ing a demand for childrearing by individuals other than the parents. Those most experienced to provide that care are members of the grandparent genera-tion. "Elders are thought to be those best equipped to transmit cultural lore across generations, thus ensuring the cultural integrity of the group" (Weibel-Orlando 1990:114).

Raising one, two, or more grandchildren has been a common experience for the elder grandmothers. Genevieve and her husband raised eight grandchil-dren as well as their six children. Two grandchildren continued to live with them after reaching adulthood.

Fannie raised several orphaned grandchildren after raising her family of 10. When the children first came to live with her, she was a widow living in the country on the farm. Finding it difficult in winter weather to get around, she sold part of her allotment and bought a house in town to be sure that her grandchildren could attend public school.

I raised those grandchildren till they went to government school here and graduated.

Grandmothers wish to teach their grandchildren about Otoe history and lore through stories and legends. But because fewer opportunities for story-telling exist in the late twentieth century, they must show the grandchildren in other, less subtle ways what is expected of them, how they should act toward others, and the values and beliefs appropriate for proper members of the community. These lessons occur when a youngster observes the grandmother greeting an elder of the tribe or participates with the grandmother in spe-cial events; grandmothers often dance around the arena with a grandbaby in their arms. They do much to teach children what it is to be an Otoe and how to act and think like an Otoe, whether or not they have full responsibility for them.

Economic independence underlies the ability of grandmothers to raise grandchildren. Owning a house provides a home for grandchildren who are in need of shelter and care. Grandmothers who have retained possession of their own allotments or have inherited land from parents or husbands usually have income from lease of the land and a percentage of the crops grown by the lessee. Some receive cash from their deceased husbands' service pensions. The tribe provides other aid: food supplies, repairs to houses, and help with winter heating bills. With continued good health, grandmothers are willing to share their few economic advantages with grandchildren. The concern of the grand-mothers for the welfare of their grandchildren is central to the continued maintenance of the family *and* the entire Otoe community.

The Keepers of Tradition—Skills, Ceremonies, and Rituals

The skills of sewing and cooking that the grandmothers pass on to their daughters and granddaughters are a combination of lessons learned at school and in on-the-spot apprenticeships in the kitchens and living rooms of their own mothers and grandmothers. One highly valued use of these skills is making dance clothes for family members. Minnie Mae Moore, for example, sewed the dance outfits her granddaughter wore when she served as the Otoe-Missouria princess in 1986.

Making dance clothes takes skill and patience. Grandmothers use family-owned ribbon-work designs handed down from *their* grandmothers to decorate broadcloth skirts, dance aprons, and shawls. They bead Otoe-style moccasins, medallions, and headdresses, often in floral designs. Grandmothers hope that their granddaughters will keep the designs and skills alive when *they* can no longer see well. But as long as they are able to sew, they are in great demand by their powwow-dancing granddaughters and grandsons.

The grandmothers are experienced cooks. On the farm they grew corn and vegetables and learned firsthand from their mothers and grandmothers how to prepare food in the ways that Otoes have done for generations. Even quite old grandmothers work in the kitchen, cutting up meat and cooking for the feast served at a peyote meeting, although usually younger women (who are probably grandmothers who learned from the elder grandmothers) prepare the meals for most special events. The skills of sewing and cooking lie at the center of an Otoe woman's traditional role as homemaker. The need and desire to learn these skills are still present today.

Some grandmothers possess the knowledge and the right to perform special ceremonies or to act in a special role. Two such skills are the naming ceremony, in which an individual is given an Otoe name, and the curing knowledge possessed by a native woman doctor. These specialties have been handed down from family members who passed on the authority to perform the rituals or practices in the proper way.

Lizzie Harper conducted a naming ceremony[16] during the annual encampment for two young members of the Otoe tribe who live on the West Coast.

She began by saying:

According to the name, the child must be instructed and told what the name means and not to disgrace it.

After bestowing the names, Lizzie explained the meanings in English: for the little boy, the name of his great-great-grandfather, "Good Fish"; for the young woman, the name of her grandmother, "The Lightning Coming." After the brief ceremony, family members gave gifts to Lizzie in recognition of her expertise and appreciation for conducting the ceremony.

Brief remarks by two tribal elders preceded the feast prepared for all the guests; the elders were invited to eat at a long table under a canvas canopy. The meal, cooked on open fires in large tubs, included corn soup with beef, fry bread, and a sweet dish of pumpkin and corn, a traditional Otoe food signifying thanksgiving.

Although the ceremony took place in a setting different from that of historic times—those who attended the naming ceremony under the big pecan trees sat in folding lawn chairs instead of on a banquette in an earth lodge, and Lizzie and the other grandmothers present were dressed in everyday cotton clothing

Lizzie Dailey Harper conducts an Otoe naming ceremony for the great-grandson of a tribal member. Photograph by Marjorie M. Schweitzer.

of the twentieth century rather than buckskin—the ceremony retained much of its customary meaning. The naming of these individuals in the presence of tribal members, on tribal ground, reinforced the connection between the tribe and its descendants who live far away. Equally important, perhaps, the ceremony publicly acknowledged the heritage of the individuals and connected them firmly to Otoe tradition.

In a very real sense, Lizzie contributed to the maintenance of culture and of the Otoe community in a world vastly different from the one she knew in her childhood. She wove elements of Otoe tradition and modern innovation into a unified whole.

Traditions and Transitions—The War Mothers

The War Mothers[17] represent, at its best, the interweaving of White culture traits with some of the deepest and most persistent concerns to Otoe people—

the importance of family and the continuation of time-honored rituals and meanings.

The grandmothers, as younger women, organized the first all-Indian chapter of the American War Mothers. They took a Euro-American organization, complete with monthly chapter meetings, state and national conventions, and red, white, and blue decorations featuring the American flag and the eagle, and blended them with Otoe cultural values, events, and actions. The organizational features of the parent organization became part of the structure of the Otoe chapter, but being an Indian organization meant much more. The women transformed the American War Mothers into an Indian phenomenon.

The Otoe women added their own paraphernalia, activities, and symbolism. They honor the soldiers and veterans with dances and feasts, hold giveaways in their honor, make and wear War Mothers' dance shawls and broadcloth blankets,[18] and are proud owners of a War Mothers' drum. The War Mothers' song, composed by one of their members, is sung on special occasions.

Modern-day Otoe "warriors," the soldiers, sailors, and marines who have served in the armed forces of the United States, are held in high esteem. The intense admiration for these soldiers and veterans derives in part from the important place of the warrior in traditional Otoe society, a sensibility that is still prevalent today. In turn, soldiers, and especially older veterans, respect and admire the War Mothers.

The ceremonies and values of the War Mothers are tied to social interactions basic to their society today—respect, reciprocity, emphasis on the individual within the family (described below), transmission of cultural traditions, and accommodation to White culture.

Reciprocity and Respect—The Grandmothers

Embedded within the traditional structure of the clans and the special concerns of the ranked groups were two fundamental features of Otoe society: (1) the family and (2) the position of the individual within the family.[19] Although the clans held certain rights and duties, they did not assume an overwhelming importance. Rather, the family was the basic unit of social organization and its prestige and prerogatives were felt in all activities. The importance of family was evident in traditional economic pursuits such as hunting, cultivating the garden, and doing daily chores, where activities took place on a face-to-face basis with extended family members.

The family was considered responsible for individual family members and made a concerted effort to ensure their proper behavior because an individual's actions and behavior reflected directly on the family's status. Families exerted control over individual members by invoking sanctions and expecting them to fulfill their obligations. It was only in the context of the family that an individual could gain appropriate recognition (Whitman 1937:35–38, 42, 63–65).

An individual's position in the family social structure dominated the perceptions that others had. A woman who was a curing doctor would be referred to by her kin name, grandmother, with the recognition that her doctoring knowledge and abilities were part of her special skills as a grandmother. The same is true today. The status of grandmother is paramount in people's perceptions of an older woman, and "older woman" is synonymous with grandmother status and a reflection of the continuing importance of the family in Otoe culture.

The most cherished relationship in the family was that between grandparent and grandchild (Whitman 1937:47). Children were taught from infancy to respect their grandparents. Since patrilocality was the most common residence pattern, grandparents on the paternal side were more likely to be involved with the enculturation of grandchildren than were the maternal grandparents.

A form of generalized reciprocity in the exchange of gifts, services, and moral support was characteristic of Otoe culture. Families of a man and woman who were to marry exchanged gifts at the time of the marriage; people seeking power or skills from another person gave gifts of clothing, blankets, or food in exchange for less tangible but potent knowledge; children gave nuts and sweets to grandparents who were going to tell stories. The giving of gifts validated an individual's knowledge, confirmed the transfer of power, or gave public recognition to an event such as marriage.

The relationship of an individual with the family, gift exchange, reciprocity, and respect continue as defining characteristics of contemporary Otoe society. Reciprocal and interdependent relationships emphasize the importance of the family while the exercise of autonomy recognizes the individual. Autonomy allows a person to take responsibility for her own actions and to make her own decisions. While these details of social interaction appear to be antagonistic, they actually complement each other by offering support for both the individual and the larger group. They are evident, for example, in the kin roles of grandparent and grandchild.

Care of a grandmother who once raised them and now needs help is frequently the responsibility of grandchildren who reciprocate when they are old enough to do so. Living with grandmother to provide aid and companionship, helping with chores, taking care of her when she is sick, taking the grandparent to visit other relatives and to attend meetings and events when she is no longer able to go by herself—all are ways of expressing family responsibility for a woman who has been a major influence and who now needs care in return.

The responsibilities and rewards of being a grandmother are set firmly within the family. While grandmothers begin by doing many things for their children, grandchildren, and other members of their extended families, it is the family that provides the securest place for grandmother, especially when she becomes frail.

The traditional sense of respect for older people continues today and is expressed on both public and private occasions. Even though some of the elders say that respect for grandparents has lessened, parents make an effort to teach children to respect and love their grandparents. Grandchildren and grandparents are quite fond of each other and spend time doing things for each other and with each other. These expressions of respect and reciprocity continue in spite of kin who live far away and family members who do not choose to follow the norms. Individuals who have living grandparents, and grandparents who have living descendants, are considered to be fortunate and to possess great wealth. By the same token, a young person who has no living grandparents, or grandparents with no living descendants, are considered to be "pitiful," that is, unfortunate, unlucky, and deprived.

Reciprocity includes not only the exchange of items but the social, financial, and psychological support that people offer as they fulfill their obligations both to their extended family network and to particular individuals. The exchange of material goods and physical help are basic to the maintenance of the family and the cultural community. Old and sometimes frail individuals are obvious benefactors in these exchanges.

Reciprocity and respect for the status of grandmother is part of the cultural heritage that the grandmothers have been instrumental in helping to preserve.

The dynamic tension that exists between the group and an individual are resolved in a complex interaction exemplified by public events in which reciprocity plays a prominent role. When a grandmother honors a grandson who is home on leave from a tour of duty as a soldier or honors a granddaughter who has been chosen as tribal princess, the attention is centered on the grandson or granddaughter who is being recognized. The grandmother may act as the representative of the family, but the extended family is necessary in order to carry out the required tasks; it is the family network in which the exchange of goods, money, services, and emotional commitment take place. The individual for whom the event is sponsored is honored in explicit and implicit ways, but as in traditional times, recognition of the individual cannot take place without the support of the family. On another occasion, the "tables will be turned" as a granddaughter or grandson will reciprocate by participating in a special event organized to honor the grandmother.

A grandmother's eighty-fifth birthday illustrates the dynamic complexity occurring between individual and group. The celebration included an all-night peyote meeting and an all-day gourd dance. At the church meeting, prayers were said for the old woman's health and for a continued long life. At the dance, friends and relatives gave her gifts and danced with her. A family representative requested the singers to sing a family honor song. During the song, the grandmother and her family led relatives and friends as they danced around the drum. After the song, the family held a giveaway in which the head staff, the dance committee, the singers, and friends were given gifts.

The speaker for the family acknowledged the birthday celebrant by saying:

Without looking back, she's always had her head forward and always said, "Don't worry, things are going to work out all right."

A peyote meeting involves the invitation of individuals to participate and the preparation of an evening meal as well as the special food served to participants at the end of the service. It may include a noon meal on the day following the meeting at which many people are fed. The dance necessitates the collection of gifts for the giveaway, the invitation to singers, the choice of a master of ceremonies and head staff, cooks to prepare the food for the evening meal, and a place to hold the dance.

Events such as these public honorings are expensive and require money and material goods to produce. Thus while an individual is honored, it is through family and friends that resources are gathered. Furthermore, the public events take place only through the participation of the peyote leader, worshipers, singers, dancers, head staff, arena director, and those who attend. Each individual receives prestige (implicit and explicit) by participating; each in his or her own way makes a contribution to the intricate design melding individual with group.

There are other less complex examples of reciprocity. Many include simple exchanges between individuals. One young woman lives with her grandmother and takes her to tribal dances. There she dances with her, as the old woman is not very steady on her feet, but she loves to dance. With the care and concern of her granddaughter, she is able to remain involved in community life.

Another instance involves a kind of "reverse" fostering; one granddaughter came to stay with her grandmother when the old woman was recovering from an operation. The grandmother was able to remain at home during her convalescence because her granddaughter shopped for her, cooked the meals, and cleaned the house. When she was in her nineties and quite frail, her grandson and granddaughter took turns caring for her, a turnabout "custodial" care reminiscent of the days when she raised them.

In recent decades the Otoe tribe has administered programs for senior citizens, assuming responsibility for the elders in ways that are reminiscent of an earlier era when care for the old was carried out by the more wealthy members of the tribe (one of the requisites for a man to become a good leader was to see that the old and the frail were given food and shelter). The grandmothers of the tribe are beneficiaries of these programs. The services (especially important for grandmothers who live alone) include a hot noon meal, transportation from home to the senior citizens center where the meal is served, and transportation to town for shopping and to the clinic for visits to the Indian Health Service doctor. Special programs such as a class to improve memory or an exercise class are occasionally offered. On both family and tribal levels, the shared belief in interdependence (mutual dependency) enhances family and tribal efforts to care for those who need it.

The examples of reciprocity, respect, and honor are values that have roots in an earlier hunting/horticultural society where the survival of the individual was, without question, dependent on interaction and exchange with the group. Today reciprocity continues to be important, especially for the survival of older people who wish to maintain an autonomous self-defining lifestyle but still retain connections with people and places important to their social life. As the old have fostered and taught the young, so the young reciprocate by providing the help and interaction that elder grandmothers want and need. Grandchildren do not just "take care" of the elders but offer friendship, companionship, and trust as well as help with needed tasks. Reciprocity and interdependence (mutual dependence) foster not only survival but well-being for old and young alike.[20]

Honorary and Spiritual Grandmothers

Today respect is shown to women for the same reasons as in the past—for raising children and grandchildren who are well thought of in the community. The respect for older women (i.e., grandmothers) is expressed not only by their families but by other tribal members and members of other tribes. Grandmothers are asked to participate at public events by family members or by other members of the tribe; they are recognized with gifts and words of praise. "Grandmother" is used as a term of address and implies respect and honor.

The respect for and inspiration from grandmothers does not stop with their deaths. Relatives and friends continue to be influenced by their grandmothers through recalling the lessons learned, wearing jewelry that once belonged to her, giving the grandmother's Otoe name to a grandchild, or invoking their names on public occasions. I refer to these women as *spiritual grandmothers*.

Each year at the beginning of the first evening's program at the summer encampment, the master of ceremonies calls out the names of the grand-mothers and grandfathers who have died during the past year and offers con-dolences to their relatives. He calls upon the tribe to remember the elders who have gone on and encourages everyone present to conduct themselves in ways that would shed honor on their departed relatives. He urges the people to follow in the footsteps of those who have gone before, to follow the paths their feet trod around the dance arena and in life.

INTRACULTURAL VARIATION AND CULTURAL LOSS

The events and individuals described here refer to the elder grandmothers who lived in and near the rural Otoe community of north-central Oklahoma, whose family members live close by and who are economically able to participate.

Intracultural variations do occur. There are families and individuals who are less involved in exchanges with others than the ones described here. Varia-tions occur because of individual personality differences and diverse family circumstances.

Even in families of elder grandmothers who remain in the Otoe community, some daughters and sons and their families live hundreds of miles away, a condition necessitated by the lack of job opportunities in their home commu-nity. For example, Indians were relocated to Los Angeles and other large cities as part of the federal job relocation plan of the 1950s. Individuals who feel the pull of the home community and are financially able return for special celebra-tions whenever they can. Some return to live in their home communities only after retirement.

Others who do not participate directly in public exchanges may not be able to do so because their finances will not allow them to be involved, except on a very limited basis. A grandmother may have few surviving family members and none who live in the area.

Another factor that affects participation in family or tribal exchanges is factionalism among different branches of the extended family or between members of the nuclear family. Factionalism may occur because there are differences of opinion about how to do things or because of personal or politi-cal rivalries.

In addition, not everyone behaves according to ideal Otoe mores and val-ues. An elder grandmother may be berated by a daughter or granddaughter because she has opinions that they don't share. They may not wish to grant her the autonomy she would like to have if she wants to do something they think she should not do. The grandmother may be an unpleasant person, or alternatively, her daughters, sons, or grandchildren may have personal problems of their own or refuse to conform to expected norms.

Arguing that Otoe people have accommodated to culture change is not meant to imply that they do not mourn the destruction of their old cultural ways. On many occasions they speak of the great loss of traditions, and they see and feel the continuing changes occurring in their own lives, especially as the elders, important sources of knowledge, die. The grandmothers often expressed anguish over the loss of their Otoe culture.

Lizzie noted, with dismay, changes in attitudes about funeral rites:

> Funerals should be sacred and serious, but they are not now. Everything is handled carelessly.

Change has not been easy, and there are Otoe elders who look with pain and distress on the difficult events of the past. But even for those individuals who experienced the troublesome times brought by acculturation, there has been a willingness to accommodate to the demands made on them to survive in the twentieth century. In some ways, it was easier for the grandmothers to adapt because role expectations for women were family oriented and, though changed, still encompassed the kinds of tasks that women have always carried out to keep families fed, clothed, and cared for. These role expectations were typical of the pre-Euro-American era and continued to be the expectations in the nineteenth and twentieth centuries.

Cultural continuity together with accommodation to change has been the foundation of success for Otoe-Missouria elder grandmothers who lived at a particular time, in a particular place, during special historical circumstances. Recognizing the difficulties that the tribe faced only emphasizes the importance of these women in facilitating the transition of the Otoe people from the past, through the present, into the future.

NOTES

1. *The Otoe-Missouria Tribe.* 1981:56.

2. The acculturation of the Otoes took several forms: (1) as simple cultural borrowing that led to a new expression of what is now considered to be traditional Otoe culture (e.g., the use of beads instead of quills in the decoration of clothing); (2) as acculturation, where White culture traits are widely accepted and used but where traditional traits continue in an attenuated form (e.g., formal schooling that has replaced much—but not all—of the traditional transmitting of history, lore, and skills through telling and showing and through the use of the Otoe language); (3) as assimilation of White traits to the exclusion of Otoe traits,

seen primarily in everyday material culture (e.g., houses and transportation) and in the economic sphere (e.g., a wage economy rather than a hunting/horticultural economy); (4) as Indianization of White culture traits (e.g., the borrowing and reinterpretation of the Anglo-originated American War Mothers Association).

3. By referring to "traditional Otoe culture" I do not imply that customs are changeless. What was considered to be traditional Otoe culture in the 1830s or the 1880s is not the same as what is considered to be traditional in the 1990s. As Bill Waters points out when writing about Otoe oral traditions, all societies are continually adapting to changing conditions. "But even through the most traumatic of events, the traditions of a people, while developing and changing, are able to continue serving their fundamental purpose: ensuring the continuity of the society" (Waters 1984:231).

Customary ways of doing things continually change. The most easily noted changes have occurred in material culture and in ways of wresting a living from the environment. Less noticeable and much slower to change are the ideologies, including beliefs, values, and mores and the behavior that is related to social relationships within the tribe. Drastic change on the surface has been accompanied by continued meaningfulness in ideas and social structure, even though the means of expressing these values is necessarily altered.

4. I am deeply indebted to all of my friends in the Otoe-Missouria tribe, especially Marjorie Hudson and the late Ennis O. Hudson, who made me feel welcome, shared information with me, and gently corrected my mistakes. Special thanks go to the Otoe-Missouria American War Mothers, Chapter 14, for their patience with my questions and their willingness to share their activities with me. I am proud to be an honorary member of Chapter 14.

While I do not expect an Otoe individual to describe the lives of the elder grandmothers in the same way that I have, I hope that I have fairly represented their lives and what they have shared with me.

I interviewed people in their homes in the small town of Red Rock, Oklahoma, in the Otoe-Missouria Cultural Center, the dance grounds, and the campground. Among the many activities I attended were dances, hand games, birthday celebrations, funerals, and War Mothers meetings.

I am particularly grateful to the Otoe grandmothers. Even though they may not be mentioned by name or quoted directly, their lives form an essential part of the observations recorded here: Fannie Moore Grant, Lizzie Dailey Harper, Sarah Hudson Kihega, Livina Dailey, Minnie Mae Moore, Genevieve Bassett, Rae Munroe, Vera Cleghorn, Susie Dailey, Vena Deroin, Lucy White Cloud, Mamie Faw Faw, Sophie Diamond, Julia Pipestem Pettit, Nora Keyes, Zelda Yeahquo, Dorcas Tohee, Frances Little Crow, and Lorena Deroin.

Special thanks go to Marjorie Hudson, Joan Weibel-Orlando, Ann Lane Hedlund, and Bruce Miller, who read earlier drafts of this chapter and made helpful suggestions. Thanks go also to Elizabeth Dressel Hoobler and Penny Raife Durant for detailed critiques and to Sherry King, Cliett Kight, and Bee Jay Zans for their comments on the first 10 pages. Although I have not heeded all of the suggestions, the chapter reads more smoothly because of their comments. I take sole responsibility for the final presentation.

5. The Missouria tribe amalgamated with the Otoe tribe in the late 1790s, and since that

time the tribe's name has been Otoe-Missouria. Even though there are members of the tribe today who can trace their ancestry directly to the Missouria, the name Otoe is frequently used by tribal members and non-Indians alike in both oral and written communication. Following common practice, I use the name Otoe to refer to the consolidated Otoe-Missouria people.

6. In the twentieth century there were seven identifiable surviving clans: Bear, Beaver, Elk, Eagle, Buffalo, Pigeon, and Owl. Even in 1987, when the functions of clans were greatly attenuated, some Otoe-Missouria elders would not publicly discuss information about their clans, saying these things could only be told to proper clan descendants (The Otoe-Missouria Tribe. 1985–1986).

In effect, the tribe was a confederation of related subunits. Each clan had an origin story, prescribed behaviors for clan members, a medicine bundle, special rituals and powers, and specific functions in the tribe as a whole. For example, designated families of the Elk clan had the power to light the sacred pipe. The leadership of the tribe rotated between the Bear clan and the Buffalo clan, depending on the seasons of the year. The separateness of the clan system may be a contributing factor in the tribal factionalism that sometimes arises in the late twentieth century.

7. I refer to the grandmothers as the "elder grandmothers" to indicate the generation that they represent. However, to avoid the use of a rather cumbersome term, in most references I use the simpler term "grandmothers."

8. The Dawes Act of 1887 mandated the division of reservation lands into individual allotments, with a plot of land (usually 160 acres) to be allotted to each individual. No reservations remained in Indian Territory after the allotment, although the tribes in Oklahoma retained ownership of small acreages of tribally owned land. These lands are used for tribal structures and activities such as business offices, dance grounds, and burial grounds. Land that was not allotted to tribal members (known as "surplus" land) was opened for White settlement, except on the Kaw, Ponca, Osage, and Otoe-Missouria reservations, where all reservation lands were divided among tribal members and not sold as surplus (Chapman 1965:220). However, through a variety of means, some of them devious and illegal, these tribes soon found that many of the allotments had been alienated from tribal members and a large percentage of the former reservations had passed into non-Indian ownership.

9. Unless otherwise indicated, the quotations and other data on contemporary Otoe life are from my field notes, 1974–1992.

10. Martha Mary McGaw, CSJ. Seeing Two Nuns in Perry Changes Her Whole Life. *The Sooner Catholic*. n.d.:16.

11. *The Ponca City News*. Sunday, November 17, 1985:5-a.

12. Schweitzer (1984).

13. *The Ponca City News*. Sunday, November 17, 1985:5-a.

14. As in any cultural community, there is intratribal variation; not all of the Otoe people share these religious beliefs in equal proportion, and there is variation in the strength of allegiance to each system. Some individuals spend more time in Christian church activities while others spend more time attending peyote meetings. Some Otoes do not attend Native

American Church meetings. Native religious practices are used in combination with both Native American Church and Christian church activities, and most Otoes find themselves involved in activities of each belief system at one time or another.

15. During my visits to Otoe country, tribal members were constantly explaining to me, "Oh, he's my uncle, even though he's younger than I am," or "Those two women over there, they're my sisters," although I knew the person speaking had only one sister born of the same father and mother and no half sisters.

Classificatory kin terms do not distinguish between lineal and (some) collateral relatives. An example is the classification of "mother's sister" with "mother" in the Omaha system (Schusky 1983:90). A further refinement identifies the Omaha kinship pattern regarding the system of cousins as bifurcate merging (1983:19). That is, mother's sister merges with mother, but mother's brother does not merge with father.

Mother's brother's daughters are referred to as "Little Mother" and distantly related fathers and mother's brothers' daughters' husbands are called "Little Father."

16. The naming ceremony is described more fully in Schweitzer (1985:4–7). Name givers tell four stories about names; the family then chooses one. The names are usually traditional clan names or related to clan names. In the ceremony described here, the family asked for the names of a great-great-grandfather and a grandmother.

17. See also Schweitzer (1983:157–171) and Schweitzer (1981:4–8).

18. War Mothers' broadcloth blankets and shawls are decorated with appliquéd or embroidered names of the sons and daughters who served in the armed forces. Other decorations include quilled medallions; red, white, and blue ribbon streamers; a beaded American eagle; an American flag (beaded or felt); and a War Mothers' shield.

19. The terms "family" or "family network" used here and in later discussions of contemporary Otoe social structure refer to the extended family, with emphasis on the patrilineage; they are more inclusive than a household or a nuclear family. These terms are used interchangeably. Because of intermarriage with Whites and other tribes, the emphasis is sometimes placed on the mother's side of the family. The use of these terms is similar to the terms "family" and "family network" defined by Miller (1994:39) as people linked by kin and reciprocity.

20. While I write of specific grandmothers and a particular tribal community, my association with and observation of the elder members of other Oklahoma tribes suggest that the behaviors and attitudes are typical of elder grandmothers in tribes of western and north-central Oklahoma.

POWWOW PRINCESSES AND GOSPELETTES

Cross-Generational Enculturation in American Indian Families

◈

JOAN WEIBEL-ORLANDO

INTRODUCTION

Much of the literature on grandmotherhood and the small body of writings specifically about Indian grandmotherhood describe the statuses and roles of aging women vis-à-vis their sons and daughters, their grandsons and grand-daughters, occasionally their great-grandchildren, and their community. These studies are concerned primarily with the social, cultural, and psychological outcomes of grandmotherhood for the women who achieve that social category. Cultural variation in expectations about appropriate grandmotherly behavior on the part of the so-labeled older woman and recognition of and deference shown that status by the labeling community has also been acknowledged and explored (Amoss 1981b, Katz 1978, Nahemow 1987, Shanas and Sussman 1981, Schweitzer 1987, Teski 1987).

The status of grandmother is at once biologically and socially achieved and ascribed. A woman becomes a grandmother when she is still alive at the time one of her children has a child. The status is a biological and cultural given. As with every status relationship there is at least one other person whose presence defines that social structure—the grandchild. Grandparental roles can include the responsibility for the caretaking, custody, socialization, and enculturation[1] of the grandchild. Both grandparent and grandchild have expectations about the set of roles associated with being a grandparent or grandchild, which may differ widely. Individuals may also choose a preferred role path from the array of possible roles associated with these statuses to the exclusion of others.

In this chapter I explore grandmothering as socialization and enculturation processes. Rather than identifying those aspects of grandmotherhood beneficial to and socially integrating for the older woman, this chapter focuses on the effects of certain types of grandmotherhood on the people who define the status—the grandchildren. In both cases presented here the grandmothers are Indian women who are the full-time caretakers of grandchildren who have lived in their homes for long periods. These grandmothers have assumed the responsibility for their young grandchildren's early socialization and enculturation in the absence of the children's parents. The effects of long-term grandparental caretaking are reciprocal. Aspects of the statuses and roles that shape experience for both the grandmother and grandchild are described.

This chapter addresses several issues of culture transmission. What kinds of sociocultural environments and modes of socialization do older Indian women provide for their grandchildren for whom they are the primary caretakers during extended periods (more than one month of each year) of the children's formative years? Are there contextual differences between the parental and grandparental environments? If so, what effects can we project for the children growing up in their grandma's world?

Based on both reflections of Sioux and Choctaw grandmothers and my own observations of their interactions with their grandchildren who spend significant parts of their childhood living in those grandmothers' care, I suggest the effect of Indian grandmothering as an enculturation process is essentially conservative. In many cases, the caretaking Indian grandmothers consciously attempt to cultivate and maintain those aspects of social experience that allow the children in their care to identify as ethnic group members in the face of and, in part, in response to powerful social, familial, and personal propensities to the contrary.

Two mechanisms by which caretaking American Indian grandmothers incorporate their grandchildren into community activities are described. Contemporaneously, powwow[2] dancing among the Sioux and gospel sings[3] among the Choctaw are appropriate and expected youth activities that promote both integration of the individual into and continuity of the culture group.

OVERVIEW OF THE ETHNICITY, CONTINUITY, AND SUCCESSFUL-AGING PROJECT

In 1983 Andrei Simič, Barbara Myerhoff, and I began a cross-cultural study of ethnicity's contribution to successful aging.[4] Myerhoff was to work with aging Jews in the Fairfax area in Los Angeles and Simič with Serbo-Croatian Americans in northern California, while I was to work with aging American Indians in Los Angeles.

When I began to contact people with whom I had talked in previous studies of the American Indian community in Los Angeles and who, in 1983, would have been at least 60 years old, I discovered approximately half of that cohort were no longer in Los Angeles. Rather, in the years since I had spoken with them, they had moved back (usually on retirement) to their childhood homelands. Feeling that the return-to-the-homelands phenomenon characterizing the experiences and career paths of at least half of the retirement-age Los Angeles Indian interviewees was too novel and anthropologically interesting a social process to be ignored, I quickly restructured my original research design to include such elder returnees.

I was particularly interested in learning the symbolic meaning of return to, and deep reemergence in, an ethnic community in later life. Was it a conscious attempt to sustain and intensify a sense of cultural continuity and belonging that we have come to associate with well-being in old age? Are there pragmatic aspects of this career path? Or, as Myerhoff and Simič (1978) suggest, are the motivations in old age primarily ideological? How are these transmigrations effected and roles negotiated in communities that have changed in ways that may not parallel the changes experienced by the returning exurbanites? In several respects the focus of this chapter is fostered by an interest in how the abstraction—cultural continuity—is expressed behaviorally in the cross-generational enculturation process.

DATA COLLECTION AND FIELD METHODS

In June 1984 I traveled to the Pine Ridge Reservation in South Dakota to obtain follow-up data for Sioux people for whom I already had collected life histories and to carry out additional life history interviews with people whom I had never interviewed but who fit the category of returning tribal member. In August 1984 I traveled to Oklahoma and completed a similar series of follow-up and life history interviews with members of the Creek, Seminole, Choctaw, and Chickasaw people, whose territorial homelands after the 1830s removal program were located in southeastern Oklahoma.

During those visits I participated as much as possible in the social life of the study participants, focusing on face-to-face interactions of the participants with members of their community. I observed the participants in interaction with their immediate families and, in particular, the enactment of their grandparental roles in the several cases in which grandchildren were in proximity to or actually living in the same household as their grandparents.

In the summer of 1985 a graduate student assistant[5] from the Center for Visual Anthropology at the University of Southern California and I returned to South Dakota and Oklahoma to do follow-up interviews and observations of the participants in both public and private (family) interactions. We video-taped the interviews as well as the interviewees' participation in several public events we attended with them and their families.

DESCRIPTION OF THE SAMPLE

Since the summer of 1984, when I began to collect and update life histories of aging Indians, I have interviewed 25 people who had lived for at least 20 years in either the West Coast urban centers of Los Angeles or San Francisco or in rural areas at least 500 miles away from their original homelands. All of the interviewees had returned to their childhood homelands less than five years before the interview.

The ages of the study participants ranged from 56 to 75 in 1984. There are 10 men and 15 women in the sample. Ten people (six women and four men) are Sioux and were living on the Pine Ridge Reservation in South Dakota when I first interviewed them in 1984. Five people (two men and three women) are members of the Creek and Seminole tribes. Six people (four women and three men) are Choctaw, and one man and two women are Chickasaw. One woman is a Caucasian married to a Creek man.

The 25 participants represent 16 families. Five women and one man were sin-gle heads of households. Of the 16 families in this study, seven families had no grandchildren living with them. Of those seven families, three couples had no biological grandchildren. Therefore, out of a possible 13 families with grand-children, only four did not have biological grandchildren living with them. Of these four couples, all had grandchildren who still lived on the West Coast with their parents. To ensure some personal contact with these grandchildren, the grandparents visit them at least once a year, or the grandchildren come to the grandparental homes for extended visits during their summer school vacations.

Fictive grandmothering is an alternative to the lack or absence of grand-children. One grandchildless woman had an informally adopted son living with her who was young enough to be her grandchild. (She was 83 and he was 25 when interviewed in 1984.) In one family in which the wife's grandchildren were living with their parents in San Francisco, the wife played a grandparental role by teaching unrelated children about "real" Choctaw traditions such as dances, beadwork, and language in a public-school-sponsored cultural enrich-ment program.

Seven families live in three-generational households. One family had at least one member from each of its four generations living under one roof. Seven sets of grandparents were the primary caretakers for at least one grandchild when interviewed. In six cases the parents of the grandchild were not included in the primary caretaking unit at the time of the interviews. In the seventh case the mother was in the home but worked full-time out of the home. The resident grandmother was responsible for the primary care of the three grandchildren in the household during the workweek.

One couple had one grandchild living with them, two had two, one had three, and five had at least four grandchildren living in the same household with them. One family had a great-grandchild living with them at least half of the day while the mother completed her high school courses.

One woman mentioned above had a foster child living with her when I first interviewed her in 1984. He subsequently followed her to Oklahoma when she decided to return to her hometown in 1985. One woman has been a foster grandmother to seven children for periods ranging from four to 18 months since her return to her hometown in 1981. At one time four foster children shared her modest two-bedroom ranch house with her husband and two biological grandchildren.

These demographic data illustrate that substantial numbers of grandparents still take on the role of primary caretaker for their grandchildren. In addition the multigenerational household still appears to be the modal family composition across the tribal groups in this study.

CASE STUDIES

Rather than attempt to discuss the entire sample in general terms, I have chosen to present and discuss the enculturation aspects of two women's grandmotherhoods. Although both women have been full-time caretakers for at least one grandchild for long periods, their grandmotherhoods represent widely different experiences and perspectives. That their grandparenthoods represent opposite ends of a motivational spectrum underscores the difficulties inherent in making broad-based statements about a general American Indian grandparenting style. Identification with and acceptance of both the grandparental status and role are influenced by the time in one's life trajectory at which and the circumstances under which grandparenthood is bestowed on an individual.

Mrs. Big Buffalo,[6] a full-blood, Lakota-speaking Sioux, exemplifies grandmother as cultural conservator. Sixty-seven years old when interviewed in 1984, she already had had three biological grandchildren and four foster grandchildren living with her at various times since she moved back to the Pine Ridge Reservation in 1981.

Primary caretaking of grandchildren is a traditional role for older Sioux women. Grandmothering is a role Mrs. Big Buffalo relishes and seeks out, even to the point of taking up fictive grandmothering (she is accredited by the South Dakota State Department of Health and Human Services as a foster-care parent) when none of her children would part with their children when she petitioned for their company.

Mrs. Bokchito, on the other hand, has assumed the role of custodial grandparent for four of her grandchildren and one great-grandchild with fatalism and resentment. At 57, this full-blood Choctaw woman feels exploited and trapped by what she describes as her eldest daughter's parental irresponsibility and her own exaggerated sense of familial loyalty and duty.

In both cases their grandmothering perspectives are illustrated by vignettes excerpted from their life history narratives. I have also known each woman for approximately 10 years, visited their homes on a number of occasions, and attended with them the ethnic community activities to which they expose their grandchildren. Their cooperation has included extensive observation of their interactions with their grandchildren in both their homes and in public community activities.

GROWING UP IN GRANDMA'S WORLD— THE CULTURAL CONSERVATOR MODEL

Being raised by one's grandparents is not a socialization pattern unique to twentieth-century Indian family life. In fact, grandmothers as primary caretakers of first and second grandchildren is a long-established Native American childcare strategy. Simmons (1970:84) tells us that "old Crow grandmothers were considered essential elements in the household, engaged in domestic chores," while helping young mothers who were burdened with work. And Schweitzer (1987) explains, "Within the framework of the extended family a special relationship existed between grandparents and grandchildren that began at birth and lasted a lifetime. Children were cared for by grandparents and, in turn, the family cared for the old when they were feeble."

Mrs. Big Buffalo recognizes the primary caretaking aspects of her grandmotherhood as not only a traditionally Indian but also as a particularly Lakota thing to do:

Traditional grandmothers are still there, but not like they were when I was growing up. The grandparents always took . . . at least the first grandchild to raise because that's just the way the Lakota did it. They think that they're [the grandparents][7] more mature and have had more experience and they could teach the children a lot more than the young parents, especially if the parents were young. . . . I'm still trying to carry on that tradition because my grandmother raised me most of the time up until I was nine years old. She was always running the tribal police off the place because they wanted me to go to school and she said that I was too young to be taken away from home. I didn't go to school until I was nine years old.

Historically the Lakota were·one of three linguistic subsections of the seven westernmost High Plains hunting tribal groups now known as the Sioux. Traditional Lakota hunting territories coincided in small part with current reservation holdings in the southwest corner of South Dakota. In 1868 a treaty mandated discontinuing their nomadic way of life and provided the mechanisms for a transition to an agricultural subsistence base. The Dawes Severalty Act in 1887 further ensured the division of lands held in common by the tribe into privately held farming parcels. Families enrolled on tribal membership lists to receive their 160-acre allotments of land and requisite stock and farming equipment.

By the second decade of the twentieth century, when Mrs. Big Buffalo was born, most of the Lakota eligible for land allotments on the Pine Ridge Reservation already had received them, sold them, leased them usually to non-Indian farmers, or were themselves trying to eke a living from their allotted tracts. Commonly held tribal lands had been greatly reduced, but wage labor was almost nonexistent on the reservation. Most people subsistence farmed, did migrant farmwork, and accepted government-sponsored assistance, a euphemism for public charity. Consequently Pine Ridge Sioux incomes were significantly below the national average.

Mrs. Big Buffalo's family seems to have fared better than their other Lakota neighbors. Her memories of a Lakota childhood include the comfort of a large, well-maintained frame farmhouse, the pride associated with racing her own pony through fields full of her grandfather's horses (then still a marker of community status), the security of a larder full of preserves from her grandmother's garden, halcyon days of unstructured prairie play with her Lakota-speaking cousins, and the status afforded her because she lived in a family wealthy enough to provide economic assistance to less well endowed neighbors.

When asked what she remembers about the things her grandparents taught to and did with her, Mrs. Big Buffalo waxes nostalgic about a childhood magically protected from external and sophisticating forces:

> Well, I knew what my grandfather did, but I didn't know about anybody else. I didn't even know there was other tribes of Indians around. I just had my own little world.

She remembers her grandparents' styles of enculturation as essentially conservative in that the things they passed on to their grandchildren were taken from traditional Sioux lore:

> My grandfather was a medicine man. . . . I saw him heal people . . . almost miraculously. . . . I used to know every one of his ceremonial songs that they sang and everything, and you know after I put them out of my mind, I forgot them. And now when I hear one, I remember.

The grandparents rarely attempted to instruct their grandchildren in strategies for coping with the dominant society or twentieth-century technology. That information and process of enculturation were better left to the parental generation or the schools.

> I was the first person on both sides of my family, of the women, to ever go out and work for a living. When I started doing it, my grandparents were dead already, so it didn't matter very much. My mother was pretty modern. She knew that's what you had to do to exist, so she never said nothing about it. But she used to say how their father never let them work for wages.

Mrs. Big Buffalo's model for cross-generational parenting and the roles she and her children should play in the enculturation of her grandchildren were and continue to be those of the parents as pragmatic exploiters of and liaisons between the workaday climate of the White man's world and the archetypically conservative and sacred character of the grandparental domain:

> My mother used to say how their father never let them work for wages. One time, at the day school, they raised a whole bunch of tomatoes and they needed to can them in a hurry, and the teacher in the summertime came over and asked my mom and her sister to help. My grandfather said they could go, but he told them not to accept wages for helping them. His wife or none of his daughters ever went to work for wages anyplace else. I

don't think he ever did either, work for anybody else but himself. It's a kind of self-sufficiency thing that they have.

If her grandparents paid any heed at all to the cultural offerings of the White world, she remembers that it was only for the purposes of fostering continuity of tribal ways:

"Granddaughter, when you learn to speak the White man's language and you learn to read it and write it," he said, "I'll tell you a story that my grandfather told me about how life was for the Lakota years ago. And you can write it down and then you can tell it to your grandchildren." I was about nine when he told me that.

And rarely did the grandparents command or require allegiance of the grandchildren to their particular worldview. Rather, instruction took the form of suggestions about or presentation of models of exemplary behavior to which Mrs. Big Buffalo admits she imperfectly attended:

Well, my grandfather always told me what a Lakota woman wouldn't do and what they were supposed to do. But he never said I had to do anything.

When I was little, I don't know, maybe a little bit bigger than Winoma [Mrs. Big Buffalo's granddaughter], my grandmother had a beaded outfit. She made me exactly the same replica in my size. So when we used to go to these powwows, she'd put hers on and I'd put mine on. At the time the women didn't walk around; they just stood stationary and danced up and down. I'd have to stand there with her then. But I'd be looking way back out of the shade where the kids were playing. I would want to be out there where they were playing and I'd stand there dancing with my grandmother. She was always telling me to not be looking way out there, to pay attention to what's going on here, but I'd stand there and dance with her and I'd be watching the kids play.

Since Mrs. Big Buffalo's mother died shortly before the family's move to Los Angeles, Mrs. Big Buffalo took on both the culturally conservative grandparental and the pragmatic parental roles in respect to her children.

When my daughter was princess[8] of these different [powwow] clubs in L.A . . . club members are expected to dress up and dance at all their own powwows. So I danced with her all the time then.

Both in dance regalia, a Plains tradition elder and her great-granddaughter join an intertribal social dance at a Saturday night powwow in Long Beach, California. Photograph by Joan Weibel-Orlando.

Mrs. Big Buffalo purposely continues to shape her grandmotherhood on the cultural conservator model of her own grandparents.

> The second- or third-generation Indian children out [in Los Angeles], most of them never get to see anything like . . . a sun dance[9] or a memorial feast[10] or giveaway[11] or just stuff that Indians do back home. I wanted my children to be involved in them and know what it's all about. So that's the reason that I always try to keep my grandchildren whenever I can.

According to Mrs. Big Buffalo she, rather than her children, initiated the long-term presence of the five grandchildren she has cared for in her home. She takes on this childcare responsibility for both ideological and pragmatic reasons:

> I ask [my children] if [their children] could spend the summer with me if there isn't school and go with me to the Indian doings so that they'll know that they're Indian and know the culture and traditions. [I'm] just kind of building memories for them.

Schweitzer (1987) further points out, "It is customary for [Indian] grandparents to raise grandchildren who have been left without a father or mother or both. . . . It is also customary for grandparents to raise grandchildren when parents work, a parent is sick, away on a job relocation or when it eased the burden of too many children." Mrs. Big Buffalo's stated motivations for having her grandchildren in her home certainly conform to this cultural model:

> And with my daughter I always thought I'd give her a rest because she worked and had children. So I thought if she didn't have children for a while . . . life would be a little bit easier for her. And I don't have nothing to do but take care of them.

Mrs. Big Buffalo describes her reservation home in relation to her children's Los Angeles homes in much the same way she remembers her own grandparental home in relation to the discrimination and socioeconomic upheaval that characterized the South Dakota wheat belt in the 1920s. Her modest prairie ranch home takes on qualities of sanctuary—a place of calm, regularity, and wholesomeness. She sharply contrasts the stability of her home with the characteristic turbulence of her children's urban social and psychological context:

> I think I have a stable home, and I can take care of them. Especially if the mother and father are having problems. This next June, Sonny [her daughter's son] will be with me two years and last November, Winoma was with me one year, so she's been with me a year and a half. That's how long I've had them. But this is an unusual situation. The parents . . . are going to get a divorce. That's why I didn't want them around there [Los Angeles] while this was going on. I think they're better off with me.

Importantly, Mrs. Big Buffalo's opinion about the optimum environment for raising her grandchildren carries considerable weight with her children. They periodically and after her insistent petitions place their children in her custody during summer school vacations and, in times of crisis, for periods of up to five years. What, then, is the cultural milieu into which these children are placed, and how does this setting differ from that of the parental generation? In Mrs. Big Buffalo's case, her grandchildren, except for the time they are in school, accompany her on her steady rounds of tribal events:

> If I can't take my grandchildren with me somewhere, I don't go. Most everywhere I go, they can go. They go with me to [church, powwows, sun dances in the summer, giveaways], even to my bingo games. They can go

on Friday night with me when there's no school the next day. And so their parents are always looking for a babysitter for them so that they can go wherever they want to go. But I don't need a babysitter.

Mrs. Big Buffalo's enthusiasm about having her grandchildren in her home is tempered by the realization that because her children have grown up in an urban environment, the spiritual magnetism of reservation life is essentially lost on them (Tefft, 1968). She regards their disdain for tribal life with consternation and ironic humor and consciously opts for taking a major role in the early socialization of her grandchildren. Mrs. Big Buffalo views her children as being just "too far gone" [assimilated] for any attempt at repatriation on her part. Her role as the culture conservator grandmother, then, is doubly important. The grandchildren are her only hope for effecting both personal and cultural continuity:

> When I was leaving Long Beach to move back to South Dakota, my second son, Brian, was really surprised that I would go back there to live. He said, "Mom, are you really going back there to live?" So I said, "Yeah, I'm gonna go back. That's where I was raised, that's where I'm from, that's where my roots are. So I'm gonna go back there and I'm gonna build a house and live there and when I die I'm gonna be buried there." And he shrugged and said, "Oh, well, I guess there ain't much else to do there." And oh, I had to laugh. That's the way they [her children] feel about South Dakota. They don't think nothing much ever goes on over here.

Schweitzer (1987) suggests that adults, especially women, welcome becoming a grandparent and are proud to claim that status. For Mrs. Big Buffalo, primary-care grandmothering is a role she eagerly negotiates with her children. Having her youngest grandchildren in her home and under her absolute custody for extended periods is just one more example of her acceptance and enactment of behaviors expected of properly traditional older Lakota women. Her active grandmotherhood fulfills what she sees as an important cultural function not only for herself but also for her future generations. She exercises that function in ways that would have been familiar to her archconservative grandparents—a cultural continuity she finds particularly satisfying:

> I think it's a privilege to keep my grandchildren. When they're grown up, they'll remember and talk about when I lived with my grandmother . . . like I talk about living with my grandmother.

GROWING UP IN GRANDMA'S WORLD—THE CUSTODIAL MODEL

As Butler and Bengtson (1985) point out, grandparenthood is not a status to which individuals universally aspire. The ease and enthusiasm with which the status is assumed depends to a great extent on timing, personal career path aspirations of both parents and new grandparents, and the relative stability of the extended family structure. Though Butler and Bengtson's findings are based on Black family studies, much the same can be said of the range of responses to grandparenthood among the Indian grandparents I interviewed.

In contrast to Mrs. Big Buffalo's eager negotiation with her children for the prolonged presence of her grandchildren in her home, Mrs. Bokchito is torn between her own personal agenda and the cultural and familial expectations of her as a grandmother:

> When is it ever going to end, that's what I would like to know? All my life I've had these kids off and on. That's why I get upset sometimes when I think this is never going to end.

Her mood swings alternate between bouts of anger, resignation, and depression and positive assessments about the role she plays in her grandchildren's lives. The custodial role essentially has been forced on her by the misconduct or disinterest of two of her children. She accepts the role as the duty of a moral Christian woman and in the best interest of her several, troubled, and often abandoned grandchildren.

> Atoka has been with me since she was a year and a half. Her mother would go out and would be partying, and someone was left with the child. But that person took off and left Atoka by herself. And the neighbors called me to tell me the child was all by herself, crying. The judge wouldn't let her [the daughter] have her back, so he gave her to me.
>
> Lahoma, she's been with me since she was born, I guess. [My daughter] had problems with drugs all these years. Lahoma, when she was left [by her mother], she had to go to McClaran Hall and then the court awarded her to me. It's been like that off and on.
>
> Pamela went with somebody. I think she was placed in a home, then she would come to stay with me for a while, then her mother would take her back and then get into trouble again and the whole thing would start all over again.

Although when I first reinterviewed her in 1984 Mrs. Bokchito's household strained from having four unruly grandchildren, an invalid husband, and an unemployed adult daughter all under one roof, Mrs. Bokchito, like Mrs. Big Buffalo, was firmly convinced her lifestyle and brand of discipline are far superior to the non-Indian and antisocial drug culture to which her grandchildren would be exposed in the parental homes:

> The father of the girls was in jail and still is in there. It must be hard for them [the children]. One time both of their parents were in jail.
>
> Pamela's kind of stubborn at times. She started working. And now [that] she has her own money, she thinks she can do just as she pleases. So I kind of had to put my foot down. I said, "You're only 15 years old. And I don't want you doing anything wrong." The first time she went out, she said she was going to be with these girls and then I found out she was someplace else. So I told her there wasn't going to be a second time. And oh, she didn't like that very much. But the next time she told me when she was going to come back in, five minutes before her time was up she came running into the house to let me know she was on time.

Recognizing that her children, and especially her drug-dependent daughter, take advantage of her nurturant nature, Mrs. Bokchito explains her reasons for accepting the moral responsibility for the welfare of her grandchildren:

> In L.A. sometimes I would go out to one of the Indian bars just to do something else besides working and taking care of kids. So I'd pay someone to watch the kids and I'd go out for a few hours. But every time I was at a party or something, in the back of my mind I'd think, "What if something happened to me? What if I get in an accident? What's going to happen to those kids?" You know, most people don't think like that.

Although the older children from her daughter's long-term but marriageless relationship suffer all the classic symptoms of neglected children (discipline problems, poor school performance, absenteeism, drug experimentation, and an early and unplanned pregnancy), Mrs. Bokchito still holds out hope for the youngest of the four grandchildren currently living with her:

> Donny is real good, he's lots of company for me. You see, his mother had died in childbirth and his father, well, he kind of blamed the child for her death. My son was really crazy about that woman. And he had to work and all that, so I thought it was better for me to take the baby. His other

grandparents, they fought us. Being that their daughter and my son weren't married. My son had to go to court to fight them. And after a while he found someone else and they got married. Now they have a new baby, and so Donny gets treated like the stepson. And since he's been with me most of his life, it's best for him to be with me. And he's no trouble, he's a real good kid, so loving and kind. He's a lot of comfort for me.

Perhaps because Donny has been with her since his birth and her care of him had not been interrupted by mercurial and often short-lived and traumatic bouts of inept parental intervention, he seems to have fared best in her care. He is clearly her favorite grandchild. And his presence in her home is seen as being as beneficial for her as it is for him. In this symbiotic relationship grandparent and grandchild share easy demonstrations of affection and interdependence when all other relationships in the family are marked by strain and/or avoidance. Her voice softens when she describes his sweet personality. The only time she laughed during our talk about grandmotherhood was when she thought of Donny joining in with her gospel choir in easy imitation of her modeling of respectable Christian/Choctaw behavior:

Donny doesn't go to school yet. He's only five years old. He's got a brain. Boy, he's smart. You know he goes with me to practicing [choir rehearsal], and he knows all these words what we're singing and he sings right along with us. And when we [the choir] get up there [in front of a congregation] to sing, he wants to sing for us. He starts tapping his feet. He looks so cute.

And so Donny, the loved, wanted, and fought-for grandchild, accompanies Mrs. Bokchito on her endless round of church sings and potluck dinners.

Ironically, membership in one of the several fundamental, Protestant Christian denominations, the very social institution designed to co-opt pre-Western European contact Choctaw social organization now sustains Choctaw community life more than any other social structure. Concerted efforts to introduce Protestantism to the tribal people of the American Southeast were initiated in the first decade of the nineteenth century (Berkhofer 1972). The impact was immediate, strong, and lasting. Within two decades Christian conversion was such that scores of Protestant pastors accompanied their flocks of Choctaw brethren on the Longest Walk, the 1830 trek from their farming villages east of the Mississippi River and into the southeastern piney forests of Oklahoma Choctaw Territory (Ronda and Axtell 1978). Parallel church-centered villages were established in Oklahoma and continue to structure Choctaw social life.

The land allotment directives of the 1880s also affected the original Choctaw

A Choctaw woman and her granddaughter share a hymnal during a Fifth Sunday Sing at the Native American and First United Methodist Church in Norwalk, California. Photograph by Robert A. Orlando.

Oklahoma land severalty arrangements. Depending on the rather arbitrary assignment of land parcels to people on the tribal enrollments, families either scratched out subsistence farms in hard-won pine forest clearings or "struck it rich" when lands leased to oil-drilling companies in the 1920s and 1930s came up wet.

Mrs. Bokchito's family was not among the lucky Oklahoma "oil" Indians. She remembers biting poverty; too many brothers and sisters sharing crowded, century-old log cabins with an assortment of cousins, aunts, and uncles; and extended family households from which parents were often absent. Unlike Mrs. Big Buffalo, who remembers her first contact with Indian boarding schools as a negative and anomic experience, Mrs. Bokchito is grateful to have been sent to a Christian Indian orphanage:

> It was real nice. For the first time in my life I had my own clothes that I wasn't supposed to share with anyone. I had my own bed—my own bed! I didn't have to share it with three other kids like I had had to all my life. . . . The teachers were real good to me. I had a good singing voice.

And I knew all of the old-time hymns because I had sung them all my life at Sunday school and at all the sings. So I was always asked to get up and do a special.[12] And they would clap. And oh, boy, did I like that. I was a real ham. . . . Then I got to take piano lessons. I learned real quick. After that I traveled all around the state with the school choir as their accompanist. I sure had a good time at that church school.

The isolation and family-centered life of the Choctaw hill people is relieved only by a crowded annual schedule of church community gatherings, services, choir practices, revivals, camp-outs, and sings. For the last 150 years Christian belief and ceremonial ritual and aboriginal Choctaw social structure have been synthesized into what is now an established Christian Choctaw ethos:

About the only thing a person like me can do to enjoy herself is to go to singings. There's a singing going on every night if you want to go to it, and there's always eating at the singing. But that's about all you can do, or go to church. Or else you go drinking, and that's about all that goes on. That's it.

Mrs. Bokchito's limited and circumspect world of the Choctaw gospel singing circuit has become the cultural reference for Donny, the sparrowlike child of a Choctaw father and a Puerto Rican mother. His beloved grandma's world is as secure and real to him as is her ample and comforting bosom, into which he nestles when tired of practicing the art of four-part harmonization, restive from night-long reiterations of old gospel favorites, or satiated by the generous and familiar potluck offerings.

Although Mrs. Bokchito freely voices her ambivalence about her custodial grandmotherhood, in Donny's case, she carries it out in ways similar to Mrs. Big Buffalo's cultural conservator model. While Mrs. Bokchito does not articulate the need to sustain continuity of Choctaw culture as Mrs. Big Buffalo does about Sioux culture, Mrs. Bokchito clearly views the milieu in which she is raising Donny and to which she has, mostly in vain, attempted to introduce her teenage granddaughters as superior to the uncaring and non-Indian urban social milieu of her Los Angeles–based children:

The Indian Center tried to get her [daughter] a job. But she just wouldn't go. The father of the baby wouldn't marry or support her. But as soon as she had the baby he'd come around again. And they would repeat the same thing all over again. And I helped in the best way I could. And then she got married. But sometimes things would pile up. And her husband went to jail and she'd be cooped up in the house with these three little kids. And then she'd get depressed and start taking all these things that she used to take. She just couldn't cope. She got help in the institutions. She hung around with a Mexican crowd. In the last few years seems like she didn't want to have anything to do with me because I am always trying to talk to her. But she won't hear it.

Like Mrs. Big Buffalo, Mrs. Bokchito has little hope for her urban-bred children's return to rural life and traditional tribal roles:

She [her daughter] says she is going to come down and take care of her grandchild. But I wonder if that is going to hold her? She's been into these drugs and alcohol all these years. I don't think a baby is going to hold her down. She had her own flesh and blood and that didn't hold her down, so I don't think [being a grandmother] is going to do it either.

For Mrs. Big Buffalo, having a houseful of grandchildren is an expected privilege of old age. In contrast, the younger Mrs. Bokchito's perceptions of her custodial grandmothering range from an appreciation of the comfort and companionship she receives from her favorite to annoyance and frustration with having to assume the extra burden of her 16-year-old granddaughter's unwanted pregnancy. She finds her custodial responsibilities particularly irksome as she feels they are inappropriate to the current stage of her life:

The only thing that gets me down is these kids. They get me so uptight. I already have high blood pressure. Anxiety . . . these kids fighting all the time. That's what gets me down mostly. I shouldn't be doing this [taking care of children]. Not at my age. I should be just taking it easy and going here and there. And then my granddaughter's going to have a baby. The 16-year-old granddaughter. Everything, they just keep multiplying.

When asked if she and her granddaughter had thought about an alternative to carrying the unplanned pregnancy to full term, Mrs. Bokchito explained the process by which the family decision to keep the baby was made:

At the beginning we thought about it [abortion]. Then the social worker up at the clinic did talk to us about it. He said if she had this abortion, then she would have the rest of her life to think about what she did. And then if she did have the baby, then she would have the rest of her life to take care of it and support it. So there was no easy way. . . . Then she felt like she wanted to keep it. So that's what she's going to do now. She's going to keep it. And guess who's going to take care of it when she's back in school?

Mrs. Bokchito's long history of accepting caretaking responsibilities for her children's children has set a precedent. Having spent major parts of her childhood in the care of her grandmother, the pregnant 16-year-old granddaughter simply assumed that Grandmother would be there to help out with her baby for as long as the young mother needed support. The bitter inflection of Mrs. Bokchito's last words underscores her resentment and sense of futility in this matter. Pressured by cultural norms and familial needs, this 57-year-old about-to-be great-grandmother felt powerless to act on her own behalf. Suffused since childhood with fundamental Christian values (charity, self-denial, motherhood, the sanctity of the family) and spurred on by the promise of heavenly rewards to those who endure an earthly martyrdom, Mrs. Bokchito resentfully accepts her custodial great-grandmotherhood as her "cross to bear."

CONCLUSIONS

The divergent perceptions of grandparenting in the cases of the two Indian grandmothers presented here are clearly consequences of the individual's sense of personal control, autonomy, choice, and initiative in shaping the role. In the first case the individual readily accepts, even exploits, the cultural tenets that guarantee the rewards of community acknowledgment and respect for the Lakota older woman who cares for her grandchildren. In the second case, the individual feels trapped by cultural tenets that to her mind force her to assume caretaking responsibilities long past the time she expected to have primary childcare responsibilities and long before the time in her life she had expected to act out a much less active grandparenthood. The status, grandmother, is imbued with considerable social-structural weight in that across cultures it automatically confers both responsibility and rewards to the individual on the birth of the grandchild. The roles associated with grandmotherhood, however, can be and are negotiated. Satisfaction with both status and role, then, is the result of the individual's sense of creating a grandmotherhood consistent with both personal and cultural expectations.

Mrs. Big Buffalo is particularly sensitive to the power of the non-Indian social environment to shape children's attitudes and ethnic orientation. She therefore takes an active role in the enculturation of her grandchildren. She consciously exposes her grandchildren to activities and cultural scenes that perpetuate the family's participation in Sioux ceremonial life. Mrs. Bokchito is less apt to express overtly concerns about cultural continuity. Nonetheless, even though Mrs. Bokchito is a reluctant and much put-upon custodial caretaker and her grandmotherhood is in sharp contrast to Mrs. Big Buffalo's sought-after caretaking responsibilities, the effects of their grandparenting on their grandchildren are remarkably similar.

Both women incorporate their grandchildren into their rounds of culturally conservative activities. In both cases the youngest of the grandchildren are the most consistently exposed to their grandmothers' worlds. Both women see their worlds as clearly superior alternatives to the assorted corruptions and instabilities of their children's multicultural urban life. Interestingly, Mrs. Big Buffalo's two and Mrs. Bokchito's youngest grandchildren are at least 50 percent Hispanic. That the grandchildren's parental social milieus are multicultural and the second set of grandparents are enmeshed in the large and vital Los Angeles Hispanic community I suspect further underscores for these grandmothers the importance of exposing their grandchildren to Indian ways.

Total immersion in the grandmothers' cultural milieus provides a clear cultural template by which the grandparents can enculturate their grandchildren into valued tribal orientations. Isolated from contrasting cultural modes of ethnically heterogeneous urban life, the enculturation process is in essence conservative. Both grandmothers recognize that their caretaking responsibilities include a mitigation of what they view as the negative aspects of their grandchildren growing up in their parents' urban homes.

The cultural conservator grandmother is acutely aware of her role in the enculturation process. Convinced her urbanized children would not know or care how "to do it right," she consciously assumes the responsibility to teach her grandchildren how to and what it means to be Sioux. For the custodial grandmother the enculturation process includes providing an alternative to her eldest daughter's seductive and ubiquitous drug and alcohol addiction subculture. In both cases the grandchildren for whom these grandmothers have taken on primary caretaking responsibilities appear to be thriving in adapting to, and thereby ensuring the continued presence of the ordered domains of, their grandmas' worlds.

EPILOGUE

In the summer of 1986, at the insistence of her youngest granddaughter, Winoma, Mrs. Big Buffalo spent her evenings painstakingly sewing row upon row of tiny, powder blue, cut glass beads onto a diminutive white buckskin dress.

The dress would match Mrs. Big Buffalo's own ceremonial outfit. Winoma, her three-year-old imagination fired by dreams of future powwow princesshood, was about to take her first steps toward a lifetime of Sioux ceremonial participation. That summer, at the side of her proud grandmother, Winoma would dance in the weekly powwows just as Mrs. Big Buffalo had danced with her grandmother 60 years before.

That summer, I am happy to report, Mrs. Bokchito's life had taken an upward turn. Her invalid husband had been institutionalized. Lahoma had had her baby, gotten married, established her own household, and returned to school. Mrs. Bokchito was responsible for her first great-grandchild's care only during the mornings, when his mother attended high school. Her second daughter had gotten a job, found a steady beau, and been living with him in Texas for almost a year. The three remaining granddaughters had decided to go back to Los Angeles and live with an assortment of aunts and uncles. The teenagers sporadically drift in and out of the Oklahoma homestead as interpersonal crises in the city dictate. Only Donny remained her full caretaking responsibility.

The last time I telephoned Mrs. Bokchito, she had only a moment to talk because Donny, resplendent in his new choir robe, was already out in the car waiting impatiently for her arrival, as the insistent honking of a car horn in the background indicated. Eager to start the 35-mile drive to that evening's sing in one of the more remote Choctaw country churches, both grandmother and grandson enthusiastically anticipated the evening's soul-satisfying entertainment. It was to be Donny's debut as a bona fide member of their home church's children's choir—The Gospelettes.

NOTES

1. The terms socialization and enculturation are associated but connotatively distinct terms commonly used in the child development, psychology, and anthropology literature. Socialization refers to the process by which a child is taught to be socially competent. Enculturation refers to the process by which an individual is taught cultural competency in a specific society.

2. A powwow is an essentially social and secular gathering of American Indians. Increasingly pan-Indian, these gatherings include the following set of activities: donning elaborate Indian ceremonial dress, participating in traditional pan-Indian social and ceremonial dances, socializing, eating ethnic foods, and trading supplies and handicrafts. The contemporary powwow is thought to have its origins in the social dances held annually during the Plains Indians' tribal convocations during the summers before and after the great communal buffalo hunts (Young 1981).

3. A sing is usually a day-long gathering of members of a Protestant denomination for the

purposes of singing gospel hymns, lay preaching, Christian testimony, and personal rededi-cation to the faith. These spiritual congregations also include secular elements—midday potluck meals, community announcements, and general socializing. A sing, singing, or Fifth Sunday Sing is not a particularly Indian activity. Rather, it is a nineteenth-century southern fundamentalist Protestant innovation that Southeastern Indians have incorpo-rated into their Christian and often interdenomination ceremonial schedule.

4. This research was funded by grant 1RO1 AGO 3794–2 from the National Institute on Aging.

5. Thomas Fleming, a graduate student in the Visual Anthropology Program of the Anthropology Department at the University of Southern California, provided much appre-ciated assistance during this field research period.

6. In all cases fictitious names have been used to protect the privacy of those people who so generously shared their life stories and current activities with us.

7. All words and phrases in brackets have been added by the author so that the verbatim translation of the narratives is intelligible to the reader. In many cases I have known the study participants for 10 years or more. They therefore assume that when they talk with me, they need not explain much of the cultural or familial particulars of their lives. I have expanded the narrative only where I felt clarification was needed to fully appreciate the full intent of the participants' words.

8. A powwow princess is an honorific title conferred upon a young Indian woman through a contest process. A powwow princess is usually responsible for attending and leading the ceremonial aspects of a particular powwow club's yearly schedule of powwows. For a full discussion of the powwow princess's selection process and roles see Weibel-Orlando 1988b.

9. A sun dance is a pan-Plains ceremony, rite of intensification, and world renewal rite. Formerly prohibited by law, the 1978 Indian Religious Freedom Act saw the public re-surgence of this most important annual ceremony throughout the Plains tribal groups but particularly among the Sioux.

For a full discussion of the sun dance phenomenon see Jorgensen 1972 and Powers 1975.

10. Conservative Lakota observe a year of mourning after the death of a family member. At the end of the mourning period members of the bereaved family will hold a memorial feast for their deceased member. A memorial headstone is often dedicated and the deceased person's personal effects may be distributed among the community members at that time (see Powers 1975, 131–34).

11. A giveaway is a secular ceremony in which goods collected by a family group are publically distributed by that group to members of their economic, political, and psycholog-ical support system. Many events stimulate giveaways: graduating from school, dancing in a powwow for the first time, moving back home, return of a veteran, receiving your Indian name, winning a powwow princess contest.

12. Most of the singing at a sing is congregational. However, people known for their fine voices, special renditions of gospel favorites, membership in a regular trio or quartet, or instrumental virtuosity may be asked to come forward and sing a "special" for the group.

DAUGHTERS OF CHURCH ROCK

◆

PATRICIA McCABE

My grandmother remembers
the first whiteman she ever saw.
She hid behind a bush and watched.
Was he terribly sick?
What was it that made his seemingly healthy body
turn White?
Later after the mission school,
she was to be one of a few who traveled
to Michigan, Grand Rapids, with the missionaries
as their guest.
They asked her to go to China too,
but she declined.
They knew she was remarkable.
I'm glad they knew, when they met her.
I have a picture of her holding me,
a tiny infant in her strong arms.
She wore a frilly apron and large, thick glasses,
the way everyone did in black-and-white photos.
She smiled down on me.
My own mother went to work after I was born,
she taught school up and down the Rio Grande
to all the Pueblos
as a Navajo. A Navajo born in Los Angeles.
I spent my infancy in the arms of my grandmother.

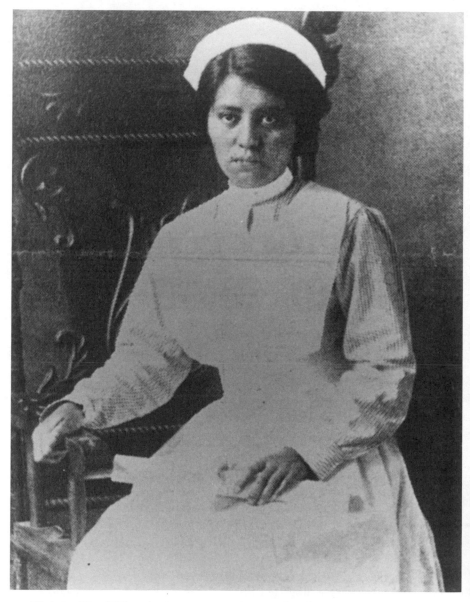

Christine Hood Whipple, Patricia McCabe's grandmother.
Photographer unknown.

I never thought to regret it. I still don't.
It wasn't in the hogan but it was
the natural course of things,
I found out much later,
for Navajos and all the living peoples of old.
We shared a bed until I was nine.
She stayed up with me when I was sick,
changed the sheets when I forgot to tell her I had to get up.
One night she took me by the hand
and marched me to the room where my parents slept,
boldly walked in and announced,
"This child can read."
I found out later, too late to find out more,
about how she and a doctor from the mission
used to make house calls all over the reservation
on horseback.
She was not only a nurse,
she also had to teach the medical staff to ride.
They didn't even know how to ride, she marveled.
She once told me when I asked her
why she didn't teach her daughters to speak Navajo
that she used to have a beautiful palomino.
She told me that she loved that horse.
Her eyes and voice told me
how beautiful the horse really was.
"They sold it when I was away. At School.
Oh, I just didn't even want a horse after that."
Sometimes I think about how it must have been
when she left the reservation in 1910 or so,
a young girl,
and moved to Los Angeles.
I don't know what that city looked like then,
probably nothing like it looks now,
but I'll bet it didn't look anything like Crownpoint.
Or Church Rock. Or Pinedale.
Grandmother, why didn't I ask these things?
I wish I could know.
What makes a woman leave her world?
And then move back again.
Was it courage and longing?

Or just the massive hand of life moving its trivial pieces?
My mother has spoken, once or twice,
about the move from Los Angeles.
She also knows what it's like to leave a world.
She was nine.
Whenever they passed Church Rock in the wagon,
on the long drive to town,
she used to look for a cathedral
with a steeple.
But she didn't see it until much later.
She found out it was only a rock.
After the mission school she went away
to college in Illinois.
I wasn't there for that.
I came along much later in life. Long after
Los Angeles and sheepherding.
And her Church Rock.
Long after the mission school
and solitude and courtship and marriage.
I came along much later in life
when things got back to normal.
I saw Church Rock the other day.
On a visit.
I was thinking I could remember
the first time I ever knew I saw a Navajo.
Grandmother was just grandma,
like everyone had,
or so I used to think.

CONCLUSIONS

◇

MARJORIE M. SCHWEITZER

When I talk to my non-Indian friends about American Indian grandmothers and aging in Indian communities, I am invariably asked two questions. The first is, "What tips can Indian grandmothers give us?" I believe the feeling behind this question has to do with a vague uncertainty about the role of grandmothers in contemporary Anglo-American society. My friends seem to suspect that Anglo-American grandmothers, while symbolically revered in children's stories, do not always have meaningful roles. Indian grandmothers, on the other hand, are believed to be wiser and more knowledgeable.

The other question is, "What have these studies of American Indian grandmothers taught us about aging?" Ideas about "old" people and what it is like to grow old have undergone many changes in the past 15 to 20 years. These ideas will continue to change, especially as "baby boomers" push their way into the over–50 age bracket and are no longer referred to as "young." They will bring new and challenging ideas about aging and "growing old." Their numbers alone will have a tremendous impact on society and on the process of aging.

My friends are concerned about what will happen when these "baby boomers" swell the ranks of "senior citizens." But most of all, they are concerned about what will happen to themselves.

TIPS FROM AMERICAN INDIAN GRANDMOTHERS?

The keys to understanding grandmotherhood and being a grandmother lie, I believe, in exploring the forms of family and community organization that are ordinarily the most resistant to change: the social organization, ideology, values, and worldview that are typical of each group.[1] Is it possible to characterize Indian and Anglo/Euro-American societies from these perspectives? Although not everyone will follow *all* of the traits, a few may not adhere to *any* traits, and the "real" culture may not necessarily mirror the "ideal" culture, it is nevertheless possible to describe a general pattern for each group.[2]

In the Introduction I described the characteristics of Indian society that affect the role of a grandmother. Briefly, they include many ways to define who is a grandmother through lineal, classificatory, fictive, and behavioral means; an emphasis on the extended family and kinship systems, which support complementarity between gender roles; ideologies (myths and stories) that are supportive of women in general and of grandmothers specifically; a focus on interdependence and reciprocity between generations; autonomy of behavior tempered by concern for the group; a positive attitude toward growing old; and a well-defined and unambiguous grandmother role. Activities tend to be intergenerational, and kin roles merge easily with public roles.

In contrast, the characteristics of Anglo-American society that affect the lives of grandmothers and the institution of grandmotherhood present a somewhat different image. They include a lineal definition of who is a grandmother; an emphasis on the nuclear family; a patriarchal heritage imbued with notions of second-class status for and possession of women; values that favor independence, self-reliance, self-determination, and individuality with an emphasis on action, democracy, and equality; a fear of growing old; and tenuous, ambiguous grandmother roles with ill-defined behavioral expectations.[3] Activities tend to be age segregated, and kin roles do not merge with public roles.[4]

In both societies women are the most active in family affairs. Indian women are often the primary socializers of grandchildren, and Anglo women are characterized as the "kin keepers," that is, the ones who make an effort to facilitate communication and keep family relationships intact.

The differences cited above in social structure, ideology, values, and worldview preclude, it seems to me, any transfer of ideas, or "tips," about grandmothering from one group to the other. Without greater structural and ideological similarities in the cultural contexts, it would be impractical, if not impossible, for women to expect the details of being a grandmother to be comparable in both societies. The behavioral imperatives in each society stem from and reflect the particular cultural context.[5]

The models I outlined are not absolute or limiting but represent one of degree. The roles we play are in part what society hands us, but intracultural variations do occur (Pelto and Pelto 1975). Individuals can and do, through their own personalities and activities, influence the direction of society, or at least the direction of their own lives. Although many Indian women raise grandchildren, some Indian grandmothers are adamant about not wishing to be involved a second time around. The end to childrearing days gives them freedom to pursue other goals. Their own personalities may not be receptive to the grandmother role.

Some Anglo women prefer grandmother roles that are strongly defined. They have close and long-lasting relationships with their grandchildren. Others are happy with an ambiguous grandmother role, as it allows them to pursue their own dreams. It fits ideas they learned when they were children and young adults. They wish close relationships with their grandchildren as long as they have the freedom to pursue other activities.

And in *both* groups, grandmothers increasingly raise grandchildren more out of necessity than desire in cases where families suffer the disruption caused by alcoholism, drug abuse, illness, or death in the parent generation.

GRANDMOTHERHOOD AND THE AGING PROCESS—
WHAT HAVE WE LEARNED?

Several conclusions about aging emerge from these studies of American Indian grandmothers and from the studies of Anglo-American grandmotherhood (grandparenthood) cited above. I state these ideas as propositions with the intention of encouraging others to ask the same or similar questions in their cross-cultural research on aging:[6]

1. Societies/communities in which the cultural definition of *grandmother* is multifaceted and complex will develop well-defined grandmother roles with specific prescriptions about duties, obligations, and behavior.

2. Societies/communities with a single definition of *grandmother* will foster a grandmother role that tends to be ambiguous, undefined, characterized by proscriptions, and in some instances roleless.

3. In societies where grandmothers are involved extensively in childrearing, the grandmother role will be characterized by specific cultural prescriptions for role behavior.

4. In societies/communities where well-defined roles with specific duties exist for grandmothers, grandmothers will be extensively involved in rearing grandchildren.

5. Societies/communities/families that are economically successful and financially secure provide contexts that make it easier for grandmothers to carry out their roles vis-à-vis their grandchildren.

6. Societies/communities/families that suffer economic instability and are

without sufficient funds for everyday living create conditions that make it difficult for grandmothers to carry out their roles vis-à-vis their grandchildren.

7. Societies that view growing old positively and/or adhere to an ideology supportive of women will provide positive role definitions for grandmothers and women will look forward to becoming grandmothers.

8. Societies that devalue the old and/or do not support an ideology with positive images of women will tend to develop a negative attitude about becoming a grandmother and toward aging in general.

9. Aging women/grandmothers whose families function well, are intact, and whose members are in good health and financially stable are more likely to receive security and care when they become frail.

10. In societies where grandmothers contribute to the economy, pass on vital knowledge and skills, and/or possess property, they are more likely to maintain an honored, secure position in the family even when frail.

11. In societies where interdependence is stressed over independence and individuality, a frail person is more willing to accept help.

SUGGESTIONS

Several opportunities exist for future research beyond testing the propositions listed above.

Much has been learned about aging in contemporary Indian communities through study of the cultural dimensions of aging and the needs of the elderly. However, recent research has for the most part ignored Simmons's admonition about the significance of gender in aging. Researchers tend to lump the aged into a single, genderless category, referring to aging Indian women and men as "the old," "the aged," "the elderly," or sometimes "the elders." It is as if, after a certain stage in life, gender ceases to exist.

Although the Indian grandmother studies represent a beginning, it is imperative that we continue our research efforts on the effects of gender on aging. It is not sufficient to describe women and men simply as "the elderly" without paying detailed attention to the gender differences in their lives.

A second requirement for understanding aging in all of its cultural and physical dimensions demands research on the social/family roles of older people.

Indian aging studies have failed to recognize or describe the importance of the grandparent role and the extent to which it intersects with, and permeates, other societal/tribal roles.[7] Instead of elucidating the behavior and attitudes associated with the roles of grandmothers and grandfathers in specific family and tribal relationships, researchers usually refer to them as an undifferentiated group, *grandparents*. The Indian grandmother studies demonstrate that exploring the familial roles of older Indian women is of utmost importance in understanding their lives.

Other questions about Indian grandmothers might be asked. How will Indian women interpret their grandmother roles in the future? How do the lives of younger Indian grandmothers differ from those of older grandmothers? Of rural grandmothers from urban grandmothers? How will continuing changes in contemporary society affect their relationships with their grandchildren? Will they continue to be the cultural conservators that many of them are today?

These portrayals of Indian grandmothers recognize the importance of family roles in the lives of Indian women. But they will remain incomplete without similar research on the roles of *grandfathers*. How do grandfathers participate in the enculturation of their grandchildren if admittedly they are less involved in the day-to-day socialization? In what ways do Indian grandfathers transmit cultural and social knowledge to boys and young men? What are the relationships of the grandfather role to men's political and religious roles?[8]

In-depth studies of gender differences and the social roles of grandmothers and grandfathers in other ethnic groups are still lacking. Knowledge of these two dimensions is equally important in comprehending the lives of Anglo-American women, even though their grandmother roles may carry some ambiguity.[9]

Qualitative research would further illuminate social and cultural influences on aging. Some studies of aging "Americans" not only lump together Blacks, Whites, and European ethnics but fail to distinguish between women's and men's responses. The effects of ethnicity and gender on the aging process are well documented, and it is time to recognize these variables. Lumping Blacks and Whites with European ethnics and men with women results in a skewed picture of the aging process.

Finally, I suggest that we look for and describe examples of "successful" aging.[10] There is no one cultural recommendation for aging that is the answer for all people. Many ways to age successfully exist, and in our rapidly changing world we should recognize new and challenging options. Our measure of what it means need not include *only* close-knit families where grandparents are well integrated but can embrace alternative options where "family" and "community" are created with people other than or in addition to family.

Self-reliance and resourcefulness can be valuable allies in creating a meaningful existence that depends more on self than on others. The use by older people of new and imaginative technological processes may offer an opportunity for "networking" with others without leaving the confines of the home.

A promising example as we near the beginning of the twenty-first century is the possibility of frequent communication with family members via e-mail and of connecting with people in distant lands, obtaining information from around the world in many languages through access to the Internet and the World Wide Web. These connections have the potential to expand the world of a person who for reasons of health and frailty can no longer travel the community, much less the world.

Modern society demands that we broaden our vision of how to age successfully, no matter what our ethnic heritage is. American Indian grandmothers have accommodated to new demands and roles while at the same time persisting in their efforts to keep traditions alive. All of us must be equally adaptive and open to yet unthought-of alternatives that may embellish the path that we, as long-lived people, travel.[11] Our future depends on it.

NOTES

1. Edward H. Spicer, in *Cycles of Conquest,* suggests that the staying power of an ethnic enclave is due as much to social structure as to other factors. "Where these [Indian forms of family and community organization] were little altered under the conditions of contact, cultural assimilation was at a minimum; where they were much altered the dominant peoples proceeded with greater success to bring about replacement of custom and belief. Where there was continuity the Indian-type family continued as the major institution for inducting children into the cultural life of the group; where there was continuity the Indian form of local community was the regulator of change and the effective mechanism of cultural adaptation" (1962:586). Spicer's comments were made in reference to Indians of the Greater Southwest. Forms of family and community organization vary widely within the Southwest as they do in all Indian communities across the United States.

2. Richard M. Burkey (1978:163) summarizes the values, beliefs, and personality traits that are subscribed to by ethnic Americans. The complete quote is: "If it is understood that no single individual must necessarily adhere to the total number of such elements, that some individuals may not subscribe to any of these traits, and that individuals do not necessarily practice what they preach, it is still possible to come up with a number of traits or elements that are typically American." This statement is equally valid for other cultural groups, although the percentage of those adhering or not adhering to the norms would likely vary depending on the structure of the society.

"Ideal" refers to a society's verbal (and/or written) expressions of standards of behavior, the norms that the society professes to live by. "Real" culture refers to the statistical expression of culture; that is, the actual behavior of individuals and groups. For example, the norms or expected (ideal) behavior toward an elderly grandmother may be one of respect and concern for her welfare. In fact, the actual (real) behavior may include benign neglect or even elder abuse.

3. Burkey (1978) summarizes the values that characterize American culture and character,

citing several authors who have studied and written on this subject (pp. 161–66). He also discusses the ethnogenesis of what he calls a new ethnic group, the "Americans." This group included immigrants from Germany, France, and Holland who merged with the English, the dominant group, around the time of the American Revolution (pp. 154–61). Other mergings have taken place since that time. It is in this broader sense that I use the term Anglo-Americans.

See Andrei Simič (1990:90–96) for a rather harsh description of American values and how they affect the lives of older Americans. To present data on Anglo-American grand-motherhood and the social characteristics associated with grandparenthood, I summarize several studies in the following paragraphs. I should note that many of the studies that I perused focused on grandparents and not on grandmothers, but there was a general consensus that women were more involved in "kin keeping" than men were.

In 1982 Helen Kivnick offered a summary critique of the studies of grandparenthood published in the second half of the twentieth century. She concluded that "grandparenthood in contemporary America is a role that exists without clear historical and social responsibilities or generally accepted behavioral norms" (p. 1).

In 1986 Cherlin and Furstenberg suggested that articles prior to the 1960s portrayed grandparents as "isolated, cut off from kin, a social problem" (p. 3). They admit, though, that even in 1985 they knew very little about the actual roles of and attitudes toward grandparents in the American family (p. 5).

Bengtson (Bengtson and Robertson 1985) argued that grandparents hold an important symbolic role in American society. He classified these roles into four domains: (1) being there in time of trouble, (2) as symbolic "family watchdogs" to protect and give aid, (3) as arbitrators in intergenerational negotiations, and (4) as participants in the social construction of a family's history. It is interesting to note that of the four symbolic functions, three are called into play under negative or difficult circumstances.

Hagestad (in Bengtson and Robertson 1985:36) summarized other authors who alternatively describe the grandparent role as lacking, "tenuous," or ambiguous.

Kornhaber and Woodward (1981:75) label the majority of the grandparents in their study as "disconnected." They describe what they call the "New Social Contract" in which the majority of grandparents choose to "keep their distance" without completely losing contact with their families.

4. As Alice Schlegel noted in her remarks as discussant for the symposium *American Indian Grandmothers: Historical and Contemporary Issues* (Schweitzer, organizer 1985), the grandmother role in Euro-American society is easily disentangled from other roles; i.e., the kin role is separate from other roles of power and prestige.

5. Bengtson (Bengtson and Robertson 1985) cautions that a wide variety of grandparent roles exist in Euro-American society that depend in part on the effect of history on a particular cohort, gender differences, and age differences (p. 19).

Hagestad (1985) relates the ambiguity of the grandparent role to the demographic shift taking place today, that is, the rapid increase in the number and age of grandparents.

I would argue that a stronger influence on grandmother roles is the cultural context (social structure, ideology, values, worldview) as well as the historical context.

6. I present these propositions in the sense that Pelto and Pelto (1991) discuss them in chapter 1, "The Domain of Methodology," as I understand their discussion. They regard propositions as low-order generalizations based on data obtained from direct observation, interviews, and other forms of information gathering.

The propositions outlined here are offered for further "refinement and investigation" as "potentially researchable statements" in other societies that share the same/similar characteristics of social organization and values (Pelto and Pelto 1991:2–6).

7. Fry (1990) regards "roles" as the building blocks of social analysis. Rubinstein (1990) notes the lack of gender role differentiation in grandparent studies. He argues that current grandparent studies lack information that would illuminate role differentiation and the effect it has on how people age.

8. The symposium *American Indian Grandfathers: Bridging the Gap* (Schweitzer 1988) explored the roles of contemporary Indian grandfathers and the effects of culture change.

In "Navajo Grandfathers: the Bridge Between Generations" Karen Ritts Benally describes grandfathers who transmit information about the roles and responsibilities of men only to their grandsons but share ceremonial knowledge with all grandchildren. In a modern-day version of grandfatherhood, grandfathers reach out to all children through a special grandparent program in the school.

In the paper "Fancy Dancers and Preachermen: Growing Up in Grandfather's World" Joan Weibel-Orlando suggests that fathers provide models of selective assimilation and maintenance of a bicultural identity while grandfathers offer models of earlier and idealized Indian male statuses and roles.

In the paper "Singers, Sailors and Roadmen: Grandfathers in Two Worlds," I explore the relationships between cultural heritage and culture change. Becoming a grandfather was an ideal in Otoe-Missouria and Iowa society. The roles of contemporary grandfathers help bridge the gap between old and new.

9. See *Someone to Lend a Helping Hand: Women Growing Old in Rural Society,* by Dena Shenk, for an in-depth study of rural Euro-American women (Gordon and Breach Publisher 1998).

10. See note 32 in the Introduction to this volume for the definition of successful aging used here.

11. The 65-and-over population in the United States has risen from 4.1 percent in 1900 to 12.5 percent in 1990 (Taeuber 1992:table 2–1, p. 2–2), and similar increases are occurring worldwide (Albert and Cattel 1994:39). See also note 18 in the Introduction to this volume.

BIBLIOGRAPHY

◆

Aberle, David F.

1961   The Navaho. In *Matrilineal Kinship*. David M. Schneider and Kathleen Gough, eds. Pp. 96–201. Los Angeles: University of California Press.

1963   Some Sources of Flexibility in Navaho Social Organization. *Southwestern Journal of Anthropology* 19:1–18.

Administration on Aging

1997   *A Profile of Older Americans: 1996.* http://www.aoa.dhls.gov/aoa/pages/profil96.html.

Albert, Steven M. and Maria G. Cattell

1994   *Old Age in Global Perspective. Cross-Cultural and Cross-National Views.* New York: G. K. Hall.

Allen, Paula Gunn

1989   *Spider Woman's Granddaughters: Traditional Tales and Contemporary Writing by Native American Women.* New York: Fawcett Columbine.

1991   *Grandmothers of the Light: A Medicine Woman's Sourcebook.* Boston, MA: Beacon Press.

Amoss, Pamela T.

1978   *Coast Salish Spirit Dancing: The Survival of an Ancestral Religion.* Seattle and London: University of Washington Press.

1981a   Coast Salish Elders. In *Other Ways of Growing Old: Anthropological Perspectives.* Pamela Amoss and Stevan Harrell, eds. Pp. 227–47. Stanford: Stanford University Press.

1981b   Cultural Centrality and Prestige for the Elderly: The Coast Salish Case. In *Dimensions: Aging, Culture, and Health.* Christine L. Fry, ed. Brooklyn, NY: J. F. Bergin, pp. 47–63.

1987   The Fish God Gave Us: The First Salmon Ceremony Revived. *Arctic Anthropology* 24(1);56–66.

1990   The Indian Shaker Church. In *The Northwest Coast.* Wayne Suttles, ed. Pp. 633–39. *Handbook of North American Indians,* Vol. 7. William Sturtevant, general editor. Washington, DC: Smithsonian Institution.

1993   Hair of the Dog: Unraveling Pre-contact Coast Salish Social Stratification.
                In *American Indian Linguistics and Ethnography: In Honor of Laurence C.
                Thompson.* Anthony Matina and Timothy Montler, eds. Pp. 3–35.
                Occasional Papers in Linguistics, #10. Missoula: University of Montana.

Amoss, Pamela T. and Stevan Harrell
1981   Introduction: An Anthropological Perspective on Aging. In *Other Ways of
                Growing Old, Anthropological Perspectives.* Pamela T. Amoss and Stevan
                Harrell, eds. Pp. 1–24. Stanford: Stanford University Press.

Association of American Indian Physicians
1979   Physical and Mental Health of Elderly American Indians. In *The
                Continuum of Life: Health Concerns of the Indian Elderly.* Pp. 123–55.
                Albuquerque: National Indian Council on Aging.

Bataille, Gretchen and Kathleen M. Sands
1984   *American Indian Women: Telling Their Lives.* Lincoln: University of
                Nebraska Press.
1991   *American Indian Women: A Guide to Research.* New York: Garland.

Bell, Duran, Patricia Kasschau, and Gail Zellman
1978   Services Delivery to American Indian Elderly. In *The Indian Elder, A
                Forgotten American.* Final Report. Juana P. Lyon, ed. Pp. 185–98. First
                National Indian Conference on Aging, 1976. Albuquerque, NM: National
                Indian Council on Aging.

Bengtson, Vern L. and Leslie A. Morgan
1987   Ethnicity and Aging: A Comparison of Three Ethnic Groups. *Growing
                Old in Different Cultures—Cross-Cultural Perspectives.* Jay Sokolovsky, ed.
                Pp. 157–67. Acton, MA: Copley. Original edition, Belmont, CA:
                Wadsworth, 1983.

Bengtson, Vern L. and Joan F. Robertson, eds.
1985   *Grandparenthood.* Beverly Hills, CA: Sage.

Berkhofer, Robert F.
1972   *Salvation and the Savage: An Analysis of Protestant Missions and American
                Indian Response, 1787–1862.* New York: Atheneum Press.
1978   *The White Man's Indian: Images of the American Indian from Columbus to
                the Present.* New York: Alfred A. Knopf.

Bernard, H. Russell
1988   *Research Methods in Cultural Anthropology.* Newbury Park, CA: Sage.

Bierwert, Crisca
1986   Tracery in the Mist Lines: Semiotic Readings of Sto:lo Culture. Ph.D.
                dissertation, University of Washington, Seattle.
1996   Lushootseed Texts: An Introduction to Puget Salish Narrative Aesthetics.
                In *Studies in the Anthropology of North American Indians.* Raymond
                DeMallie and Douglas Parks, eds. Lincoln and London: University of
                Nebraska Press.

Blackman, Margaret B.

1989   *Sadie Brower Neakok, An Iñupiaq Woman.* Seattle, WA: University of
        Washington Press and Vancouver, BC: Douglas & McIntyre.

1992   *During My Time, Florence Edenshaw Davidson: A Haida Woman.* Revised
        edition. Seattle: University of Washington Press.

Brown, Judith K.

1985   Introduction. In *In Her Prime: A New View of Middle-Aged Women.* Judith
        K. Brown and Virginia Kerns, eds. Pp. 1–11. South Hadley, MA: Bergin
        and Garvey.

Burkey, Richard M.

1978   *Ethnic and Racial Groups: The Dynamics of Dominance.* Menlo Park, CA:
        Cummings.

Butler, Linda M. and Vern L. Bengtson

1985   Black Grandmothers: Issues of Timing and Continuity in Roles. In
        Grandparenthood. Vern L. Bengtson and Joan F. Robinson, eds. Pp. 61–78.
        Beverly Hills, CA: Sage.

Chapman, Berlin B.

1965   *The Otoes and Missourias: A Study of Indian Removal and the Legal
        Aftermath.* Oklahoma City, OK: *Times Journal.*

Cherlin, Andrew J. and Frank F. Furstenberg, Jr.

1986   *The New American Grandparent: A Place in the Family, a Life Apart.* New
        York: Basic Books.

Chiñas, Beverly

1973   *The Isthmus Zapotec: Women's Roles in Cultural Context.* New York: Holt,
        Rinehart & Winston.

Clifford, James

1988   *The Predicament of Culture: Twentieth-Century Ethnography, Literature,
        and Art.* Cambridge, MA: Harvard University Press.

Clifton, James A.

1989   Alternate Identities and Cultural Frontiers. In *Being and Becoming Indian:
        Biographical Studies of North American Frontiers.* James A. Clifton, ed. Pp.
        1–37. Chicago: The Dorsey Press.

Collins, June McCormick

1974   *Valley of the Spirits: The Upper Skagit Indians of Western Washington.*
        Seattle: University of Washington Press.

Cool, Linda

1980   Ethnicity and Aging: Continuity Through Change for Elderly Corsicans.
        In *Aging in Culture and Society, Comparative Viewpoints and Strategies.*
        Christine Fry, ed. Pp. 149–69. Brooklyn, NY: J. F. Bergin.

1981   Ethnic Identity: A Source of Community Esteem for the Elderly.
        Anthropological Quarterly 54:179–89.

1987   The Effects of Social Class and Ethnicity on the Aging Process. In *The*

Elderly as Modern Pioneers. Phillip Silverman, ed. Pp. 263–82. Bloomington, IN: Indiana University Press.

Counts, Dorothy Ayers

1985   *Tamparonga:* "The Big Women" of Kaliai (Papua New Guinea). In *In Her Prime, A New View of Middle-Aged Women.* Judith K. Brown and Virginia Kerns, eds. Pp. 49–64. South Hadley, MA: Bergin and Garvey.

Cruikshank, Julie

1990   *Life Lived Like a Story.* Lincoln: University of Nebraska Press and Vancouver, BC: University of British Columbia Press.

Deloria, Vine, Jr. and Clifford M. Lytle

1983   *American Indians, American Justice.* Austin, TX: University of Texas Press.

Densmore, Frances

1920   Chippewa Customs. *Bulletin of Bureau of American Ethnology,* Vol. LXXXVI.

The Denver Post

1997   *The Denver Post.* February 14, p. 4B.

Donaldson, Laurie

1985   Change in the Economic Roles of Suquamish Men and Women: An Ethnohistoric Analysis. M.A. thesis, Department of Anthropology, Western Washington University.

Dowd, J. J. and Vern L. Bengtson

1978   Aging in Minority Populations: An Examination of the Double Jeopardy Hypothesis. *Journal of Gerontology* 33(3):427–36.

Dozier, Edward

1966   *Hano: A Tewa Indian Community in Arizona.* Holt, Rinehart & Winston.

Dyk, Walter and Ruth Dyk

1980   *Left Handed: A Navajo Autobiography.* New York: Columbia University Press.

Eggan, Fred

1950   *The Social Organization of the Western Pueblo.* Chicago: University of Chicago Press.

Farella, John R.

1984   *The Main Stalk: A Synthesis of Navajo Philosophy.* Tucson: University of Arizona Press.

Fletcher, Alice C. and Francis La Flesche

1905–06   The Omaha. *AR Bureau of American Ethnology,* Vol. XXVII.

Fox, Richard G.

1991   For a Nearly New Culture History. In *Recapturing Anthropology, Working in the Present.* Richard G. Fox, ed. Pp. 93–113. Santa Fe, NM: School of American Research.

Frank, Gelya and Rosamond M. Vanderburgh

1986   Cross-Cultural Use of Life History Methods in Gerontology. In *New Methods for Old Age Research.* Christine L. Fry and Jennie Keith, eds. Pp. 185–207. South Hadley, MA: Bergin and Garvey.

Frisbie, Charlotte J.
1982   Traditional Navajo Women: Ethnographic and Life History Portrayals.
              American Indian Quarterly 6(1/2):11–33.
Fry, Christine L.
1980   Toward an Anthropology of Aging. In *Aging in Culture and Society,*
              Comparative Viewpoints and Strategies. Christine L. Fry, ed. Pp. 1–20.
              Brooklyn, New York: Bergin and Garvey.
1990   The Life Course in Context: Implications of Comparative Research. In
              Anthropology and Aging, Comprehensive Reviews. Robert L. Rubinstein, ed.
              Pp. 129–52. Boston: Kluwer.
Fry, Christine L., Jennie Keith and Contributors
1986   *New Methods for Old-Age Research: Strategies for Studying Diversity.* South
              Hadley, MA: Bergin and Garvey.
Geiger, Susan N. G.
1986   Women's Life Histories: Method and Content. *Signs: Journal of Women in*
              Culture and Society. 11(2):335–38.
Gelfand, Donald E.
1994   *Aging and Ethnicity, Knowledge and Services.* New York: Springer.
Gelfand, Donald E. and Charles M. Baresi, eds.
1987   *Ethnic Dimensions of Aging.* New York: Springer.
Glascock, Anthony P.
1990   By Any Other Name, It Is Still Killing: A Comparison of the Treatment of
              the Elderly in America and Other Societies. In *The Cultural Context of*
              Aging: Worldwide Perspectives. Jay Sokolovsky, ed. Pp. 43–56. Westport,
              CT: Bergin and Garvey.
Green, Rayna
1979   The Pocahontas Perplex: The Image of Indian Women in American
              Culture. *Massachusetts Review* 16:698–714.
1980   Native American Women: A Review Essay. *Signs.* Winter 248–67.
1983   *Native American Women: A Contextual Bibliography.* Bloomington, IN:
              Indiana University Press.
1988   The Indian in Popular American Culture. In *History of Indian-White*
              Relations, Wilcomb E. Washburn, ed. Pp. 587–606. *Handbook of North*
              American Indians. Vol. 4. William Sturtevant, general editor. Washington:
              Smithsonian Institution.
Green Rayna, ed.
1984   *That's What She Said.* Bloomington, IN: Indiana University Press.
Guemple, D. Lee
1969   Human Resource Management: The Dilemma of the Aging Eskimo.
              Sociological Symposium 2:59–74.
Guilmet, George M. and David L. Whited
1989   The People Who Give More: Health and Mental Health Among the
              Contemporary Puyallup Indian Tribal Community. *American Indian and*

Alaska Native Mental Health Research Monograph Series, Vol. 2, No. 2. Denver.

Haeberlin, Herman and Erna Gunther

1930   *The Indians of Puget Sound.* University of Washington Publications in Anthropology 4(1):1–83. Seattle: University of Washington Press.

Hagestad, Gunhild O.

1985   Continuity and Connectedness. In *Grandparenthood.* Vern L. Bengtson and Joan F. Robertson, eds. Pp. 31–48. Beverly Hills, CA: Sage.

Hedlund, Ann Lane

1978–1990   Field notes, Navajo Indian Reservation, Arizona and New Mexico. Files of the author.

1983   Contemporary Navajo Weaving: An Ethnography of a Native Craft. Ph.D. dissertation, Department of Anthropology, University of Colorado at Boulder.

1985   Give and Take: Contributions to Household Economics by Elderly Navajo and Pueblo Women. Paper presented at symposium *American Indian Grandmothers: Historical and Contemporary Issues.* Eighty-fourth annual meeting of the American Anthropological Association, Washington, DC.

1989   Designing Among the Navajo: Ethnoaesthetics in Weaving. In *Textiles as Primary Sources: Proceedings of the First Symposium of the Textile Society of America.* John Vollmer, ed. Pp. 86–93. Minneapolis: Minneapolis Institute of Arts.

1992   *Reflections of the Weaver's World: The Gloria F. Ross Collection of Contemporary Navajo Weaving.* Denver, CO: Denver Art Museum (distributed by University of Washington Press).

Hess, Thom

1976   *Dictionary of Puget Salish.* Seattle: University of Washington Press.

1995   Lushootseed Reader with Introductory Grammar. *Four Stories from Edward Sam,* Vol. 1. University of Montana Occasional Papers in Linguistics, 11. Missoula.

Hilbert, Violet

n.d.   *Yehaw: Lushootseed Literature in English.* Privately printed.

1980   *Huboo: Lushootseed Literature in English.* Privately printed.

1985   *Haboo: Native American Stories from Puget Sound.* Seattle and London: University of Washington Press.

1990   *Lushootseed Texts.* Seattle: Lushootseed Research.

1995a   x̌ǝc̓usǝdǝʔ ʔǝ gʷǝqʷulc̓ǝʔ: *Aunt Susie Sampson Peter: The Wisdom of a Skagit Elder.* Seattle: Lushootseed Research.

1995b   x̌ǝc̓usǝdǝʔ ʔǝ siastǝnu: *Gram Ruth Sehome Shelton: The Wisdom of a Tulalip Elder.* Seattle: Lushootseed Research.

1996   *Haboo: Lushootseed Literature in English.* Seattle: Lushootseed Research.

Hoebel, E. Adamson
    1954   *The Law of Primitive Man.* Cambridge, MA: Harvard University Press.

Holmes, Ellen Rhoads and Lowell D. Holmes
    1995   *Other Cultures, Elder Years.* 2nd edition. Thousand Oaks, CA: Sage.

Howard, James H.
    1981   *Shawnee!* Athens, OH: Ohio University Press.

Hungry Wolf, Beverly
    1980   *The Ways of My Grandmothers.* New York: William Morrow.

Hyde, Jeffrey C.
    1990   *American Indian Elders: A Demographic Profile.* National Resource Center on Minority Aging Populations. San Diego State University: University Center on Aging.

Indian Health Service
    1997   *Health Services for American Indians in Great Plains Remain Intact Through Blizzard, January 21, 1997.* Internet site: http://www.ihs.gov/2Comm/Jan97ma.html

Jacobs, Sue-Ellen
    1982   *Ethnohistorical and Contemporary Factors Affecting Land Tenure and Water Rights at San Juan Pueblo.* San Juan Pueblo Tribal Council.

Jeffries, W. R.
    1972   Our Aged Indians. In *Triple Jeopardy—Myth or Reality?* Washington, DC: National Council on Aging.

Jilek, Wolfgang G.
    1982   *Indian Healing: Shamanic Ceremonialism in the Pacific Northwest Today.* Blaine, Washington: Hancock House Publishers.

John, Robert
    1993   *Brief Bibliography: A Selective Annotated Bibliography for Gerontology Instruction. American Indian Aging.* 2nd edition. Washington, DC: Association for Gerontology in Higher Education.

John, Robert et al.
    1993   *Increasing the Supply of Paraprofessional Home-care Workers to Serve At-Risk Indian Elders.* Final Report: Grant #90AT0511, Washington, DC: Administration on Aging.

John, Robert and Dave Baldridge
    1996   *The NICOA Report, Health and Long-Term Care for Indian Elders.* Washington, DC: National Indian Policy Center.

Joos, Sandra K. and Shirley Ewart
    1988   A Health Survey of Klamath Indian Elders 30 Years After the Loss of Tribal Status. *Public Health Reports.* 103(2):166–73.

Jorgensen, Joseph G.
    1972   *The Sun Dance Religion: Power for the Powerless.* Chicago: University of Chicago Press.

Katz, Solomon H.
  1978   Anthropological Perspectives on Aging. *Annals of the American Academy of Political and Social Sciences,* 438:1–27.
Keesing, Roger M.
  1975   *Kin Groups and Social Structure.* New York: Holt, Rinehart & Winston.
Kent, Donald P.
  1971   The Elderly in Minority Groups: Variant Patterns of Aging. *The Gerontologist* 11(2):26–29.
Kent, Kate Peck
  1985   *Navajo Weaving: Three Centuries of Change.* Santa Fe, NM: School of American Research Press.
Kew, Michael
  1970   Coast Salish Ceremonial Life: Status and Identity in a Modern Village. Ph.D. dissertation, University of Washington, Seattle.
Kivnick, Helen
  1982   *The Meaning of Grandparenthood.* Ann Arbor, MI: UMI Research Press.
Kluckhohn, Clyde
  1944   *Navajo Witchcraft.* Cambridge, MA: Harvard University Press.
  1949   The Philosophy of the Navaho Indians. In *Ideological Differences and the World Order.* F. S. C. Northrup, ed. New Haven: Yale University Press.
Kluckhohn, Clyde and Dorothea Leighton
  1946   *The Navaho.* Cambridge, MA: Harvard University Press.
Kornhaber, Arthur, M.D. and Kenneth L. Woodward
  1981   *Grandparents/Grandchildren: The Vital Connection.* Garden City, NY: Anchor Press.
Kramer, B. Josea
  1991   Urban American Indian Aging. *Journal of Cross-Cultural Gerontology* 6(2):205–17.
Kramer, Josea, Donna Polisar and Jeffrey C. Hyde
  1990   *Study of Urban American Indian Aging.* Final Report: Research Grant #ARO118, Washington, DC: Administration on Aging.
Kunitz, Stephen J. and Jerrold E. Levy
  1991   *Navajo Aging: The Transition from Family to Institutional Support.* Tucson, AZ: University of Arizona Press.
LaFromboise, Teresa D. and Elizabeth Anne Parent
  1985   Book Reviews. *Signs.* Summer 782–85.
LaFromboise, Teresa D. and Anneliese M. Heyle
  1990   Changing and Diverse Roles of Women in American Indian Cultures. *Sex Roles* 22(7/8):455–76.
Lamphere, Louise
  1977   *To Run After Them: Cultural and Social Bases of Cooperation in a Navajo Community.* Tucson: University of Arizona Press.

Lancaster, Jane B. and Barbara J. King

1985   An Evolutionary Perspective on Menopause. In *In Her Prime: A New View of Middle-Aged Women.* Judith K. Brown and Virginia Kerns, eds. Pp. 13–20. South Hadley, MA: Bergin and Garvey.

Langen, Toby

1982   Personal communication.

1988   Mrs. Peter's Bluejay Story: Narrative Modes. In *Proceedings of the 23rd International Conference on Salish and Neighboring Languages.* Jay Miller, ed. Pp. 50–77. History of the American Indian Occasional Papers. Chicago: Newberry Library.

1989   The Organization of Thought in Puget Salish Narrative: Martha Lamont's "Mink and Changer." *Multi-Ethnic Literatures of the United States* 16(1):77–94.

Langness, L. L. and Gelya Frank

1981   *Lives: An Anthropological Approach to Biography.* Novato, CA: Chandler & Sharp.

Lee, Dorothy

1959   *Freedom and Culture.* Englewood Cliffs, NJ: Prentice Hall.

Leighton, Dorothea C. and Clyde Kluckhohn

1947   *Children of the People: The Navaho Individual and His Development.* Cambridge, MA: Harvard University Press.

Lomawaima, K. Tsianina

1994   *They Called It Prairie Light.* Lincoln: University of Nebraska Press.

Lurie, Nancy Oestreich, ed.

1961   *Mountain Wolf Woman, Sister of Crashing Thunder: The Autobiography of a Winnebago Indian.* Ann Arbor, MI: University of Michigan Press.

Lyon, Juana P., ed.

1978   *The Indian Elder: A Forgotten American.* Final Report. First National Indian Conference on Aging, 1976. Albuquerque, NM.

Manson, Spero M. and Donald G. Callaway

1988   Health and Aging Among American Indians: Issues and Challenges for the Biobehavioral Sciences. In *Behavioral Health Issues Among American Indians and Alaska Natives: Explorations on the Frontiers of the Biobehavioral Sciences.* Vol. 1, Monograph No. 1, Pp. 159–209. Denver, CO: University of Colorado.

Martinez, Esther

1983   *San Juan Pueblo Tewa Dictionary.* Portales, NM: Bishop Publishing Co.

Maxwell, Eleanor Krassen and Robert J. Maxwell

1980   Contempt for the Elderly: A Cross-Cultural Analysis. *Current Anthropology* 24:569–70.

1992   Insults to the Body Civil: Mistreatment of Elderly in Two Plains Indian Tribes. *Journal of Cross-Cultural Gerontology* 7(1):3–23.

Maxwell, Robert J. and Phil Silverman
    1970   Information and Esteem. *Aging and Human Development* 1:361–92.

McBeth, Sally
    1983   *Ethnic Identity and the Boarding School Experience of West-Central Oklahoma American Indians.* Washington, DC: University Press of America.

McGaw, Martha Mary, CSJ
    n.d.   Seeing Two Nuns in Perry Changes Her Whole Life. *The Sooner Catholic.*

McNeley, James
    1981   *Holy Wind in Navajo Philosophy.* Tucson: University of Arizona Press.

Medicine, Bea
    1981   American Indian Family: Cultural Change and Adaptive Strategies. *Journal of Ethnic Studies* 8:13–23.

Metcalf, Leon
    1951–1958   Messages Recorded by Leon Metcalf. Audio tapes in Burke Museum, Seattle, WA. Transcriptions and translations in the possession of Violet Hilbert, Seattle, WA.

Miller, Bruce G.
    1989   A Sociocultural Explanation of the Election of Women to Formal Office: The Upper Skagit Case. Ph.D. dissertation, Department of Anthropology, Arizona State University, Tempe.
    1990   An Ethnographic View: Positive Consequences of the War on Poverty. *American Indian and Alaska Native Mental Health Journal* 4(2):55–71.
    1992   Women and Politics: Comparative Evidence from the Northwest Coast. *Ethnology* 31(4):367–84.
    1994   Women and Tribal Politics: Is There a Gender Gap in Indian Elections? *American Indian Quarterly.* Winter 18(1):25–41.
    1995   Folk Law and Contemporary Coast Salish Tribal Code. *American Indian Culture and Research Journal* 19(3):141–64.

Miller, Jay
    1988   *Shamanic Odyssey: The Lushootseed Salish Journey to the Land of the Dead.* Menlo Park, CA: Ballena Press.

Miller, Jay and Warren Snyder
    n.d.   Suquamish Ethnographic Notes. MS.

Milner, Clyde A., II
    1982   *With Good Intentions: Quaker Work Among the Pawnees, Otos, and Omahas in the 1870s.* Lincoln: University of Nebraska Press.

Mitchell, Marjorie and Anna Franklin
    1984   When You Don't Know the Language, Just Listen to the Silence: An Historical Overview of Native Women in BC. In *Not Just Pin Money: Selected Essays on the History of Women's Work in BC.* B. K. Latham and R. J. Pazdro, eds. Pp. 17–35. Victoria: Camouson College.

Mooney, Kathleen A.
    1976   Social Distance and Exchange: the Coast Salish Case. *Ethnology* 15(4):323–46.
Myerhoff, Barbara
    1987   Number Our Days. In *Growing Old in Different Cultures—Cross-Cultural Perspectives.* Jay Sokolovsky, ed. Pp. 179–85. Acton, MA: Copley. Original edition, Belmont, CA: Wadsworth, 1983.
Myerhoff, Barbara and Andrei Simič, eds.
    1978   *Life's Career-Aging—Cultural Variations on Growing Old.* Beverly Hills, CA: Sage.
Nahemow, Nina
    1987   Grandparenthood among the Baganda: Role Option in Old Age. In *Growing Old in Different Societies, Cross-Cultural Perspectives.* Jay Sokolovsky, ed. Pp. 104–15. Acton, MA: Copley. Original edition, Belmont, CA: Wadsworth, 1983.
National Indian Council on Aging
    1979   *The Continuum of Life: Health Concerns of the Indian Elderly.* Albuquerque, NM: National Indian Council on Aging.
    1981   *American Indian Elderly: A National Profile.* Albuquerque, NM: National Indian Council on Aging.
    1993   *National Indian Aging Agenda.* National Indian Council on Aging White House Conference on Indian Aging, Green Bay, WI.
    1996a   *Mapping Indian Elders.* Albuquerque, NM: National Indian Council on Aging.
    1996b   *Honoring Indian Elders.* 20th Anniversary Conference on Indian Aging. Albuquerque, NM, August 29–30.
Nelson, Charles M.
    1990   Prehistory of the Puget Sound Region. In *The Northwest Coast.* Wayne Suttles, ed. Pp. 481–84. *Handbook of North American Indians,* Vol. 7. William Sturtevant, general editor. Washington, DC: Smithsonian Institution.
The New York Times
    1992   *The New York Times.* September 26, p. 26.
Nowell, Kenneth L.
    1996   Respecting Their Elders. *Modern Maturity* May-June:20.
Ohoyo Resource Center Staff
    1981   *Words of Today's American Indian Women: OHOYO MAKACHI.* Wichita Falls, TX: Ohoyo Resource Center.
Oneida Senior Center
    n.d.   Oneida, WI.
Ortiz, Alfonso
    1969   *The Tewa World: Space, Time, Being and Becoming in a Pueblo Society.* Chicago: University of Chicago Press.
    1986   Personal communication.

The Otoe-Missouria Tribe

1981   *The Otoe-Missouria Elders: Centennial Memoirs 1881–1981*. Red Rock, OK:
            The Otoe-Missouria Tribe.

1985–1986   *Otoe Tribal Heritage—The Preservation and Transmission of Cultural Values
            Through Videotape*. Administration on Aging, Office of Human
            Development Services, Department of Health and Human Services. HDS
            FY 1985 Coordinated Discretionary Funds Program, Priority No. 1.07A.

Paisano, Edna L.

1997   *The American Indian, Eskimo, and Aleut Population*. U.S. Census Bureau.
            Internet site: http://www.census.gov/ftp/pub/population/www/pop-
            profile/amerind.html.

Pelto, Pertti J. and Gretel H. Pelto

1975   Intra-Cultural Diversity: Some Theoretical Issues. *American Ethnologist*
            2(1):2–18.

1991   *Anthropological Research: The Structure of Inquiry*. 2nd edition. New York:
            Cambridge University Press.

The Ponca City News

1985   November 17, p. 5-a.

The Philadelphia Inquirer

1991   *The Philadelphia Inquirer*. July 10, 1991.

Powers, Marla

1986   *Oglala Women*. Chicago: University of Chicago Press.

Powers, William K.

1975   *Oglala Religion*. Lincoln: University of Nebraska Press.

Press, Irwin and Mike McKool, Jr.

1972   Social Structure and Status of the Aged: Toward Some Valid Cross-
            Cultural Generalizations. *Aging and Human Development* 3(4):297–306.

Rainer, Howard

1996   Taos Pueblo/Creek. *Native Peoples*. Fall/Winter, p. 5.

Red Horse, John G.

1980a   American Indian Elders: Unifiers of Indian Families. The Phoenix from
            the Flame: The American Indian Today. Special Issue. *Social Casework:
            The Journal of Contemporary Social Work* 61(8):490–93.

1980b   Family Structure and Value Orientation in American Indians. The
            Phoenix from the Flame: The American Indian Today. Special Issue.
            Social Casework: The Journal of Contemporary Social Work 61(8):462–67.

1982   American Indian and Alaskan Native Elders: A Policy Critique. In *Trends
            and Status of Minority Aging*. E. P. Stanford and S. A. Lockery, eds. Pp. 15–
            26. San Diego, CA: San Diego State University.

Reinharz, Shulamit and Graham D. Rowles, eds.

1988   *Qualitative Gerontology*. New York: Springer.

Ritts (Benally), Karen

1989   Turnings: From Life History to Group Biography—Four Generations of

Change in a Navajo Family. Ph.D. dissertation, Northwestern University, Evanston, IL.

Rix, Sarah E., ed.

1987   *The American Woman 1987–88: A Report in Depth.* New York: W. W. Norton.

Roach, Mary

1987   Survival Cost Analysis. Ms. prepared for the Upper Skagit Tribal Council.

Robbins, Lynn A.

1980   Fishing Households: Location, Composition and Multiple-Family Compositions. Ms. prepared for the Upper Skagit Tribal Council.

1984   Upper Skagit Survey. Ms. prepared for the Upper Skagit Tribal Council.

Roberts, Joan L.

1990   *Bibliography of American Indian Elders.* National Resource Center on Minority Aging Populations. San Diego, CA: San Diego State University.

Roberts, Judy

1987   Low-Income Needs and Community Resources Assessment. Ms. commissioned by the Skagit County Community Action Agency.

Roessel, Ruth

1981   *Women in Navajo Society.* Rough Rock, AZ: Navajo Resource Center, Rough Rock Demonstration School.

1983   Navajo Arts and Crafts. In *Southwest.* Alfonso Ortiz, ed. Pp. 592–604. *Handbook of North American Indians,* Vol. 10. William Sturtevant, general editor. Washington, DC: Smithsonian Institution.

Ronda, J. P. and J. Axtell.

1978   *Indian Missions: A Critical Bibliography.* Bloomington, IN: Indiana University Press.

Rubinstein, Robert L.

1990   Nature, Culture, Gender, Age: A Critical Review. In *Anthropology and Aging, Comprehensive Reviews.* Robert L. Rubinstein, ed. Pp. 109–25. Boston: Kluwer.

Rubinstein, Robert L., ed.

1990   *Anthropology and Aging, Comprehensive Reviews.* Boston: Kluwer.

Russell, Gail

1993   *Adopt-a-Grandparent Program.* Taos, NM: Mountain Light Center.

The Santa Fe New Mexican

1997   *The Santa Fe New Mexican.* January 27, pp. A1, A3.

Schaefer, Richard

1997   *Racial and Ethnic Groups.* 7th edition. New York: Longman.

Schlegel, Alice

1973   The Adolescent Socialization of the Hopi Girl. *Ethnology* 12:449–62.

1984   Hopi Gender Ideology of Female Superiority. *The Quarterly Journal of Ideology* 8:44–52.

1988   Hopi Widowhood. In *On Their Own: Widows and Widowhood in the*

American Southwest, 1848–1939. Arlene Scadron, ed. Pp. 42–46. Urbana, IL: University of Illinois Press.

1989   Fathers, Daughters, and Kachina Dolls. *European Review of Native American Studies* 3:7–10.

Schusky, Ernest L.

1983   *Manual for Kinship Analysis.* 2nd edition. New York: University Press of America.

Schweitzer, Marjorie M.

1974–1992   Field Notes. In possession of author.

1978   The Power and Prestige of the Elderly in Two Indian Communities. Ph.D. dissertation, University of Oklahoma.

1981   The Otoe-Missouria War Mothers: Women of Valor. *Moccasin Tracks.* September 7(1)4–8.

1983   The War Mothers: Reflections of Space and Time. *Papers in Anthropology* 24(2)157–71.

1984   Joseph and Genevieve Bassett: A Traditional Wedding and Traditional Values. *Moccasin Tracks.* October 10(2)10–11.

1985   Giving Them a Name: An Otoe-Missouria Ceremony. *Moccasin Tracks.* April 10(8):4–7.

1987   The Elders: Cultural Dimensions of Aging in Two American Indian Communities. In *Growing Old in Different Cultures—Cross-Cultural Perspectives.* Jay Sokolovsky, ed. Pp. 168–78. Acton, MA: Copley. Original edition, Belmont, CA: Wadsworth, 1983.

Schweitzer, Marjorie, Organizer and Chair

1985   *American Indian Grandmothers: Historical and Contemporary Issues.* Eighty-fourth annual meeting of the American Anthropological Association, Washington, DC.

1986   *American Indian Grandmothers II: Status, Tradition and Change.* Eighty-fifth annual meeting of the American Anthropological Association, Washington, DC.

1988   *American Indian Grandfathers: Bridging the Gap.* Eighty-seventh annual meeting of the American Anthropological Association, Phoenix, AZ.

Schweitzer, Marjorie M., General Editor

1991   *Anthropology of Aging: A Partially Annotated Bibliography.* Westport, CT: Greenwood Press.

Shanas, Ethel and M. Sussman

1981   The Family in Later Life: Social Structure and Social Policy. In *Aging: Social Change.* Sara Kiesler, James Morgan and Valerie K. Oppenheimer, eds. Pp. 211–31. New York: Academic Press.

Shomaker, Dianna

1981   Navajo Nursing Homes: Conflict of Philosophies. *Journal of Gerontological Nursing* 7(9):531–36.

1989   Transfer of Children and the Importance of Grandmothers Among the
            Navajo Indians. *Journal of Cross-Cultural Gerontology* 4(1):1–18.
1990   Health Care, Cultural Expectations and Frail Elderly Navajo
            Grandmothers. *Journal of Cross-Cultural Gerontology* 5(1):21–34.
Simič, Andrei
1978   Introduction: Aging and the Aged in Cultural Perspective. In *Life's
            Career—Aging Cultural Variations on Growing Old.* Barbara G. Myerhoff
            and Andrei Simič, eds. Pp. 9–22. Beverly Hills, CA: Sage.
1990   Aging, World View, and Intergenerational Relations in America and
            Yugoslavia. In *The Cultural Context of Aging, Worldwide Perspectives.* Jay
            Sokolovsky, ed. Pp. 89–107. New York: Bergin and Garvey.
Simmons, Leo, ed.
1942   *Sun Chief: The Autobiography of a Hopi Indian.* New Haven: Yale
            University Press.
Simmons, Leo W.
1970   *The Role of the Aged in Primitive Society.* Reprint. Archon Books. Original
            edition, New Haven, CT: Yale University Press, 1945.
Smith, Marian W.
n.d.   Field notes of Marian W. Smith. Notebooks and papers in the collection
            of the Royal Anthropological Institute of Great Britain, London.
1940   *The Puyallup Nisqually.* New York: Columbia University Press.
1949   *Indians of the Urban Northwest.* New York: Columbia University Press.
Snyder, Sally
1964   *Skagit Society and Its Existential Basis: An Ethnofolkloristic Reconstruction.*
            Ph.D. dissertation, Department of Anthropology, University of
            Washington, Seattle.
Snyder, Warren
1968   *Southern Puget Sound Salish: Texts, Place Names and Dictionary.*
            Sacramento Anthropological Society, #9. Sacramento, CA.
Spicer, Edward H.
1962   *Cycles of Conquest.* Tucson, AZ: University of Arizona Press.
Spradley, James P.
1979   *The Ethnographic Interview.* New York: Holt, Rinehart & Winston.
1980   *Participant Observation.* New York: Holt, Rinehart & Winston.
Sunset Magazine
1987   The Land of the Navajo and the Hopi. *Sunset* 178(5):96–109.
Suttles, Wayne
1958   Private Knowledge, Morality and Social Classes Among the Coast Salish.
            American Anthropologist 60(3):497–507.
Swinomish Tribal Mental Health Program
1991   *A Gathering of Wisdoms.* La Conner, WA: Swinomish Tribal Mental
            Health Program.

Taeuber, Cynthia M.

1992   U.S. Census Bureau. Current Population Reports, Special Studies P23–
178RV, *Sixty-five Plus in America*. Washington, DC: United States
Government Printing Office.

The Taos News

1993   *The Taos News*. November 4.

Tefft, Stanton K.

1968   Intergenerational Value Differentials and Family Structure Among the
Wind River Shoshone. *American Anthropologist* 70:330–33.

Teski, Marea

1987   The Evolution of Aging, Ecology, and the Elderly in the Modern World.
In *Growing Old in Different Societies: Cross-Cultural Perspectives*. Jay
Sokolovsky, ed. Pp. 14–23. Acton, MA: Copley. Original edition,
Belmont, CA: Wadsworth, 1983.

Trennert, Robert A.

1982   Educating Indian Girls at Nonreservation Boarding Schools, 1878–1920.
Western Historical Quarterly 13(3):271–90.

Tsosie, Rebecca

1988   Changing Women: The Cross-Currents of American Indian Feminine
Identity. *American Indian Culture and Research Journal* 12(1):1–37.

Underhill, Ruth M.

1979   *Papago Woman*. Reprint. New York: Holt, Rinehart & Winston. Original
edition, Memoir 46 of the American Anthropological Association, 1936.

1983   *The Navajos*. Norman: University of Oklahoma Press. Original edition,
1956.

U.S. Department of Education

1980   *Proceedings of the Conference on the Educational and Occupational Needs of
American Indian Women, October 12–13, 1976*. Washington, DC: U.S.
Department of Education.

Vogt, Evon Z. and Ethel M. Albert

1966   *People of Rimrock: A Study of Values in Five Cultures*. Cambridge: Harvard
University Press.

Waterman, Thomas T.

1973   *Notes on the Ethnology of the Indians of Puget Sound*. Indian Notes and
Monographs, Miscellaneous Series #59. New York: Museum of the
American Indian.

Waters, William T.

1984   *Otoe-Missouria Oral Narratives*. Master's thesis, University of Nebraska.

Watson, Lawrence C. and Maria-Barbara Watson-Franke

1985   *Interpreting Life Histories*. New Brunswick, NJ: Rutgers University Press.

Weibel-Orlando, Joan

1986   *Going Home: A Grandmother's Story*. Video recording.

1988a   Indians, Ethnicity as a Resource and Aging: You Can Go Home Again. *Journal of Cross-Cultural Gerontology* 3(4):323–48.

1988b   Miss America and Powwow Princess: Icons of Womanhood. *Urban Resources* 70(3):LA 1–8.

1989   Elders and Elderlies: Well-Being in Indian Old Age. *American Indian Culture and Research Journal* 13:(3&4)149–70.

1990   Grandparenting Styles: Native American Perspectives. In *The Cultural Context of Aging: Worldwide Perspectives.* Jay Sokolovsky, ed. Pp. 109–25. Westport, CT: Bergin and Garvey.

1991   *Indian Country, L.A. Maintaining Ethnic Community in Complex Society.* Urbana, IL: University of Illinois Press.

Weltfish, Gene

1965   *The Lost Universe, Pawnee Life and Culture.* Lincoln: University of Nebraska Press.

Wheat, Joe Ben

1977   Documentary Basis for Material Changes and Design Styles in Navajo Blanket Weaving. In *Ethnographic Textiles of the Western Hemisphere,* Proceedings of the Irene Emery Roundtable on Museum Textiles. Irene Emery and Patricia Fiske, eds. Pp. 420–40. Washington, DC: The Textile Museum.

1981   Early Navajo Weaving. *Plateau* 52(4):2–9. Museum of Northern Arizona, Flagstaff, AZ.

Whitman, William

1937   *The Oto.* New York: Columbia University Press.

Williams, Gerry C.

1980   Warriors No More: A Study of the American Indian Elderly. In *Aging in Culture and Society, Comparative Viewpoints and Strategies.* Christine L. Fry, ed. Pp. 101–11. Brooklyn, New York: Bergin and Garvey.

Witherspoon, Gary

1975   *Navajo Kinship and Marriage.* Chicago: University of Chicago Press.

1977   *Language and Art in the Navajo Universe.* Ann Arbor: University of Michigan Press.

1983   Navajo Social Organization. In *Southwest.* Alfonso Ortiz, ed. Pp. 524–35. *Handbook of North American Indians,* Vol. 10. William C. Sturtevant, general editor. Washington, DC: Smithsonian Institution Press.

Wright, Mary C.

1981   Economic Development and Native American Women in the Early Nineteenth Century. *American Indian Quarterly* 33(5):525–36.

Wyman, Leland

1970   *The Blessingway.* Tucson: University of Arizona Press.

Young, Gloria

1981   *Powwow Power: Perspectives on Historical and Contemporary Intertribalism.*

Ph.D. dissertation, Indiana University, Ann Arbor, MI: University Microfilm International, DDJ81 28084.

Young, Robert and William Morgan
    1980   *The Navajo Language: A Grammar and Colloquial Dictionary.*
                Albuquerque: University of New Mexico Press.

ABOUT THE AUTHORS

◆

PAMELA T. AMOSS is one of the increasing numbers of anthropologists who works outside the academy. After teaching for 10 years at the University of Washington, where she earned her M.A. and Ph.D., she left academe to become an independent consultant and researcher. She has done fieldwork among the Coast Salish Indians of Washington and British Columbia and the Hazara of Afghanistan. Her publications include *Coast Salish Spirit Dancing* (Washington 1978) and *Other Ways of Growing Old: Anthropological Perspectives* (Stanford 1981).

KAREN RITTS BENALLY holds a Ph.D. in cultural anthropology (Northwestern University, 1989). Her research centers on "story"; that is, on the interdigitation of individual life histories, family histories, community histories, stories of place, the history of a people (the Navajo), and events in the larger world. Born and raised in Michigan, she has lived and worked on the Navajo Nation since 1984. She makes her home in Red Valley, Arizona, where through marriage she has become a member of a large Navajo family and an "adopted" member of the *Tábąąhá* (Edge of Water) clan. Dr. Benally currently is employed as an anthropologist with the Navajo Nation Historic Preservation Department, specializing in the identification and protection of Navajo sacred sites, traditional cultural properties, and historic properties.

ANN LANE HEDLUND is associate professor of anthropology and director of the Museum Studies Program at Arizona State University, Tempe. She also directs the Gloria F. Ross Center for Tapestry Studies, founded in 1997. She received her doctorate from the University of Colorado at Boulder and is the author of numerous books and articles, as well as curator of exhibitions about craft production in the American Southwest. Since the mid-1970s she has conducted ethnographic fieldwork among Navajo weavers in northern Arizona and New Mexico.

SUE-ELLEN JACOBS received her Ph.D. in anthropology from the University of Colorado in 1970. She is currently professor of women studies and adjunct professor of anthropology and music at the University of Washington. She has written numerous publications, based on extensive fieldwork, on the Pueblo Southwest. She is an authority on issues of sex and gender variation, reflected in her most recent book, *Two-Spirit People: Native American Gender Identity, Sexuality and Spirituality* (Illinois 1997), coedited with Wesley Thomas and Sabine Lang. She coauthored *Winds of Change: Women in Northwest Commercial Fishing* (Washington 1989) and published *Women in Perspective* in 1974 (Illinois).

PATRICIA MCCABE, a Navajo woman born to the *Táchii'nìi* (Red Running into Water) clan, is a writer and mother of four beautiful children living in Taos, New Mexico. She was born in Gallup, New Mexico, but has lived abroad, that is, outside Dinétah, most of her life. She shares her writing at various readings in Taos. At present she is working on a publication of an adult picture book called *Magpie*.

BRUCE G. MILLER received his Ph.D. in anthropology from Arizona State University in 1989. He is associate professor of anthropology in the Department of Anthropology and Sociology at the University of British Columbia in Vancouver. His research concerns politics, law, and gender in contemporary aboriginal North America. Recent publications include articles in the *American Indian Culture and Research Journal* and the *American Indian Quarterly*. He is the editor of *Culture,* the journal of the Canadian Anthropology Society.

ALICE SCHLEGEL is professor of anthropology at the University of Arizona. Her areas of research include gender, social organization, and adolescence. She is the author of *Male Dominance and Female Autonomy* (1972), editor of *Sexual Stratification* (1977), and coauthor of *Adolescence: An Anthropological Inquiry* (1991). The articles she has written on the Hopi are based on more than 20 years of fieldwork.

MARJORIE M. SCHWEITZER received her Ph.D. from the University of Oklahoma in 1978. Her interests include American Indian culture history, with a special focus on the interconnections between the life histories of individuals and the cultural-historical context in which they occur and on the cultural dimensions of aging. She has carried out fieldwork since the mid-1970s in American Indian communities of Oklahoma as well as with descendants of Oklahoma land rush pioneers. She is the general editor of *Anthropology of Aging: A Partially Annotated Bibliography* (Greenwood 1991).

JOAN WEIBEL-ORLANDO began working with the Los Angeles Native American community in 1973. At that time she was a first-year graduate student in anthropology at the University of California at Los Angeles. Receiving a doctorate in 1977, her dissertation is an analysis of urban Indian adjustment strategies. Since that time she has published over 30 articles and a book, *Indian Country, LA,* about contemporary American Indian life. An associate professor of anthropology at the University of Southern California, she continues (when not conducting fieldwork in the Italian region of Tuscany) to be a student of the Los Angeles Native American community and its attempts to balance tribal identities, ethnic community concerns, and the demands of twenty-first-century life.

INDEX

◈

accommodation, 160, 165, 176

acculturation, 176–77n2

adaptation, 159–60

adolescence, Coast Salish, 83; Hopi, 150

"Adopt-a-Grandparent" program, 23n27

adoptions, 9; informal, 184; Navajo, 26, 44, 69; Otoe-Missouria, 166

advisory roles, 61, 62, 68–71

age, functional definition, 12

age-as-leveler theory, 14

aging: baby boomers, 207; contemporary studies, 13; ethnicity and studies of, 182–83; first comparative, cross-cultural analysis, 12; gender issues in studies of, 210; propositions about, 209–10; paradox of, 18; power and authority, 109; prestige-generating components, 61; studies of, 4; "successful," 16, 54, 211; suggested research on, 76n3, 210–12; as topic of inquiry, 12; weaving's role, 54

ancestors, 95

anecdotes, personal, 81

Anglo/Euro-American grandmothers, 208–10, 212–13nn3, 5

anthropology of aging, 4, 23n31

attitudes towards grandmothers, 98; Coast Salish, in stories, 89, 90, 93–94; negative, in stories, 90, 91, 93–94

attitudes toward women, 116–17, 210

autonomy, 11; Navajo, 57, 58; Otoe-Missouria, 171, 174

baptism, 131, 132, 134

behavior of grandmothers, 7, 17; Coast Salish, in stories, 88–91, 92–93; Hopi, 148–54, 156; Navajo, 55–59

bilateral, defined, 142n6

birth, seclusion following, 148, 150, 153

Blackfoot Indians, 20n2

boarding schools, 16–17; Choctaw, 196–97; Lakota, 187; Navajo, 27; Otoe-Missouria, 162–63, 165

Boldt decision, 106

bone dolls, 150

ceremonials (ceremonies): Coast Salish, 119; Navajo, 26, 39; Otoe-Missouria, 162, 164–65, 168–70; puberty, 72; Tewa, 130, 139

child care, 8–10, 182, 185; Choctaw, 186, 193–99; Coast Salish, 21n10, 111; collectivism, 114; Crow, 186; different attitudes about, 209; Hopi, 150, 156, 157; Lakota Sioux, 186–92; Navajo, 42–43,65; of necessity, 209; Otoe-Missouria, 166; Sioux, 186–92; Tewa, 126, 129, 131, 132, 134, 139; tribal subsidies, 129